ATHEISM,

MORALITY,

—— a n d ——

MEANING

OTHER BOOKS IN THE PROMETHEUS LECTURE SERIES

Atheistic Humanism
Antony Flew

Naturalism without Foundations
Kai Nielsen

Philosophy in Crisis: The Need for Reconstruction
Mario Bunge

Problems of Life and Death: A Humanist Perspective
Kurt Baier

The Vanquished Gods: Science, Religion, and the Nature of Belief
Richard H. Schlagel

ATHEISM, MORALITY, —and— MEANING

MICHAEL MARTIN

PROMETHEUS LECTURE SERIES

Prometheus Books

59 John Glenn Drive
Amherst, New York 14228-2197

Published 2002 by Prometheus Books.

Inquiries should be addressed to
Prometheus Books
59 John Glenn Drive
Amherst, New York 14228–2197
VOICE: 716–691–0133, ext. 207
FAX: 716–564–2711
WWW.PROMETHEUSBOOKS.COM

06 05 04 03 02   5 4 3 2 1

Library of Congress Cataloging-in-Publication Data

Martin, Michael, 1932 Feb. 3–
    Atheism, morality, and meaning / Michael Martin.
        p. cm. — (Prometheus lecture series)
    Includes bibliographical references and index.
    ISBN 1–57392–987–5 (alk. paper)
    1. Religious ethics. 2. Christian ethics. 3. Atheism. I. Title. II. Series.

BJ1188 .M37 2002
211'.8—dc21

2002070512

Printed in Canada on acid-free paper

To Jane

CONTENTS

PART TWO: THE CHRISTIAN
FOUNDATION OF MORALITY

PART THREE: THE MEANING OF
LIFE WITHOUT GOD

PART FOUR: CHRISTIANITY
AND THE MEANING OF LIFE

PREFACE

I gratefully acknowledge the help of three people in bringing this volume to completion. I am indebted first and foremost to Paul Kurtz, who invited me to give the Prometheus Lecture which is based on several themes from part 4 of this volume and who has been not just encouraging but inspirational throughout; second, to Steven L. Mitchell, the editor in chief of Prometheus Books, who was a paragon of patience while waiting for me to complete the manuscript and then skillfully guided it through the publication process; and finally to my wife, Jane Roland Martin, who, as well as being a constant source of support, read the manuscript several times and made invaluable editorial and philosophical suggestions.

I wish to thank the editors and publishers of the books, journals, and Web sites from which previously published materials have been taken for granting their permission to reemploy those materials in the present volume. Parts of previously published works of mine have been incorporated into the following chapters: chapters 7, 9, 16, and 17 include material from chapters 6 and 7, and appendices 1 and 2 from *The Case against Christianity* (Temple University Press, 1991); and chapters 2 and 13 include material from the introduction to *Atheism: Philosophical Justification* (Temple University Press, 1990). This material is reprinted by per-

9

mission of Temple University, who holds the copyright and who reserves all rights. Chapter 18 includes material from from my exchange with Steven Davis that was published in *Philo* ("Why the Resurrection Is Initially Improbable," *Philo* 1 [spring–summer 1998]; "Reply to Davis," *Philo* 2 [spring–summer 1999]; "Christianity and the Rationality of the Resurrection," *Philo* 3 [spring–summer 2000]. In chapters 2 and 8 I use material from my exchange with Paul Copan ("Atheism, Christian Theism, and Rape," http://www.infidels.org/library/modern/michael_martin/rape.html; "A Response to Paul Copan's Critique of Atheistic Morality," *Philosophia Christi* 2 [2000]; and "The Naturalistic Fallacy and Other Mistaken Arguments of Paul Copan," http://www.infidels.org/library/modern/michael_martin/nat_fallacy.html). Chapter 15 borrows material from "Problems with Heaven," http://www.infidels.org/library/modern/michael_martin/heaven.html.

INTRODUCTION

The idea that objective morality and the meaningfulness of life are impossible without belief in God has a long history in Western religious thought and is still used by Christian apologists to argue against atheism. Indeed, many religious believers and even some atheists hold the view that atheism has two implications. First, it is alleged that atheism leads to the nonobjectivity of morality; in consequence, it is held that atheists must embrace some form of moral relativism or skepticism or nihilism. Second, it is claimed that if atheism is true, then life is meaningless. Moreover, according to this view, only belief in God can provide the basis for objective ethics and a meaningful life.

These are serious charges. Indeed, theists argue that these implications are grounds for rejecting atheism while atheists try to defend the truth of atheism in spite of them. In particular, the critics hold that if atheism is committed to moral subjectivism, there is no nonarbitrary reason for a person to refrain from rape, murder, theft, and torture. In fact, they go so far as to say that atheists probably engage in actions such as rape, murder, theft, and torture more frequently than religious believers do since there are no nonprudential reasons to prevent them performing atrocities. On the other hand, religious believers in our culture allege that belief in God provides a justification for an objective, nonarbitrary reason

11

for not engaging in murder, rape, theft, and torture. In addition, critics claim that if atheism is committed to the meaninglessness of life, then there is no point in living; and that being aware of this meaninglessness should result in a bleak, depressing, and pessimistic outlook. On the other hand, they say that belief in God gives a point to living and provides for an optimistic outlook.

This book will challenge the view that atheism leads to a nonobjective ethics and the meaninglessness of life. In it I will not only show that objective ethics and a meaningful life are possible without God, I will show that from the dominant religious point of view of our culture there are serious obstacles to developing an objective ethics and having a meaningful life.

Ordinary language and common sense assume that morality is objective. Yet many ordinary religious men and women suppose that if God does not exist, morality is not objective, and some famous religious thinkers hold a similar view. For example, Emil Brunner, the twentieth-century Swiss theologian, held that the only unquestionable basis for morality is religion. He argued that "the believer alone clearly perceives that the Good, as recognized by faith, is the sole Good and all that is otherwise called good cannot lay claim to this title, at least in the ultimate sense of the word."[1] Hastings Rashdall, an early twentieth-century English philosopher, theologian, and historian maintained in turn that the "belief in God . . . is the logical presupposition of an 'objective' and absolute morality."[2]

Interestingly enough, some atheists agree that without God morality is nonobjective. Thus, John L. Mackie, an important late twentieth-century English atheist philosopher, argued that objective morality is ontologically queer from an atheistic point of view[3] and advocated a nonobjective approach to morality. To be sure, Mackie admitted that our ordinary moral notions presume the objectivity of morality. However, he maintained that this presumption is an error that must be corrected in any adequate account of morality. According to Mackie, human beings create morality; it is not found in the nature of the universe.

The doctrine that morality is impossible without belief in God was often combined with the view that atheists must be without a strong moral character. Thus, for example, in 1724 Richard Bentley, an English Christian apologist, maintained, "no atheists as such can be a true friend, an affectionate relation, or a loyal subject."[4] John Locke, who was famous for his advocacy of religious tolerance, maintained in *A Letter Concerning Tolerance*, "promises, covenants, and oaths, which are the bonds of human society can have no effect on an atheist."[5] Locke's belief was enshrined in legal rules that prevented atheists from testifying in court. For example, until the passage of the Evidence Amendment Act of 1869, atheists in England were considered incompetent to give evidence in a court of law.[6] Similar legal restrictions were found in the United States. For instance, in 1856 one Ira Aldrich was disqualified as a witness in an Illinois case after he testified that he did not believe in a God that "punishes people for perjury, either in this world or any other,"[7] and as late as 1871 the Supreme Court of Tennessee maintained

> The man who has the hardihood to avow that he does not believe in a God, shows a recklessness of moral character and utter want of moral sensibility, such as very little entitles him to be *heard or believed* in a court of justice in a country designated as Christian.[8]

Although this view is no longer enshrined in our laws, many religious people still hold the opinion that religious belief is closely related to moral action. But is there any reason to suppose that lack of religious belief and lack of moral character are intimately associated?

In addition to believing that God provides that foundation of objective morality, many religious believers suppose that God's existence gives life a point and significance, and that without a God nothing has any meaning. Consequently, they link atheism to a senseless existence and associate belief in God with a life full of significance and purpose. To be sure, the reasons given for this position vary from the atheists' alleged lack of an objective morality to their belief that human life is finite.

Typical is the position of William Lane Craig, a well-known contemporary Christian apologist and debater, who argues that life is absurd without God and immortality and that there is no ultimate meaning without immortality and God:

> If God does not exist, then both man and the universe are inevitably doomed to death. Man, like all biological organisms must die. With no hope of immortality life leads only to the grave . . . And the universe

faces death too. . . . The entire universe is plunging towards its inevitable extinction—death is written throughout its structure. There is no escape. There is no hope. If there is no God, then man and the universe are doomed. Like prisoners condemned to death, we wait our unavoidable execution. There is no God, and there is no immortality. And what is the consequence of all of this? It means life itself is absurd. It means that the life we have is without ultimate significance, value, or purpose.[9]

Craig goes on to argue that atheism is in practice impossible because it is impossible to live consistently and happily without belief in God. If one lives consistently one will not be happy and if one is happy it is only because one is not consistent.[10]

Some atheists have agreed that human life is meaningless in a world without God. Thus, G. L. Romanes, a nineteenth-century biologist and nonbeliever, confessed at the end of *A Candid Examination of Theism* that "with this virtual denial of God, the universe has lost to me its soul of loveliness."[11] And Bertrand Russell, perhaps the most famous nonbeliever of the twentieth century, argued that "all the labors of the ages, all devotion, all the inspiration, all the noonday brightness of human genius, are destined to extinction in the vast death of the solar system, and the whole temple of man's achievement must inevitably be buried beneath the debris of a universe in ruins."[12]

Despite these widespread charges against atheism, there are some thinkers who maintain that atheism is compatible with objective morality. For example, Richard Swinburne, perhaps the most famous contemporary Christian philosopher, argues that many moral statements are true independently of God's commands. Swinburne says, "Genocide and torturing children are wrong and would remain so whatever commands any person issued."[13] Furthermore, although he believes that if God had issued commands on a given topic, these commands would be morally relevant, he assumes that if God did not exist it would still be possible to settle moral disputes objectively.

Moreover, even some prominent religious leaders disagree that morality is impossible without God. For example, Richard Holloway, presently Bishop of Edinburgh and Primus of the Scottish Episcopal Church, has defended a godless morality. Because of the difficulty of deciding moral issues by recourse to religious considerations, Bishop Holloway recommends leaving God out of moral debates and finding good human reasons for supporting the moral system we advocate.[14] In addition, not all philosophical ethicists share Mackie's view that morality without God must be nonobjective.[15]

Moreover, some well-known humanists and philosophical atheists reject the meaningless thesis. Thus, Julian Huxley, a twentieth-century humanist biologist and writer, wrote that although he did not believe in the existence of a god or gods,

> I believe that life can be worth living. I believe that in spite of pain, squalor, cruelty, unhappiness, and death. I do not believe that it is necessarily worth living but only for most people it can be.
>
> I believe that man, as individual, as group, and collectively as mankind, can achieve a satisfying purpose in existence. I believe this in spite of frustration, aimlessness, frivolity, boredom, sloth, and failure. Again I do not believe that a purpose inevitably inheres in the nature of the universe or in our existence, or that mankind is bound to achieve a satisfying purpose, but only that such a progress can be found.[16]

And Kurt Baier, a well-known contemporary ethical philosopher, has said,

> My main conclusion is that the acceptance of a scientific worldview picture provides no reason for saying that life is meaningless, but on the contrary every reason for saying that there are many lives which are meaningful and significant. My subsidiary conclusion is that one of the reasons frequently offered for retaining the Christian world picture, namely, that its acceptance gives us a guarantee of a meaningful life, is unsound.[17]

It is clear from this brief survey that opinion is divided on whether atheism is committed to a nonobjective morality and to the meaninglessness of life. To be sure, some religious apologists try to support their antiatheistic position by citing atheists who agree with them on these issues. However, they fail to mention that many atheists do not agree and that there are even some theists who would disagree with them.

Nothing is to be gained then in regard to the issue of nonobjectivism in ethics and the meaninglessness of human life by citing atheists such as Mackie and Russell. What is needed is a detailed critical analysis of the arguments. This book provides such analysis. In part 1 a nonreligious foundation of morality is developed and defended. Part 2 provides a critique of the foundations of theistic morality in general and of Christian morality in particular. Part 3 defends the possibility of the meaning of life without God and part 4 maintains that there are difficult problems in establishing the meaningfulness of the religious life in general and the Christian life in particular.

NOTES

1. Emil Brunner, *The Divine Imperative*, trans. Olive Wyon (London: Littleworth Press, 1947), chap. 9. Quoted by Kai Nielsen in *Ethics without God* (Amherst, N.Y.: Prometheus Books, 1972), p. 1.

2. Hastings Rashdall, *Theory of Good and Evil* (Oxford, 1907), vol. II, p. 212. Quoted by Patrick H. Nowell-Smith in "Religion and Morality," in *The Encyclopedia of Philosophy*, ed. Paul Edwards (New York: Macmillan, 1967), vol. 7, p. 157.

3. John L. Mackie, *Ethics: Inventing Right and Wrong* (New York: Penguin Books, 1979).

4. Richard Bentley, *Eight Sermons* (Cambridge, 1724). Quoted by Paul Edwards in "Atheism," in Edwards, *The Encyclopedia of Philosophy*, vol. 1, p. 174.

5. John Locke, *A Letter on Religious Tolerance*. Quoted by Edwards in "Atheism."

6. Edwards, "Atheism," p. 175.

7. *The Central Military Tract Railroad Co.* v. *A. Rockafellow*, 17 Ill. 541 (1856). Quoted in Frank Swancara, *Separation of Religion and Government* (New York: Truth Seeker Company, 1950), p. 136.

8. *Odell* v. *Koppee*, 5 Heisk. (Tenn) 91. Quoted in Swancara, *Separation of Religion and Government*, p. 140.

9. William Lane Craig, "The Absurdity of Life without God," in *The Meaning of Life*, ed. E. D. Klemke (New York: Oxford University Press, 2000), pp. 40–42.

10. Ibid., p. 47.

11. G. L. Romanes, *A Candid Examination of Theism* (1879), quoted in Edwards, "Atheism," p. 187.

12. Bertrand Russell, *A Free Man Worship*. Quoted by Paul Edwards in "Meaning and Value of Life," in *The Meaning of Life*, ed. Steven Sanders and David R. Cheney (Englewood Cliffs, N.J.: Prentice Hall, 1980), p. 89.

13. Richard Swinburne, *The Coherence of Theism* (Oxford: Oxford University Press, 1977), p. 204.

14. Richard Holloway, *Godless Morality* (Edinburgh: Canongate, 1999), p. 20.

15. See, for example, Roderick Firth, "Ethical Absolutism and the Ideal Observer," in *Readings in Ethical Theory*, 2d ed., ed. Wilfrid Sellars and John Hospers (Englewood Cliffs, N.J.: Prentice-Hall, 1970); Richard Boyd, "How to Be a Moral Realist" and Peter Railton, "Moral Realism," in *Moral Discourse and Practice*, ed. Stephen Darwall, Allan Gibbard, and Peter Railton (Oxford: Oxford University Press, 1997); David O. Brink, *Moral Realism and the Foundations of Ethics* (Cambridge: Cambridge University Press, 1989), pp. 37–39, 197–203.

16. Julian Huxley, "The Creed of a Scientific Humanist," in Klemke, *The Meaning of Life*, p. 78.

17. Kurt Baier, "The Meaning of Life," in Klemke, *The Meaning of Life*, pp. 129–30.

THE NONRELIGIOUS FOUNDATION OF MORALITY

1

INTRODUCTION TO THE NONRELIGIOUS FOUNDATION OF MORALITY

In order to maintain that atheism is compatible with objective morality it is important to develop a nonreligious foundation of morality. Unless one can show that an objective basis of morality need not presuppose God, a defense of atheism against one of the charges raised against it in the introduction will not be successful. The best way to show this is to argue successfully for a basis for morality that is not dependent on God.

Part 1 of this book is about a nonreligious foundation of morality. In this chapter preliminary concepts necessary to understanding a nonreligious foundation of morality will be introduced and clarified. In later chapters objections to a nonreligious foundation of morality will be posed and a nonreligious foundation of morality will be developed and defended.

Although I use the expression "nonreligious foundation of morality," I do not presuppose that God does or does not exist. In my sense of "nonreligious foundation of morality," then, theists and other believers can consistently embrace a nonreligious foundation of morality. This usage is perfectly consistent with the purposes of this work since I am arguing that belief in God is not essential for the foundations of objective morality. But this is precisely what establishing a nonreligious foundation of objective morality would show.

In a narrow sense another expression for "a nonreligious foundation of morality" is "a nonreligious metaethics." Metaethical issues are second order issues; that is, issues *about* ethics, rather than *within* ethics. Typically, metaethics is concerned with metaphysical, epistemological and semantical, and psychological questions connected with ethics. For example, Are there moral truths? Can we justify moral judgments? This second order discipline of metaethics is usually contrasted with the first order discipline of normative ethics which considers both general and particular questions within ethics, for example, what sort of things are right and wrong and is the death penalty immoral?[1]

In contrast to this narrow sense that there is a broader sense that the foundations of ethics considered include metaethics as well as the more theoretical aspects of normative ethics. For example, How are rightness and goodness related? What ideal of a person should we accept? The foundations of ethics in this broader sense would exclude particular ethical questions such as, Is war ever morally justified and if so, under what conditions? Should Dr. Jones not tell Ms. Smith the truth about her condition in order to prevent her from worrying? In part 1 we will be concerned mainly with the foundation of nonreligious morality in the narrow sense, that is, in terms of the second order discipline of metaethics.[2]

In order to defend a nonreligious metaethics it is necessary to accomplish three interrelated tasks. First, it is necessary to meet general arguments that purport to show that morality without God is impossible. Second, it is essential to present a plausible metaethics that does not presuppose God. Third, it is important to meet objections to this metaethics. The first task will be accomplished in chapter 2, the second in chapters 3 and 4, and the final one in chapter 5.

The claim that a nonreligious foundation of morality is possible is not a historical thesis. For example, atheists are not saying that, historically speaking, morality developed independently of religious beliefs and institutions. The question of the historical origins of moral notions is a complicated one that atheists need not take a stand on, except to deny that morality has a supernatural origin. It should be noted that to deny that morality has a supernatural origin is compatible with the belief that moral obligation has its historical origins in the doctrines of Christian theism. Indeed, it is compatible with the belief that without the existence of Christianity moral obligation would not exist.

Although the claim that a nonreligious foundation of morality is possible has psychological aspects, it is not reducible to a psychological claim. Thus, an atheist can admit that some people are psychologically incapable of being moral without religious belief, or even that for many people possessing religious beliefs makes engaging in moral activities easier. An atheist need only maintain that for many people ethical motivation is possible without a belief in God.

The crucial questions for an atheist are not primarily historical and psychological but ontological and epistemological: Are there moral facts if God does not exist? If there are, can these facts be known? If there are no moral facts and no God, can moral advice, prescriptions, ideals, and the like be rationally justified?

Nonreligious metaethics can take three forms corresponding to the three leading schools of metaethics: naturalism, intuitionism, and noncognitivism. First, atheists might claim that there are moral facts that are identical or constituted by natural facts. In recent times Roderick Firth, Richard Boyd, Peter Railton, and David Brink have advocated this metaethical position.[3] Second, atheists might argue that there are moral facts that are ontologically unique; that is, are not identical with or constituted by natural or supernatural facts. This theory has usually been combined with the view that these moral facts are known by some sort of moral intuition. Although classical intuitionists such as G. E. Moore,[4] Henry Sidgwick,[5] and W. D. Ross[6] advocated such a view in the early part of the twentieth century, intuitionism is no longer a popular metaethical theory and, to my knowledge, is not now defended by any well-known atheistic thinkers. Third, atheism is compatible with a noncognitive view of ethics. According to this position there are no moral facts and ethical language is used not to state facts but to give advice and make recommendations, prescriptions, and proposals. Originally formulated by such philosophers as C. L. Stevenson in a very narrow, noncognitive way—ethical language was thought to be a form of emotive language used to express emotions and to influence others by its emotional force[7]—this approach was later developed by R. M. Hare,[8] William Frankena,[9] and others into a sophisticated theory in which reason and logic play crucial roles.

Closely related to these three metaethical positions are different positions on the relationship holds between science and ethics. According to ethical naturalism, moral facts are a subclass of scientific facts and moral inquiry is continuous with scientific inquiry. In ethical intuitionism, although there are moral facts, these facts and inquiry concerning them are discontinuous with scientific facts and inquiry. In noncognitivism, since there are no moral facts and therefore no moral inquiry aimed at discovering moral truths, the discontinuity between morality and science seems the sharpest. Nevertheless, advocates of some forms of noncognitivism maintain that there are rationally justified moral advice, prescriptions, and recommendations just as there are rationally justified scientific beliefs, theories, and predictions.[10]

One important question that must concern us has to do with the relationship between the truth of nonreligious metaethics and the truth of atheism. The latter does not entail any specific nonreligious metaethics. Thus, atheism is compatible with naturalism, intuitionism, and noncognitivism. On the other hand, the truth of atheism means that a metaethics that assumes God cannot be accepted even if it is desirable in other respects. However, there is one peculiar sense in which atheism is compatible with a religious metaethics. For example, an atheist might hold that in theory moral obligations must be based on God's command. But since atheism holds that there is no God, such an atheist would in effect be holding there is no such thing as moral obligation. In such a case, acceptance of a religious metaethics is combined with rejection of God. Some atheists might hold this position,[11] but it is safe to say that such a view is at best very rare.

In any case, let us assume, as Christian theists allege, that only a metaethics that presupposes God provides a firm objective basis for our deepest moral convictions. Notice that this would not be an argument for the truth of belief in God, for atheists could simply say that, unfortunately, our deepest moral convictions have no objective basis. In a similar way, problems with a nonreligious metaethics have no bearing on the falsehood of atheism. Let us assume, as some theists argue, that a metaethics that does not presuppose God is subjective and relativistic. This would have no bearing on the truth of atheism and could not be used as an argument against it. If a nonreligious metaethics were subjective and relativistic, this might be cause for regret but it is something that would have to be accepted and lived with. It would show nothing about the truth or falsity of atheism. Regrettably, the implications of the truth are sometimes hard to accept. However, as will be shown in the chapters that follow, there is no reason to believe that objective morality presupposes God or that atheists have to accept a moral position that leads to moral relativism or skepticism or nihilism. On this score, at least, atheists should have no regrets.

NOTES

1. See David O. Brink, *Moral Realism and the Foundations of Ethics* (Cambridge: Cambridge University Press, 1989), p. 1. See also Stephen Darwall, Allan Gibbard, and Peter Railton, "Toward *Fin de siècle* Ethics: Some Trends," in *Moral Discourse and Practice*, ed. Stephen Darwall, Allan Gibbard, and Peter Railton (New York: Oxford University Press, 1997), p. 7.

2. This restriction seems justified since there are several normative ethical systems compatible with atheistic metaphysics and none have gained dominance. As we shall see, this, contrasted with theistic normative ethics, is where Christian ethics holds prominence.

3. See, for example, Roderick Firth, "Ethical Absolutism and the Ideal Observer," in *Readings in Ethical Theory*, 2d ed., ed. Wilfrid Sellars and John Hospers (Englewood Cliffs, N.J.: Prentice-Hall, 1970); Richard Boyd, "How to Be a Moral Realist" and Peter Railton, "Moral Realism," in Darwall, Gibbard, and Railton, *Moral Discourse and Practice*; Brink, *Moral Realism*, pp. 37–39, 197–203.

4. G. E. Moore, *Principia Ethica* (Cambridge: Cambridge University Press, 1903).

5. H. Sidgwick, *The Methods of Ethics*, 7th ed. (Chicago: University of Chicago Press, 1907).

6. W. D. Ross, *The Right and the Good* (New York: Oxford University Press, 1930).

7. C. L. Stevenson, *Ethics and Language* (New Haven, Conn.: Yale University Press, 1944).

8. See R. M. Hare, *Moral Thinking* (New York: Oxford University Press, 1981).

9. William Frankena, *Ethics*, 2d ed. (Englewood Cliffs, N.J.: Prentice-Hall, 1973), pp. 105–14.

10. There is another position that could be taken. One might argue that in common sense terms strictly speaking there are neither scientific facts nor moral facts. Consequently, science and morality are in the same boat. This could be

understood as either global subjectivism or a sophisticated view of scientific and moral facts. On this point see Brink, *Moral Realism*, pp. 6–7.

11. John Mackie may have held this position as well as the fictional character Smerdyakov in Dostoyevsky's novel *The Brothers Karamazov*.

2

OBJECTIONS TO MORALITY WITHOUT RELIGION

INTRODUCTION

In this chapter I will consider three types of arguments that are used to show that objective morality is impossible without God.[1] In each instance I will show that the argument fails. The first kind assumes that nonbelievers do not have adequate motivation to uphold objective morality. The second sort maintains that if one doubts the truth of God's existence, one must doubt objectivity of morality; in other words, objective morality can only be derived from the truth of God's existence. The third type assumes that the worldview presupposed by atheists posits a world without objective morality.

ARGUMENTS FROM MOTIVATION

Historically it has been claimed that atheists do not follow an objective moral code where this can be understood as a code based on moral facts. Atheists, it is said, either cannot hold that there are moral facts and thus cannot follow a code based on such facts or, if they do believe that there are moral facts, they do not have sufficient motivation to obey a code based on them. If someone does believe there are moral facts, let us say that the person has an objective morality. If someone has an objective morality and yet is not motivated to follow it, let us say that he or she has an unmotivated objective morality. Accordingly, atheists are deficient either in having an objective morality or in having a motivated objective morality. Furthermore because of this deficiency they lack moral character and consequently cannot be honest or truthful. However, is there any reason to suppose that religious belief and either lack of objective morality or unmotivated objective morality is closely connected?

To answer this question a number of different theses need to be distinguished. Someone holding the view that religion and morality are connected might be maintaining that belief in God is a necessary condition for having a high moral character. This thesis can be stated as follows:

1. It is impossible to have a high moral character without belief in God.

That person might, however, simply be arguing that, although it is possible to have a high moral character without belief in God, this state of affairs is unlikely. This thesis can be formulated as

2. It is more probable than not that a person without a belief in God will not have a high moral character.

Or our critic of the moral character of atheists may be maintaining that people who do not believe in God are less likely to have a high moral character than people who do believe. Consider:

3. It is more probable that a person without a belief in God will not have a high moral character than that a person with a belief in God will.

Now it seems clear that thesis (1) is false. Members of the Jainist religion are atheists yet they follow a strict ethical code that forbids injuring any living creature.[2] David Hume, one of history's most distinguished atheists, was called the Saintly Infidel.[3] Percy Shelley, another famous atheist, has been described as driven by principles and high ideals and his life has been characterized as one of generosity and integrity.[4] A theist might of course disagree with these judgments, but then one must ask if he or she is using the sentence "X is a person of high moral character" in such a way that it entails "X believes in God." If so, then no possible evidence could refute (1). However, since this is surely not the way the expression "has a high moral character" is normally understood, the onus to say what possible evidence could refute (1) is on the theist.

Now it must be understood that an atheist could readily admit the truth of (2). He or she could maintain that high moral character is a rare trait, one that is distributed at approximately the same low rate of frequency both among theists and atheists. That is, an atheist could argue that in addition to (2) the following thesis is true:

2'. It is more probable than not that a person with a belief in God will not have a high moral character.

Is (2') correct? If it is, then (3) is mistaken. Is it? The empirical research on the topic is vast and difficult to interpret. Certainly some studies suggest that religion may have little to do with criminal activity,[5] delinquency,[6] and humanitarian behavior[7] and that, statistically speaking, atheists are morally at least as well off as theists. For example, a review by Gorsuch and Aleshire of the empirical research up to 1974 on the relationship between Christian belief and ethnic prejudice indicated that moderately active church members were more prejudiced than highly active members and nonmembers and that highly active members were as tolerant as nonmembers. This review concluded that "holding a strong value position which allowed one to stand outside the value tradition of society at large was crucial in adopting a nonprejudiced position and was typical of nonreligious and highly religious people."[8] Thus, Gorsuch and Aleshire suggest that, at least as far as ethnic tolerance is concerned, nonbelievers are just as moral as the most devout religious believers and more are moral than the less devout believers. Moreover, as Adolf Grünbaum has pointed out, in the United States 90 percent of the population professes a belief in God in comparison to the countries of Western Europe and Scandinavia where less than 50 percent of the population profess this belief. Yet the United States has a higher incident of homicide and other crimes than these other countries.[9]

Although reviews such as those by Gorsuch and Aleshire and the crime statistics cited by Grünbaum should give theists pause, at the present time there does not seem to be any clear and definite evidence showing (3) to be false. On the other hand, there is no clear and definite evidence that supports (3). Thus, the truth of (3) cannot at present be conclusively determined. However, one can say that in the light of available evidence (3) seems dubious.

Without better evidence than we have now, the criticism that atheism has an adverse influence on moral character is unwarranted. For the sake of the argument, however, let us assume that (3) is true. One still cannot immediately leap to the conclusion that there is a causal relation between nonbelief in God and low moral character. After all, atheists might have other traits that causally account for the supposed differential rate of high moral character between them and theists.

In terms of our three interpretations of the connection between religion and morality there is no reason to question the view that atheists can have high moral characters. Consequently, there is no reason to suppose that atheists cannot have a motivated objective morality. But why would anyone suppose that motivated objective morality is closely connected with belief in God? One reason traditionally given is that human beings have motivated objective morality only because they believe that they will be rewarded for good action and punished for bad action. Stated more formally, the Argument from Rewards and Punishment is this:

1. If people do not believe God exists, they have no grounds for supposing that acting in terms of objective morality will consistently be rewarded and acting against such a morality will consistently be punished.
2. If people have no good grounds for believing that acting in terms of objective morality will consistently be rewarded and acting against such a morality will consistently be punished, people will not be motivated to act according to objective morality.
3. If people are not motivated to act according to objective morality, they will not follow objective morality.
4. Hence, if people do not believe God exists, they will not follow objective morality.

Since the conclusion of this argument conflicts with the fact that atheists exist who have a motivated objective morality there must be something wrong with one or more of the above premises. One dubious premise is (2). Surely some people have a motivated objective morality not because of belief in divine rewards and punishments but by virtue of their belief in the inherent value of moral action. Thus, a medical researcher might devote her life to finding a cure for cancer because she has a strong desire to eliminate evil and believes that cancer is a natural evil that should be eliminated. Moreover, some people may be motivated by secular rewards and punishments. For example, a social benefactor may give millions to charities because it adds to his prestige and a greedy person may refrain from stealing for fear of getting caught.

Premise (3) is also questionable. People may not be motivated in any explicit or conscious way to act according to objective morality and yet many are moral out of habit. In addition, it is obvious that religious believers who believe in divine rewards and punishments are not always moral. Indeed, some believers are murderers, rapists, thieves, child abusers, and traitors. Even when believers are moral it is not obvious that they are moral *because* they are motivated by a belief in divine rewards and punishments. Is Mr. Jones, a devout Methodist, faithful to his wife because of the fear of divine punishment of adultery or because of his deep love and respect for her? His behavior may not reveal his true motive; indeed, he may not even be aware of it. There is one further reason that indicates that the Argument from Rewards and Punishment is problematic. In some views of Christianity moral behavior is not rewarded or punished at all. What is rewarded or punished is whether the person has accepted Jesus.

The Argument from Rewards and Punishment is, however, just one Argument from Motivation. In the eyes of some religious ethicists it has seemed too naïve and simple and they accordingly have constructed far more sophisticated arguments.[10] One such argument is that a secular moralist must regard the lack of the ultimate justice of life in a godless world as a tragedy that leaves the pursuit of the moral life pointless.[11] According to this argument, in a secular world good people do not always triumph over injustice and evil people are often victorious. Indeed, it is alleged that nonbelievers have their own problem of evil. While believers have the problem of reconciling evil with an all-good, all-powerful God, atheists have the problem of reconciling the pervasiveness of injustice with a commitment to being virtuous. If leading a good life does not promote the welfare of others, then part of the motive for leading a good life is taken away. Only God, an undefeatable agency for justice who will complete the purpose of a virtuous life, can provide this assurance. If someone has an objective morality and yet has no good reason to follow it, let us say she or he has an unreasonable objective morality.

Stated more formally, the Argument from Culmination can be reconstructed as follows:

1. If there is no God, then there is no assurance that justice will triumph over evil.
2. If there is no assurance that justice will triumph over evil, then objective morality is pointless.
3. If objective morality is pointless, then objective morality is unreasonable.
4. Therefore, if there is no God, then objective morality is unreasonable.

The conclusion of the Argument from Culmination, unlike that of the Argument from Rewards and Punishments, is not contradicted by the existence of virtuous atheists for (4) is compatible with virtuous nonbelievers who have no good reason to be virtuous. However, although the Argument from Culmination may be more sophisticated than the Argument from Rewards and Punishment, it is still problematic. First of all, there is a worry about making sense of the background assumptions of the argument, which seem to assume that our earthly existence is completely unjust and that this injustice can be reconciled only in the afterlife. Premise (1) calls into question God's motives for creating or at least permitting such an unjust world, yet why is the secular world so unjust when the afterlife is not? The existence of heaven shows that moral choice is compatible with a better world than ours, so why did not God make Earth more like heaven? Premise (2) should make religious believers question the necessity of trying to eliminate injustice in our secular lives. If complete justice will be achieved after death, why try to eliminate evil now?

Putting aside these background issues there are problems with premise (2). One assumes that "no assurance" means that it is uncertain that just action will triumph over evil. But why demand certainty? Why is it not enough that the triumph of justice is possible? For example, secular reformers fighting social injustice typically do not suppose that their success is certain. Thinking that they have some chance of success, they often work against what seems to them like overwhelming odds. This does not mean that their behavior is unreasonable. A social reformer may value her goals so much that even a small chance of success would provide a very strong reason for action. Given the vagaries of life it is seldom the case that we can know with any certainty that the secular moral triumph of justice is impossible. This uncertainty combined with the great value of the triumph is surely enough motivation for virtuous action.

However, suppose that atheists could know with absolute certainty that evil will triumph in the next millennium. Suppose, for example, we know that a series of dictators who make Hitler and Stalin seem mild in comparison will rule Earth and that during this thousand-year period torture, death, and slavery will prevail. Moreover, let us suppose we know with certainty that all life will end with a nuclear holocaust in the year 3000. Why should this mean that people should not be virtuous? Would not courage be essential for a morally dignified survival in such a desperate time? Would not mutual compassion and charity among the victims help people cope with the reign of terror? Would not wisdom of how to live in such a hell on Earth be needed? Further, despite the fact that, by hypothesis, justice would not triumph in the end and society in general would be incredibly unjust, virtuous humans might create enclaves of justice in the larger unjust whole. Surely, no one would deny that a basically unjust society containing pockets of justice and isolated incidents of goodness is better than an unjust society without them.

One more consideration is relevant to the Argument from Culmination. It can be argued that although virtue has some inherent value, it must be considered as part of a larger whole that is only completed when it is integrated with other things, and that this completion is only guaranteed in a religious view of the world. For example, theists could be maintaining that although a virtuous life has inherent value it is part of a larger whole and is only completed with the vision and perfect love of God achieved in the afterlife. An atheist could admit that the value of virtue would be increased if God exists but this would not show that virtue would be pointless without the existence of God.[12]

I conclude that virtue can have a point without assurances that justice will triumph. Even in a worst-case scenario where we have certain knowledge of the triumph of evil until the extinction of human life, virtuous action could still have a point. Moreover, in more realistic scenarios virtuous action can be motivated simply by the possibility of success when that is combined with the belief that success will be of great value. Furthermore, even if virtue is more valuable when it is part of a theistic whole, it is valuable enough in itself to motivate moral action.

ARGUMENTS FROM DERIVATION

Theists might grant that if objective morality were available to atheists, they could be motivated to follow it and it could be reasonable for them to do so. But they might argue that objective morality can only be derived from belief in God. Let us consider five arguments adduced in support of this view.

According to the Argument from Expediency there are certain actions—for example, torture, slavery, and punishment of the innocent—that should be morally forbidden come what may.[13] This argument alleges further that there would be such prohibitions in a theistic ethics but that a secular ethics must either rely on subjective intuitions for the feeling that these actions should never be done or else proceed to calculate the probable consequences. The argument goes on to maintain that since this latter strategy is simply a stark version of utilitarianism in which anything can be morally justified given the right circumstances, in the final analysis the position is based on expediency. So whereas the reliance on intuitions is based on subjective feelings, the appeal to consequences relies on expediency. The Argument from Expediency can be formulated as follows:

1. If objective morality without God is possible, then firm principled restrictions on certain evil acts are necessary.
2. If firm principled restrictions on certain evil acts are necessary, then secular morality must not be based on either subjective intuitions or utilitarianism.
3. But secular morality must be based on either subjective intuitions or utilitarianism.
4. Hence, objective morality without God is impossible.

Let us grant the assumption of the argument that subjective intuitions would not be an acceptable basis for an objective morality and concentrate on the utilitarian aspect of the argument. So understood, the Argument from Expediency has several problems, the first of which is that it seems irrelevant to the issue of objective morality. The argument seems to assume implicitly that utilitarianism is not based on moral facts and consequently that utilitarians do not have an objective morality. However, questions of utility are based on moral facts although these may not be the sort of moral facts that theists assume. According to utilitarians the morality of a fact is purely in terms of its consequences. This argument must assume that morality of facts is a matter based on consequences. This assumption may or may not be true but it shows nothing about whether moral facts are compatible with atheism.

utilitarian morals

The second problem with the Argument from Expediency is that it seems to equate principled moral reasoning with reasoning that is not dependent on the calculation of consequences. But utilitarian reasoning is based on principles. For example, a utilitarian moral principle might be that every action should bring about more pleasure than pain. To be sure, such a principle may not be compatible with the principles of theistic ethics. However, this shows nothing about whether or not atheistic morality is based on principles.

The third problem is that the argument assumes that torture, slavery, and punishment of the innocent are always wrong. But despite what critics claim, such actions can be morally right in certain circumstances. Anyone who denies this must account for the strong moral appeal of the following hypothetical example: Suppose a powerful evil alien orders you to perform a morally horrible act such as the torture of a small child. The alien gives you the following choice: Either you torture the child, or he will destroy Earth. Would it not be morally right to torture the child?

Although I have used a science fiction example to challenge the claim that any act is wrong in all circumstances, utilitarianism can give an account of moral reasoning that is not dependent on direct calculations of consequences. Utilitarian theorists might use two different strategies for showing that consequences are not always directly calculated. First, distinguishing between utilitarianism as a decision procedure for ethics and as a criterion of moral rightness,[14] they could admit that utilitarianism, as a decision procedure, would result in reasoning in which the consequences are always calculated, but deny that utilitarianism, as a criterion of right, would have this problem. Indeed, there might well be excellent utilitarian justification for refraining from such calculations in the vast majority of situations. For example, in the vast majority of cases there could be good utilitarian reasons for unquestioned reliance on common sense moral principles such as "It is always wrong to torture."

So far we have talking about the objectivity of morality in the sense of there being moral facts. The second strategy would consist of utilitarians adopting an objective theory of value according to which value is based not on subjective psychological states such as pain, pleasure, and desires but on such things as the possession of certain character traits, the exercise of certain capacities, and the development of certain relations with others and the world.[15] Thus, one example of an objective value is a character trait that refrains as a matter of principle from torturing infants and punishing the innocent.

Another problem with the Argument from Expediency is that it mistakenly assumes that all secular ethicists are utilitarians. Peter Byrne has argued that a virtue ethics admits "goodness and badness, right and wrong, in the structure of the moral relationships and it can see them embodied in the acts themselves (arising out their relationship of habits of choice in life as a whole)."[16] In such a system of virtue ethics there need be no calculation of consequences; rather moral choice would be a manifestation of virtue.

Finally, the Argument from Expediency fails to address the problems theistic ethics itself faces in justifying its absolute prohibitions against torture, slavery, and the like. For example, on a simple divine command theory, since there is nothing intrinsic in an act of torture that makes it wrong, torture is wrong simply because God forbids it. The command not to torture seems arbitrary and hence does not provide moral grounds for obeying it. If there is something intrinsically wrong with torture, then surely it is not to be done even if God does not exist.

Three Arguments from Derivation are based on the work of Mackie, who maintains that without belief in God objective morality in the sense of moral facts would be "queer," that is, strange or odd. He says that this queerness has both an epistemological and a metaphysical aspect. According to him, claims about moral facts must be based on moral intuitions, which are epistemologically problematic. In addition, objective morality has a metaphysical aspect in that if there were moral facts, they would by their very nature be prescriptive. But then a person's behavior would not be motivated by the contingent fact that he or she desires such and such an end. The motivation would be intrinsic to the fact itself, which means in turn that the prescriptive quality would be an inherent aspect of the fact and not something external to it.[17] However, Mackie argues that this built-in or intrinsic prescriptive quality is strange and incongruous with a naturalistic view of the world. This Argument from Queerness can be stated in the following way:

1. If there were moral facts, they would have an intrinsic prescriptive quality.
2. If moral facts have an intrinsic prescriptive quality, then naturalism is not true.
3. Naturalism is true.
4. Hence, there are no moral facts.
4a. Therefore, objective morality is impossible.

One way to meet this argument is to challenge premise (2) by arguing that the inherently prescriptive nature of moral facts is compatible with a nontheistic view of the world.[18] Another more plausible way is to challenge (1) by arguing that moral facts are not inherently prescriptive. If a moral fact is motivational, this is contingent both on what the moral fact is and the psychological state of the agent.[19]

Now according to Peter Byrne's reading of Mackie's theory, Mackie says that values are not independent of human collective choice.[20] The only other alternative envisaged by Mackie is a divinely inspired purpose behind human nature that will determine our good independent of our choice or our desire. In other words, in this view humans have a proper function. However, since Mackie was an atheist he rejected this alternative as false. Stated more formally, Mackie's Argument from Proper Function is this:

1. If objective morality is possible, then human beings must have a proper function.
2. If human beings must have a proper function, then God must exist.
3. God does not exist.
4. Hence, objective morality is impossible.

One problem with the Argument for Proper Function is premise (1), for there seems to be no reason to suppose that objective morality presupposes that human beings have a proper function. There are many ways to argue for objective morality. Although an argument from proper function certainly could be one way to support objective morality, there is no reason to suppose it is the only way.[21]

Moreover, premise (2) is also dubious in that the proper function approach to objective morality need not be based on God. Thus, for example, Byrne has argued that there is a characteristic good for human beings because there is a characteristic form of activity that is human. He describes this characteristic good as graspable by reason and as real in the only sense that matters; namely, that it can be used to explain phenomena (for example, the convergence of moral opinion after proper argument) that cannot be explained without it. However, Byrne develops his view without any obvious reliance on God.[22]

Another Argument from Derivation based on Mackie's work rests on the fact of ethical disagreement. Mackie realized that disagreement in science does not undermine our belief in scientific objectivity, but he held that there is a basic difference between science and ethics. Most scientific disputes are resolvable in principle, he believed, whereas many ethical disputes are not. Mackie's position seems to have been that ethical disputes would only be resolvable in principle if there were antecedent agreement concerning general moral principles and the disagreement were the result of different applications of these principles. But his position was that there are genuine disputes. The Argument from Disagreement can be stated as follows:

1. If there were moral facts, then there would not be widespread ethical disagreement.
2. There is widespread ethical disagreement.
3. Hence, there are no moral facts.
3a. Hence, there is no objective morality.

This argument is unsound and the problematic premise is (1). First of all, in order for all disputes to be reconcilable in principle the people engaged in them must be fully informed, fully rational, and have sufficient time for deliberation. In many cases, there is no reason to suppose that these conditions have been met. For example, many moral disputes may be the result of nonculpable ignorance of nonmoral facts, such as whether a particular economic policy would increase the standard of living. Second, in science one can imagine cases in which agreement is not even possible in principle because of systematic error. For example, a person in a factual dispute over some scientific or historical occurrence may start off with false psychological hypotheses about human nature. In this case one would hardly expect agreement in principle to be possible. Systematic error may also occur in moral disputes, thus precluding agreement in principle. Third, even barring systematic error, the existence of moral facts does not require that all ethical disputes are reconcilable in principle. There can be moral ties where one position does not have any overall advantage over another. Moreover, the existence of moral facts is compatible with some moral considerations being incommensurable with others. In such cases, two moral positions are not equal but incomparable. In addition, Mackie is mistaken to think that agreement in principle must be based on antecedent agreement on general ethical principles. In one well-known model (the coherentist model) of moral agreement, agreement is brought about by the mutual adjustment of general moral principles and judgments in particular cases. David Brink, a contemporary ethical philosopher, puts it in this way:

> Ideally, we make trade-offs among the various levels of generality of beliefs in such a way as to maximize initial commitment, overall consistency, explanatory power and so on. The fact that we disagree about some moral issues at the beginning of the process of adjustment gives no compelling reason to suppose the adjustment will not, in the limit, resolve our disagreement.[23]

In addition, Mackie maintains that in order to explain moral disputes, moral realists must assume that many moral facts are contingent. Necessary moral facts would only be associated with the common moral principles that allegedly underlie disputes. For reasons that are unclear, Mackie supposed that advocates of objectivity are committed to *necessary* moral facts. However, there is no reason to suppose that this is so.

Finally, the existence of widespread disagreement on ethical matters is a problem for theists and can be used against such ethics. Consider the following modification of the Argument from Disagreement:

1. If a theistic-based ethics were possible, there would be moral facts.
2. If there were moral facts, then there would not be widespread ethical disagreement among theists.
3. There is widespread ethical disagreement among theists.
4. Hence, a theistic-based ethics is not possible.

To be sure, theistic ethical theorists could attempt to answer this argument by raising objections to premise (2) just as I have done. Whether or not this defense would be successful, such a defense is surely necessary. Without it this argument would undermine the attempt to base ethics on God.

The fifth Argument from Derivation, based on the Transcendental Argument for the Existence of God, purports to show that logic, science, and objective morality presuppose the existence of the Christian God. Many theistic apologists have maintained that morality is impossible without God. The Transcendental Argument takes this argument one step further and maintains that atheists *presuppose the Christian worldview* when they assume objective morality. This was the position taken by the Christian apologist Greg Bahnsen, who argued that atheists "have a problem of evil" in that they assume that there is evil in the world, which is incompatible with God's goodness and power, yet they can give no account of evil in terms of objective morality. But then, atheists cannot assert that there is objective evil in the world since in their view evil must be subjective and relative.[24]

The ethical part of Bahnsen's argument can be stated as follows:

1. If there is objective morality, then the Christian worldview is true.
2. Atheists assume objective morality.
3. Therefore, atheists assume that the Christian worldview is true.

However, supposing that the above argument is sound, at best the argument shows that atheists are inconsistent: that they profess not to believe in the Christian God but tacitly assume his existence. In order to avoid this presumed inconsistency they have two choices, not one: They can convert to Christianity or they can give up objective morality. Bahnsen tries to make the latter choice difficult by maintaining that atheists cannot hold the views that they want to hold if they reject moral objectivity. But Bahnsen provides no reasons for giving up moral objectivity.

One of Bahnsen's main arguments for maintaining that atheists cannot appeal to objective morality without presupposing the Christian world-view is that atheism is committed to materialism, the view that matter in motion is all there is. Because he holds that materialism is incompatible with the absolute and unchanging normative character of ethical principles, he claims that atheists cannot coherently appeal to such principles.[25]

Of course, even if Bahnsen's argument from materialism is unsound this does not show that atheism is compatible with objective morality. However, one factual reason for thinking that it is compatible is that ethical systems based on objective morality have been formed that are independent of religion in general and of Christian theism in particular and these systems have not been refuted. Another reason is an a priori one. The Transcendental Argument is supposed to show that objective morality logically presupposes the existence of the Christian God. In other words, premise (1) purports to be necessarily true. But in that case the following would be a contradiction.

~1. Objective morality exists and the Christian worldview is false.

However, this statement seems completely consistent, and until it is shown otherwise we are justified in supposing it is.

ARGUMENTS FROM MATERIALISM AND NATURALISM

It is taken for granted by many religious apologists that atheism is committed to materialism; that is, to the theory that physical matter is the only reality and that everything including thought, feeling, mind, will, and the abstract objects of logic and mathematics can be explained in terms of matter and physical phenomena. Moreover, religious apologists assume that physical matter is valueless. Given these assumptions it is easy to conclude that an atheistic world must be a world without moral facts. Stated more formally, the Argument from Materialism is this:

1. If atheists are committed to materialism, then they cannot assume that there are moral facts.

2. Atheists are committed to materialism.
3. Hence, atheists cannot assume that there are moral facts.
3a. Hence, atheists cannot assume an objective morality.

There are two basic problems with this argument. First, premise (2) is false. Not all atheists are committed to materialism. Many modern atheists have a pluralistic ontology in which material entities comprise only one kind of entity in their ontology. Bertrand Russell, for example, believed in abstract mathematical entities. To be sure, many atheists do embrace naturalism; that is, the system of thought holding that all phenomena can be explained in terms of natural causes and laws without attributing spiritual or supernatural significance to them. However, naturalism does not entail materialism: That a phenomenon is natural does not mean it is material. Moreover, some atheists even reject naturalism in favor of intuitionism. They believe that moral properties are *sui generis* and thus not identifiable with either natural or supernatural properties.

In addition, to the falsehood of premise (2) premise (1) is questionable. It is certainly not obvious that moral facts are incompatible with materialism. One need not suppose that values are reducible to matter in any important senses of "reducible." One need only assume that matter constitutes moral properties. In this case, morally wrong, although constituted by physical properties, is not identical with them since the property of being morally wrong could be, but is not, exemplified in nonmaterial entities.[26] For example, the compassion is exemplified in material objects. But if supernatural objects existed, it could be exemplified in them.

Religious apologists give no well-articulated argument to support their view that materialism is incompatible with objective morality. The only plausible argument that I have been able to construct for them seems to commit the fallacy of composition—the fallacy of arguing that every part of whole has a property to the conclusion that the whole has this property. Thus, they might be arguing from the materialistic premise

M_1. The ultimate elements of the world (material particles) are in constant flux.

to the conclusion

M_2. Ethical principles, which are composed of material particles, are in constant flux.

Since M_2 is incompatible with unchanging ethical standards and also presumably with objective morality one concludes that materialism is incompatible with such standards. However, the argument is fallacious in that the conclusion M_2 no more follows from premise M_1 than the conclusion that the army is weak follows from the premise that the members of the army are weak.

Arguing not from materialism but from naturalism other apologists for theism maintain that naturalism is committed to assumptions that make moral facts impossible. For example, Christian apologist David Beck presents this argument to support his position:

1. Morality is an objective feature of our universe.
2. Naturalistic "explanations" of the objectivity of morality are inadequate.
3. Therefore, there must be a universal personal authority that is the source of morality.

He argues:

This point [premise (2)] is not especially controversial. Most naturalists concede it. Since any form of naturalistic evolution denies human freedom, it must deny responsibility, and hence it cannot be that my actions have any value. For B. F. Skinner, all that remains is a "technology of behavior." Our values are arbitrary judgments. They are decisions that we make. Only persons who have the freedom to select views and actions can have the requisite right to make moral choice possible and to actually decide on moral values or actions for themselves.

Social explanations of moral objectivity do not account for moral value. While it is often asserted that values derive from our society, culture, religion, parents, school and friends, at least two arguments show this to be wrong. First, we often think it plausible to make evaluative moral judgments about our own peers, as well as other societies. We could not, for example, evaluate Hitler's Germany if this were not so. Second, the fact that as free persons we are all equal makes it impossible for any one finite person to determine value for any other person.

No other human person has the moral authority to make decisions about right or wrong for me. This, however, leads to a dilemma. Only persons can be the source of values, yet no finite and socially conditioned person is in a position to determine authoritatively the values appropriate for other persons. So, if there really are objective values, there must be some "ultimate" person who has the moral authority to set the standards of right and wrong.[27]

There are many things wrong with Beck's argument. First, assuming that Beck means objective morality in the sense of moral facts premise (2) is controversial. The only naturalist he cites is Skinner, whose views most naturalists reject. Naturalists who believe in objective morality would reject Beck's claim. Second, few forms of naturalism deny human freedom. To be sure, Skinner did but he is hardly representative. Of course, naturalists reject contracausal freedom (freedom in which human choices are uncaused by prior events in the brain or nervous system), but most naturalists have defended the compatibilist sense of freedom (freedom which is based on the absence of coercion). This and not the contracausal sense is relevant to our ordinary judgments of responsibility in morality and law. For example, in the law a person is not responsible for a choice made under the threat of physical harm. The fact that the choice was caused by an event in the person's brain is irrelevant.

Third, Beck argues that no finite actual person can determine authoritatively another finite person's values. If he simply means that Mr. Jones has no moral or legal right to dictate Mr. Smith's values, this is true but irrelevant. Jones has no right to dictate Smith's factual beliefs either. But from this it does not follow that without belief in God Smith's values and factual beliefs and Jones's values and factual beliefs are equally valid. With respect to moral values, there might be good reason to believe that Smith is wrong and Jones right. For example, Jones's view about values might be based on solid evidence, an impartial appraisal of the situation, and an empathetic identification with the relevant moral actors while Smith's view is not. Notice that our judgment about Jones and Smith has nothing to do with there being an ultimate person who sets the standards of value.

CONCLUSION

As I said in the last chapter, although it would be regrettable if atheism were committed to the lack of an objective morality, this would not count against the truth of atheism. But the results of this chapter indicate that atheists should have no regrets, because the arguments adduced by religious critics fail to show either that atheists have no motive or reason to follow an objective morality or that atheists cannot have an objective morality.

In this chapter I have shown that three of the main arguments for rejecting an atheistic objective morality are unsound. Two Arguments from Motivation fail because there is no reason why secular considerations cannot provide motivation or reasons for atheists to be moral. In addition, five Arguments from Derivation are unsound. Finally, two Arguments from Materialism and Naturalism are also unsuccessful. On the one hand, atheism is not committed to materialism and even if it were, there would be no a priori reason why in an objective morality values could not be constituted by matter. On the other hand, naturalism need not deny moral facts or human freedom.

Yet despite the failure of these arguments two major tasks of defending atheistic ethics remain. First, there is the positive job of developing and defending an atheistic metaethics and second, there is the negative labor of showing the difficulties of a theistic-based ethics. Completion of the first task will show that it is possible in principle to have a viable non-religious metaethics and that such a metaethics exists. Completion of the second task will indicate the superiority of a nonreligious foundation of ethic to a religious one.

NOTES

1. See Peter Byrne, *The Philosophical and Theological Foundations of Ethics*, 2d ed. (New York: St. Martin's, 1999), chap. 7.

2. Umakant Premanand Shah, "Jainism," in *Encyclopaedia Britannica*, 15th ed., (Chicago: Encyclopedia Britannica, Inc., 1984), vol. 10, pp. 8–14; Ninian Smart, "Jainism," in *The Encyclopedia of Philosophy*, ed. Paul Edwards (New York: Macmillan and Free Press, 1967), vol. 4, pp. 238–39; E. Royston

Pike, *Encyclopaedia of Religion and Religions* (New York: Meridian Books, 1958), pp. 203–205; Herbert Stroup, *Four Religions of Asia* (New York: Harper and Row, 1968), pp. 81–114.

3. Jim Herrick, *Against the Faith* (London: Glover and Blair, 1985), p. 96.

4. Terry L. Meyers, "Percy Bysshe Shelley," *Encyclopedia of Unbelief*, ed. Gordon Stein (Amherst, N.Y.: Prometheus Books, 1985), vol. 2, p. 621.

5. Philip M. Smith, "Organized Religion and Criminal Behavior," *Sociology and Social Research* 33 (1949): 632–37.

6. See, for example, Philip M. Smith, "Role of Church in Delinquency Prevention," *Sociology and Social Research* 35 (1951): 183–90; Travis Hirschi and Rodney Stark, "Hellfire and Delinquency," *Social Problems* 17 (1969): 202–13. A more recent study commissioned by the National Catholic Educational Association of 16,000 public and nonpublic high school seniors shows that students in Catholic high schools are more likely to use alcohol, cocaine, and marijuana and are more likely to steal. See Edd Doerr, "Bashing Public Education," *Humanist* (July/August 1987): 43.

7. Clifford Kirkpatrick, "Religion and Humanitarianism: A Study of Institutional Implications," *Psychological Monographs* 63, no. 9 (1949). Indeed, Kirkpatrick found a negative relation between religious belief and a humanitarian attitude.

8. Richard L. Gorsuch and Daniel Aleshire, "Christian Faith and Ethnic Prejudice: A Review and Interpretation of Research," *Journal for the Scientific Study of Religion* 13 (1974): 281.

9. Adolf Grünbaum, "The Poverty of Theistic Morality," http://www.infidels.org/library/modern/adolf_grunbaum/poverty.html. This essay was originally published in *Science, Mind and Art: Essays on Science and the Humanistic Understanding in Art. Epistemology, Religion, and Ethics in Honor of Robert S. Cohen*. Boston Studies in the Philosophy of Science, vol. 165 (Dordrecht, The Netherlands: Kluwer Academic Publisher, 1995), pp. 203–42.

10. See Byrne, *Philosophical and Theological Foundations*.

11. An argument similar to this has been developed by George I. Mavrodes in "Religion and the Queerness of Morality," in *Rationality, Religious Belief, and Moral Commitment*, ed. Robert Audi and William J. Wainwright (Ithaca, N.Y.: Cornell University Press, 1986), pp. 213–26.

12. Byrne, *Philosophical and Theological Foundations*, pp. 136–37.

13. Ibid., p. 138.

14. David Brink, *Moral Realism and the Foundations of Ethics* (New York: Cambridge University Press, 1989), pp. 216–17.

15. Ibid., pp. 217–37.

16. Byrne, *Philosophical and Theological Foundations*, p. 138.

17. J. L. Mackie, *Ethics: Inventing Right and Wrong* (New York: Penguin Books, 1979), p. 40.

18. See, for example, Thomas Nagel, *The Possibility of Altruism* (Princeton, N.J.: Princeton University Press, 1970); J. McDowell, "Are Moral Requirements Hypothetical Imperatives?" *Proceedings of the Aristotelian Society* (1979): supp. vol. 13–29.

19. See Brink, "Moral Realism and the Skeptical Arguments from Disagreement and Queerness," *Australasian Journal of Philosophy* 62 (1984): 111–22, and Brink, *Moral Realism and the Foundations of Ethics*.

20. Byrne, *Philosophical and Theological Foundations*, p. 141.

21. See, for example, Roderick Firth, "Ethical Absolutism and the Ideal Observer," *Readings in Ethical Theory*, 2d ed., ed. Wilfrid Sellars and John Hospers (Englewood Cliffs, N.J.: Prentice-Hall, 1970); Richard Boyd, "How to Be a Moral Realist," and Peter Railton, "Moral Realism," in *Moral Discourse and Practice*, ed. Stephen Darwall, Allan Gibbard, and Peter Railton (Oxford: Oxford University Press, 1997); Brink, *Moral Realism*, pp. 37–39, 197–203.

22. Byrne, *Philosophical and Theological Foundations*, chap. 6 and pp. 142–43.

23. Brink, *Moral Realism*, p. 204.

24. On the other hand, according to Bahnsen, believers have no logical problem of evil. There is no logical contradiction between the propositions that God is all-powerful and all-good and there exists evil in the world. For if God is all-good, He has a sufficient moral reason for evil although we do not know what it is. We must trust God. However, I have argued in detail in *Atheism: A Philosophical Justification* (Philadelphia: Temple University Press, 1990), chap. 14, that this solution to the problem of evil is mistaken for although there is no formal logical contradiction between the existence of evil and the existence of an all-good, all-powerful God, one can construct a strong inductive argument that there is no morally sufficient reason for God to allow evil.

25. See his taped lecture "The Debate That Never Was," available through the Covenant Tape Ministry, 22005 N. Vend Drive, Sun City West, AZ 85375. Bahnsen uses a similar argument to show that logic is incompatible with atheism.

26. See Brink, *Philosophical and Theological Foundations*, pp. 156–68.

27. David Beck, "God's Existence," in *In Defense of Miracles*, ed. Garry Habermas and R. Douglas Geivett (Downers Grove, Ill.: Intervarsity Press, 1997), pp. 160–62.

3

THE
IDEAL
OBSERVER
THEORY

INTRODUCTION

I n the last chapter one crucial step in the defense of nonreligious metaethics was completed: It was shown that the major arguments against nonreligious ethics can be answered. However, this defense would be strengthened by two additions. First, my defense would be more powerful if a positive account of the meaning of ethical expressions that is not committed to religion could be provided. By this I mean an analysis of ethical terms such as "morally obligated," and "morally forbidden" that does not use theological terms in the analysis. Assuming that such an analysis is impossible, however, my account would be helped if one could provide an account of the conditions under which ethical statements are true that does not presuppose God. Second, my position needs a positive account of how ethical judgments can be rationally justified in a way that does not assume religious beliefs. For example, my account needs a way of justifying ethical decisions that does not assume knowledge of God's desires and wants. In this chapter these challenges will be met.

THE IDEAL OBSERVER THEORY

In my opinion the Ideal Observer Theory is the most plausible theory there is to explain the meaning of ethical expressions. This theory has a long and distinguished history. Adam Smith accepted a version of it in the eighteenth century, and according to some interpretations of his philosophy, David Hume also held this theory. In the twentieth century Frank Chapman Sharp, C. D. Broad, Roderick Firth, Thomas Carson, and William Frankena espoused the Ideal Observer Theory in various forms.

The basic idea behind the Ideal Observer Theory is simple. The meaning of ethical expressions such as "It was morally wrong of Jones to steal the book," "There is a prima facie moral duty to keep promises," and "Gratuitous torture is morally wrong" is analyzed in terms of the ethically significant reactions of an observer who has certain ideal properties such as being fully informed and completely impartial. Thus, for example, the expression "morally wrong" is analyzed along the following lines:

1. X is morally wrong = If there were an Ideal Observer, it would contemplate X with a feeling of disapproval.

Although there are some commonalties, precisely what nonethical properties constitute the properties of an Ideal Observer will vary to some extent with the different Ideal Observer theorists. Note, however, that in order to avoid circularity the ethically significant reactions of an Ideal Observer are certain moral feelings or other experiences and not moral beliefs. Otherwise the analysis would contain the very ethical terms it is supposed to define, and so would be circular.

Note also that the theory does not suppose that Ideal Observers actually exist. Rather, the analysis is stated in terms of a contrary-to-fact conditional: if there *were* an Ideal Observer, it *would* react in certain way. Moreover, the term "ideal" is not to be taken in some ethical sense. On the contrary, the phrase "ideal observer" is used in approximately the same way as "perfect vacuum" or "frictionless machine." In other words, an Ideal Observer's properties of being fully informed and being completely unbiased are in principle reducible to empirical properties and are not ethical ideals on a par with being completely just or fully benevolent.

The basic idea of the Ideal Observer Theory as a theory of justification follows directly from the Ideal Observer Theory as a theory of meaning. It is that in order to be rationally justified in one's ethical judgments about some action or event one must base these judgments on one's estimate of the reaction of an Ideal Observer. One way of doing this would be to approximate to the characteristics of Ideal Observer and see what one's own reaction would be. For example, to be ethically justified in holding that it is morally wrong for John to lie to Mary, one could become well informed with respect to the relevant facts, be impartial, and so on and determine if one had a feeling of disapproval. The more one approximates to these and other ideal characteristics the more one's reaction would be morally trustworthy.

This theory has strong initial plausibility as both a theory of meaning and theory of justification for several reasons. For one thing, it coheres with our ordinary views about what qualifies people as moral judges. For example, we might reject someone's moral judgments on the grounds that he lacked certain relevant information. Here we seem to be appealing to one property of an Ideal Observer: being fully informed. We might accept a person's ethical views because he or she is unbiased. In this case we seem to be appealing to another property of an Ideal Observer: impartiality. In addition, our common sense observations seem to confirm what one would expect if the Ideal Observer Theory were true. Ethical opinion tends to converge as people approximate to Ideal Observers. For example, as people become well informed and less biased, their ethical opinions tend to come together. Moreover, one version of Ideal Observer Theory, namely Roderick Firth's, has several attractive features: It allows for moral facts, excludes ethical relativism, coheres with a naturalistic worldview, and fits into a widely accepted way of justifying ethical and scientific judgments.

FIRTH'S IDEAL OBSERVER THEORY

General Remarks

Here I will consider the most fully developed and best-known contemporary version of the Ideal Observer Theory, that developed by Roderick Firth.[1] Firth's Ideal Observer Theory is a form of ethical cognitivism, the position that ethical statements are either true or false. This is so because in his theory ethical statements have the same meaning as hypothetical statements about the reactions of an Ideal Observer. Since these latter are either true or false, so are ethical statements. Firth's Ideal Observer is also a form of ethical naturalism, the position that ethical statements are either identical with or constituted by natural facts. This is so because the hypothetical statements about an Ideal Observer are just as much about natural facts as are the hypothetical statements about a frictionless machine.

In addition, Firth's Ideal Observer Theory is a semantic thesis concerning the meaning of ethical expressions. In particular, it holds that ethical statements are identical in cognitive meaning with statements that are in principle capable of empirical verification. Firth was not saying, however, that when ethical terms such as "morally right" are analyzed they are prima facie or "intuitively" equivalent to the terms used in the analysis. After all, he said, his analysis is complex and it may not be immediately obvious to the typical speaker of English that a moral expression is synonymous with an expression about the reactions of an Ideal Observer. Moreover, since the Ideal Observer analysis attempts to capture only the *cognitive* meaning of ethical expressions, the language used in the analysis may not have the same *emotional* meaning as the ethical term being analyzed.

Firth's Ideal Observer Theory also makes ethical expressions absolute rather than relative. An analysis of an ethical expression is absolute, he says, if it does not contain egocentric terms. An expression is, in turn, egocentric if its meaning varies systematically with the speaker. Such expressions include personal pronouns ("I," "you," etc.), the corresponding possessive adjectives ("my," "your," etc.), words which refer to spatial and temporal locations ("this," "that," "here," "there," "now," "then," "past," "present," "future"), and reflexive expressions such as "the person who is speaking." Clearly the analysis given in (1) above is absolute in this sense since it contains no egocentric particulars. On the other hand, the analysis provided in the following is not absolute but relative:

2. X is morally obligatory = X is approved of in *this culture*

One consequence of a relativistic analysis like (2) is that it would be possible for one person to say correctly that an act is morally obligatory and another to say correctly that it is not without contradicting each other.[2] In contrast, an Ideal Observer analysis of ethical expressions such as (1) entails that Ideal Observers would agree in their ethical reactions, indeed, that it would be impossible for them to disagree.

Firth's Ideal Observer Theory provides for objective morality in two of the senses introduced earlier. Since there are moral facts, it entails moral objectivity in this sense. In addition, it is compatible with, although it does not require, moral objectivity in the sense of nonsubjective values. That is, instead of moral value being based on subjective psychological states such as pain, pleasure, and desires, moral value is based on non-subjective states. These would include character traits, the exercise of certain capacities, the development of certain relations with others and the world. In addition, his theory is objective in a third sense for a proposed analysis of ethical statements is objective if it could be true even if there were no actual experiencing subjects past, present, and future. The truth of (1) depends on the reactions of Ideal Observers and although Ideal Observers are experiencing subjects they are hypothetical, not actual.

Firth pointed out that if his analysis were correct, ethical statements would have the same form that statements about secondary qualities such as colors are often thought to have. For example, many philosophers have maintained that to say that a daffodil is yellow is to say that it would appear yellow under certain conditions. Here yellow is a *relational* property of physical objects. Moral properties on Firth's analysis are also relational properties for moral wrongness is what brings about a feeling of disapproval in an Ideal Observer under certain conditions. Of course, the term "yellow" might also have a nonrelational sense: for example, it might refer to a property of sense data (apparent yellowness) which is simple and unanalyzable. Now, Firth argues that ethical terms can have the same ambiguity. The term "morally right" might have a nonrelational meaning that refers to a characteristic of human experience (apparent rightness) that is just as simple and unanalyzable as yellow.

Firth's analysis is also empirical. In the first place, the characteristics of an Ideal Observer are idealized psychological properties that are capable of empirical verification. Moreover, the ethically significant reactions of an Ideal Observer are feelings of approval and disapproval and other psychological states and these are empirical experiences. Finally, the Ideal Observer Theory asserts that there is a relation between the characteristic of Ideal Observers and these feelings and other psychological states. This relation is also capable of empirical verification by extrapolation from actual cases. Just as we can confirm how frictionless machines would react by extrapolating from machines that approximate to a frictionless state, so we can confirm how an Ideal Observer would react by extrapolating from human beings that approximate to Ideal Observers.

How exactly do these morally significant reactions manifest themselves in consciousness as moral data? Firth's analysis is compatible with alternative phenomenological accounts. In one such account, the moral data are the feelings or emotions or other elements of experience in the judge's consciousness. These would appear as states of the judge herself and not as an objective property of an act or object the judge is conscious of. For example, the moral data for the moral wrongness of murder would be the subjective feeling of disapproval manifested in the judge's consciousness and not an objective property of the murder. However, in an alternative account, moral data appearing in the consciousness of a moral judge would seem to be one of the objective properties of the envisaged goal or act and not just a subjective feeling. For example, moral wrongness of murder would appear as an objective property of the act of murder. Both of these accounts, Firth said, are compatible with an Ideal Observer analysis.

The epistemic function of moral data when understood in either way is analogous to the function of color sensations in justifying one's belief that an object is really yellow. If one were in doubt about the correct solution to a moral problem or were attempting to justify a moral belief, one would appeal to the subjective feeling or to an apparent property of the act. Such an appeal would carry little weight, however, unless it was made under conditions that approximated to an Ideal Observer. When justifying one's belief that an object is really yellow something similar is true. Unless a color sensation were experienced under certain conditions, for example, in good lighting conditions, it would carry little weight in justifying the belief that the object is really yellow.

Content

So far I have said nothing about the specific content of Firth's Ideal Observer analysis; that is, about the specific properties that in this view constitute an Ideal Observer. According to Firth an Ideal Observer has the following characteristics: omniscience with respect to nonethical facts, omnipercipience (which will be discussed shortly), disinterestedness, dispassionateness, consistency, and normalcy in other respects. Firth argued that in determining the characteristics of an Ideal Observer we must examine the procedures that we either implicitly or explicitly actually regard as rational in deciding ethical questions. He selected these characteristics by a method he described as pragmatic. For example, we regard the procedures of gathering factual information and suppressing emotions we think are prejudicial as rational in making ethical decisions. These may suggest certain characteristics of an Ideal Observer such as being all-knowing and being dispassionate.

Now Firth argued that to arrive at a satisfactory analysis of ethical terms one must experiment with various concrete formulations, but that it would be a serious error to suppose that any inadequacies of particular formulations indicate that the general idea of the analysis is wrong. For example, ethical terms, like all terms, are used in different ways in different contexts. So a correct analysis of an ethical statement in one context is not necessarily a correct analysis of an ethical statement in another context although the two sentences are symbolized in exactly the same way. Firth distinguished this accidental and unsystematic ambiguity of ethical statements from the systematic ambiguity characteristic of relativism. To be sure, it may prevent philosophers from agreeing on a concrete analysis of ethical statements, but it should not prevent them from agreeing on the general form of an absolutist dispositional analysis. In what follows I will take Firth's warning seriously and will not hesitate to modify concrete formulations of Firth's analyses while trying to preserve his general formulations.

1. Omniscience with Respect to Nonmoral Facts

Firth pointed out that we sometimes disqualify ourselves as a judge of a particular moral question on the ground that we are not sufficiently familiar with the facts of the case. We also believe that one person is a better moral judge than another if, other things being equal, the one has more relevant factual information than the other. This suggests that the Ideal Observer must be characterized in part by its knowledge of nonmoral facts. To be sure, the Ideal Observer could know moral facts but such knowledge, according to Firth, is not essential to being an Ideal Observer.[3]

How then is one to characterize the knowledge required of an Ideal Observer? One might be tempted to say that an Ideal Observer has all relevant knowledge, but Firth argued that this will not do: One cannot without circularity *define* an Ideal Observer as having all relevant factual knowledge. To be sure, one could try to define factual information as being irrelevant to the morality of act A by saying that the reaction of the Ideal Observer would be the same whether or not Ideal Observer had this information. But this assumes the concept of an Ideal Observer in definition of relevant knowledge and consequently is circular.

Because of this problem Firth insisted that the Ideal Observer must be omniscient with respect to nonmoral facts. He maintained that this requirement is neither extravagant nor mysterious. There is no point where one can be logically certain that further information would be irrelevant. Consequently, a satisfactory ethical analysis must be formulated in which no nonmoral facts are irrelevant *by definition*. However, this requires that an Ideal Observer know all nonmoral facts.

Firth stressed that the Ideal Observer must have complete knowledge of the past as well as of the future. Thus the Ideal Observer analysis of ethical terms is compatible with both deontological and teleological ethical theories; that is, with theories that maintain that past events are morally relevant to evaluating present action and with those theories that deny this.

As I have argued elsewhere, however, it is dubious that omniscience is a coherent notion.[4] For example, it is dubious that an Ideal Observer could know of certain indexical knowledge. An Ideal Observer could not know that I spilled my soup although it could know that Michael Martin did. Moreover an Ideal Observer could not know the set of all truths since the set of all truths is an incoherent notion.

How then should an Ideal Observer's knowledge be characterized? Some attempts have been made to characterize the knowledge of an Ideal Observer in less than the omniscient terms so as to avoid Firth's circularity objection. However, whether these are completely adequate is uncertain.[5] Nevertheless, one has a pretty good idea of how in negative terms an Ideal Observer's knowledge should be characterized in order to avoid the incoherence of omniscience. For example, if what I have just said is correct, the Ideal Observer could not have all indexical knowledge and could not know the set of all truths. Excluding these sorts of problems leaves us with an Ideal Observer who, although not omniscient with respect to all nonmoral facts, is as knowledgeable as coherence allows.

In addition, it seems possible to exclude from the knowledge of an Ideal Observer certain irrelevant facts without begging any questions. By definition morality has to do with moral agents and other living beings. But there is good reason to suppose in terms of our background information that there are an infinite number of nonmoral facts that will exist billions of years *after* the extinction of moral agents and other living things. Ignorance of these facts would by definition be irrelevant to the reaction of an Ideal Observer since it would not affect the attitudes and feelings of an Ideal Observer. For example, suppose life becomes permanently extinct in the universe at time t. What happens a billion years after t will not affect the Ideal Observer's reactions. If the Ideal Observer were a pure deontologist, such knowledge of the future would be irrelevant to the feelings the Ideal Observer would have about moral issues at or before time t. Even if the Ideal Observer were a teleologist, knowledge of the universe after t plus one billion years would be irrelevant. What happens after t plus one billion years could not possibly affect the welfare of living things.

Moreover, although the requirement that an Ideal Observer be omniscient is too strong, it can be argued that in other respects the knowledge requirement must be strengthened. Thus, Thomas Carson, an American philosopher, has suggested that it is possible to interpret the knowledge requirement of an Ideal Observer so as to insure consistent reactions of different Ideal Observers. For example, he says that an Ideal Observer must be free from self-deception. Although this would seem to follow from any plausible account of an Ideal Observer's knowledge, it is not clear that his other suggested additions do. Carson argues that one should stipulate that an Ideal Observer must be an Ideal Observer during its entire lifetime and thus during its lifetime always be well informed. Firth does not explicitly require this, but it seems compatible with his views and might help to solve the following problem. One might argue that if an Ideal Observer only became an Ideal Observer in its adult life, it might have been indoctrinated to accept some false views in its early years that resulted in its being emotionally scarred and in its having irrational desires. This requirement would block this possibility. Similarly, according to Carson, one should require that an Ideal Observer only be influenced by other Ideal Observers. This would prevent an Ideal Observer from being influenced by parents, peers, and role models who were laboring under irrational beliefs and desires.[6] Again although this requirement is not stated by Firth, it is compatible with his views.

Whether Carson's additions are necessary is uncertain. However, if they are not, adding them will cause no harm, whereas if they are necessary, their addition will strengthen the Ideal Observer Theory. I will therefore adopt them here.

I conclude that although it is not absolutely clear how the knowledge of an Ideal Observer should be defined in positive terms, we have a good idea what knowledge an Ideal Observer cannot have. Moreover, defining an Ideal Observer in terms of omniscience with respect to all nonmoral facts is unnecessary.

2. Omnipercipience

Whether or not an Ideal Observer needs to be omniscient with respect to nonmoral facts, the Ideal Observer must have more than factual knowledge. As Firth says, we sometimes disqualify ourselves as judges of moral questions on the grounds that we cannot sufficiently imagine or visualize some of the relevant facts. We also regard one person a better moral judge than another if, other things being equal, he or she is better able to imagine or visualize the relevant facts. In other words, an Ideal Observer must be omnipercipient. This means that the Ideal Observer must be able to visualize simultaneously all actual facts and the consequences of all possible acts just as vividly as if "he were actually perceiving them all."[7] The attribution of such characteristics to the Ideal Observer, Firth says, is necessary since it guarantees that the Ideal Observer's "ethically significant reactions are forcefully and equitably stimulated."[8]

Now it is not clear if Firth's characterization of omnipercipience includes empathy; that is, the ability to identify with other sentient beings and feel their pain, terror, pleasure, and so on. But whatever his intentions, let us understand omnipercipience to include perfect and unlimited powers of empathy.[9] This construction is justified in terms of Firth's pragmatic method. As noted above, he argued that in determining the characteristics of an Ideal Observer we must examine the procedures that we either implicitly or explicitly actually regard as rational in deciding ethical questions. Empathizing is one of these procedures. We deem that one person is a better moral judge than another if, other things being equal, the one is better able than the other to empathize with the affected parties.

3. Disinterestedness

Firth pointed out that we sometimes disqualify ourselves as judges of moral questions on the grounds that we cannot make ourselves impartial. Moreover, we believe that one person is a better moral judge than another if, other things being equal, he or she is more impartial. This suggests, he said, that the Ideal Observer must be characterized as completely impartial.

But how is impartiality to be understood? Firth attempted to define impartiality in terms of disinterestedness. An ideal judge, he said, is impartial when he or she is not influenced by particular interests. Let us suppose the sole reason Crito wanted Socrates to escape from prison was that he believed Socrates was the wisest man who ever lived and did not want the wisest man who ever lived to be killed by his fellow human beings. In this case Crito's action was not determined by a particular interest for it was characterized without using proper names or terms such as "I," "here," "now," and "this." On the other hand, suppose Crito wanted Socrates to escape because he believed that Socrates was the wisest friend of Crito. Then Crito's action would have been based on a particular interest.

The problem with this interpretation of impartiality is that Firth's attribute of disinterestedness allows for morally objectionable consequences. Suppose that a racist or an anti-Semite is completely disinterested in his attitude toward African Americans or Jews in the sense that none of his interests are in terms of particular persons. For example, he desires to kill all African Americans and all Jews—not particular African Americans or Jews designated by proper names such as "Jefferson" or "Goldberg." Cannot "African American" or "Jews" be construed as proper names? This suggestion seems to run counter to Firth's Crito example. He assumed "Crito" was a proper name because it refers to a particular individual. But "African American" and "Jew" refer not to particulars but to a property or class. Indeed, if "African American" and "Jew" are considered proper names, it is unclear what is not a proper name.

Rather than employing an unduly expansive account of proper names one could expand Firth's example by characterizing impartiality as being uninfluenced by interests of the kind which are directed toward a specific person *and* displaying an attitude that would not be changed if positions were reversed.[10] Presumably the racist would not want to kill all African Americans if all whites (including him) were to become African Americans. This conclusion is strengthened when it is recalled that since the Ideal Observer has complete powers of empathy, the Ideal Observer would put himself in the place of the victims and would feel their pain and terror as if it were his own. Let us then understand disinterestedness to include a reversal requirement: An Ideal Observer could put itself in the place of others and feel what they would experience.

4. Dispassionateness

Firth pointed out that we sometimes disqualify ourselves as judges of moral questions on the grounds that we cannot make ourselves dispassionate. Moreover, we believe that one person is a better moral judge than another person if, other things being equal, the one is more dispassionate than the other. This suggests, he said, that the Ideal Observer must be characterized as completely dispassionate.

But how is dispassionateness to be understood? One possibility that Firth considered is to understand dispassionateness on the model of disinterestedness. Thus, an Ideal Observer is dispassionate in the sense that he is incapable of experiencing emotions such as jealousy, self-love, and personal hatred that are directed toward particular individuals as such.[11] But what about emotions that are not directed to particular individuals as such? Firth says that he has no a priori objections to attributing general emotions such as compassion for all-sentient beings and universal love to an Ideal Observer so long as these attributions are *not* justified by reference to the fact that these are moral virtues. Justifying them in this latter way would be circular since one would be using moral concepts to define something that is itself supposed to define moral notions.

Firth is skeptical that, other things being equal, the attributes of love and compassion make for better moral judges. However, if one excludes these as defining properties of the Ideal Observer, then his proposed analysis of dispassionateness is problematic in just the same way as his analysis of disinterestedness. A racist's hatred can be nonpersonal and directed toward all African Americans—not particular African Americans. Again a different interpretation of Firth's analysis of dispassionateness seems warranted in terms of reversibility. Consider, then, that an Ideal Observer is dispassionate in the sense that he is incapable of experiencing emotions that are directed toward particular individuals as such; moreover, his emotions would not be changed under appropriate conditions of reversal. Thus, presumably the racist would not hate all African Americans if the situation were reversed—that is, if all African Americans became white and all whites (including him) became African Americans. Again this conclusion is reinforced if one recalls that Ideal Observer has complete powers of empathy and would therefore experience the hatred directed at African Americans; that is, he would know directly what it is like to be an object of racial hatred.

Thomas Carson has suggested that there is another aspect of being an ideal observer as well: An Ideal Observer's attitude cannot involve emotional displacement. Now on one obvious reading this requirement is implicitly included under the rubric of dispassionateness. An Ideal Observer could not displace pent-up emotions such as hatred or anger from one group to another in order to achieve emotional gratification. Such displacement could not be part of the responses of an Ideal Observer since in this theory the correctness of action is based on the attitude that *it* would arouse in someone under ideal conditions. But in emotional displacement the action in question does not arouse the attitude; instead it is aroused by something else and displaced onto the action in question. Of course, not all moral judgments involving emotional displacement are mistaken; only those are that can only be maintained by someone who displaced emotion. In any case, let us understand a dispassionate person as someone who does not displace emotion in this inappropriate way.[12]

5. Consistency

Firth pointed out that consistency is ordinarily regarded as a characteristic of a good moral judge. Yet it is hard to define consistency without circularity and independently of the other characteristics of an Ideal Observer. Consider circularity. The consistency or inconsistency of any two ethical decisions depends on their relationship to certain general ethical principles. But then in order to define consistency we must already have ethical knowledge. Since ethical knowledge is analyzed in terms of the Ideal Observer, this attempt to define consistency is circular.

Now consider independence. Suppose one attempts to characterize consistency in more limited terms. For example, one might partly define the consistency of an Ideal Observer by saying that its ethically significant reaction to any particular act is always the same. But according to Firth, this definition is not independent of the other characteristics of an Ideal Observer. In attributing omniscience, disinterestedness, and other characteristics to the Ideal Observer one is attempting to eliminate factors that would cause people to have different reactions to the same act. Consequently, the consistency of the reaction of an Ideal Observer to the same act is a consequence of the Ideal Observer having these other attributes rather than independent of them. Firth concludes that consistency is not an independent property but is to be understood in terms of the other properties of an Ideal Observer.

6. Normalcy in Other Respects

Firth argues that aside from the ideal attributes mentioned above, an Ideal Observer is a normal human being. The concept of normalcy is not capable of precise definition, but nevertheless it is clear that an Ideal Observer is very different from the theistic God. God is necessarily all-powerful, all-good, and disembodied. Not only does an Ideal Observer not necessarily have any of these attributes, it could not have these attributes. Normal human beings are not all-powerful, all-good, and disembodied. Moreover, Ideal Observers are psychologically normal; for example, they have normal desires for friendship. In addition, normal human beings live in different societies and cultures.[13] Let us call Firth's understanding of normalcy *the standard interpretation* of the normalcy condition.

However, Charles Taliaferro has argued that Firth's restriction of Ideal Observers to the human species is puzzling since Firth himself wanted his theory to apply to other intelligent creatures, for example, extraterrestrial intelligences.[14] He suggests that Firth's normalcy qualification means only that an Ideal Observer's reactions are based solely on its ideal attributes. Let us call this interpretation *the modified interpretation* of the normalcy condition.

Carson has objected that in this modified interpretation Ideal Observers could have no reactions at all. "These highly abstract and indeterminate characteristics [of an Ideal Observer] generate the morally relevant attitudes of moral approval and disapproval only by interacting with the complex psychological characteristics and dispositions of moral appraisers."[15] Carson also infers from this that different complexes found in different species, for example, humans and Martians, would result in different reactions of human and Martian Ideal Observers. That this objection is sound is not obvious. It is not clear that the ideal attributes of an Ideal Observer could not generate morally relevant attitudes without interaction with other psychological characteristics and dispositions.

However, if this criticism is accepted, it suggests a still different interpretation. In what might be called the *necessary condition interpretation*, complex psychological characteristics and dispositions are necessary for the reactions of moral approval and disapproval of an Ideal Observer in the sense that without some complex set of characteristics and dispositions no moral reaction of an Ideal Observer would be possible. So on this point Carson is correct. But Carson may be mistaken to suppose that human and Martian Ideal Observers would react differently. It still may be the case that different sets would not have different effects on the reactions of approval of an Ideal Observer. Given any such set it is conceivable that the reactions of different Ideal Observers would be the same to the same moral situation.

How then in the necessary condition interpretation is the psychology of Ideal Observers to be understood? Although the ideal attributes of an Ideal Observer are not sufficient for moral approval, they are overriding and conclusive. They transform and modify the complex psychological innate and learned dispositions, irrational tendencies, and desires of members of any intelligent species in such a way that a feeling of moral approval is in the final analysis not determined by these dispositions. This would be a contingent fact about Ideal Observers and not true by definition. The supposition that it is true would be based on extrapolation from existing evidence. Thus, on the necessary condition interpretation Firth was mistaken to limit Ideal Observers to humans and Taliaferro is correct not to limit them. On the other hand, Taliaferro is wrong to suppose that the reaction of Ideal Observers is entirely a function of their ideal attributes and Carson is correct to challenge this. But Carson has erred in supposing that denying Taliaferro's point results in making the Ideal Observer's reaction relative.

MAKING ETHICAL DECISIONS

Although Firth did not say so explicitly, his Ideal Observer Theory suggests the following method of making ethical decisions: Approximate to the characteristics of an Ideal Observer by becoming well informed, empathetic, impartial, and so on. Obviously, it would be impossible to fulfill the characteristics of an Ideal Observer completely since they are ideal properties. But it is possible to approximate to these characteristics. This approximation need not be conscious or explicit. Indeed, sensitive moral individuals would tend to embody this approximation implicitly and automatically for their moral training would have instilled these characteristics in them as habitual tendencies. Consequently, their ordinary moral judgments would tend to be discerning and wise. However, even morally sensitive people who implicitly tend to approximate to the characteristics of an Ideal Observer might need to try explicitly to approximate these characteristics on occasions. When morally sensitive people disagree and discerning moral judgments pull in different directions, morally sensitive people may have to become more reflective and explicitly reexamine their evidence and biases. Less morally sensitive people may, in turn, have to make a conscious and deliberate effort in order to transcend their reliance on unreflective common sense moral intuitions.

This is not to suggest that the only way for a person to estimate the reaction of an Ideal Observer is to approximate to the characteristic of an Ideal Observer. Another way would be to rely on the judgments of people who approximate to an Ideal Observer.

FIRTH'S IDEAL OBSERVER THEORY MODIFIED

The Firthian Ideal Observer Theory can be modified in at least three ways so that criticisms of the original Firthian Ideal Observer do not apply to them. These modifications are important because they show that Ideal Observer Theory is wedded neither to naturalism nor to a semantic interpretation nor to just the original attributes of an Ideal Observer specified by Firth.

A Nonsemantic Analysis

The original theory was intended to be an analysis of the *meaning* of ethical terms in naturalistic terms. Let us call this *the semantic interpretation* of Ideal Observer Theory. However, the theory can be construed so that "disapproval by an ideal observer under ideal conditions" and "moral wrongness" do not *mean* the same thing but always *refer* to the same thing. In other words, although ethical terms do not mean the same thing as naturalistic terms, they refer to natural properties.

Thus, a naturalist who embraces the theory construed in this way could maintain

D$_1$. Act A is morally wrong if and only if, were there an Ideal Observer under ideal conditions, Act A would be disapproved of by this Ideal Observer

and hold that, although the two locutions separated by "if and only if" refer to the same thing, they do not *mean* the same thing.

Some identity naturalists would maintain that D$_1$ expresses a necessary truth. Thus, they would claim that:

D$_2$. It is necessary that Act A is morally wrong if and only if, were there an Ideal Observer under ideal conditions, Act A would be disapproved of by this Ideal Observer.

Such naturalists would hold that D$_2$ is necessary not because of the meaning of the terms involved but because D$_2$ is true in all logically possible worlds. Moreover, they would not say that this necessity could be determined a priori. Just as properties like water and H$_2$O are necessarily identical although the identity cannot be known a priori, so the properties of being morally obligatory and being approved of by an Ideal Observer are also identical although the identity cannot be known a priori. In both cases the identities are simply empirical facts.

These *nonsemantic interpretations* of the Ideal Observer Theory eliminate one possible problem with the semantic interpretation, namely that the definition of an ethical term in naturalistic terms does not seem synonymous with the ethical term defined. To be sure, it could be objected that there is nothing self-contradictory in saying that X would not be approved by an Ideal Observer and yet is morally obligatory. But this objection, if valid, would be irrelevant if the Ideal Observer Theory were construed in terms of D_2.

Adding the Attribute of Compassion

Another way to modify Ideal Observer Theory is reminiscent of theistic amendments to the Divine Command Theory. Some theists have developed a Modified Divine Command Theory which maintains that what is morally forbidden is identical with what is contrary to what a *loving* God commands. Thus, for example, R. M. Adams has developed a nonsemantic version in which the property of contrariety to a command of a loving God is necessarily identical with the property of moral wrongness, although this is not something one can know a priori, but only a posteriori.[16] One advantage of this theory has over the nonmodified divine command theory is that a loving God would not presumably command cruelty for its own sake. Thus, the theory would not have some of the outrageous moral implications often associated with the Divine Command Theory.

A similar modification of the Ideal Observer Theory can be made. In addition to the standard properties of an Ideal Observer such as omnipercipience, disinterestedness, and dispassionateness, the Ideal Observer can be defined as having complete compassion for all sentient beings. As we have seen, Firth did not have any a priori objections to such an addition so long as it does not make the analysis circular and is really needed for characterizing an Ideal Observer.

Firth argued that such an addition would be circular if it were added simply *because* being compassionate is a moral virtue. Presumably it would not be circular if compassion were added because it is a necessary attribute of a moral judge. As he indicated, one discovers the characteristics of moral judges by examining the procedures we actually regard either implicitly or explicitly to be the rational ones in *deciding* ethical questions. However, this approach suggests that compassion is a necessary condition of a moral judge. We sometimes reject someone as a judge of a particular moral question on the grounds that he is not sufficiently compassionate and we believe that one person is a better moral judge than another person if, other things being equal, the one has more compassion than the other.

But is compassion an independent property? Perhaps, like circularity, it is a property based on other properties of an Ideal Observer. Certainly compassion is related to empathy. Putting oneself in the place of other people and feeling their emotions and experiences is often a necessary condition of being compassionate with them. However, is it a sufficient condition? One might argue that it is not since empathizing with others may generate not compassion but only moral outrage and indignation. For example, putting oneself in the place of a torturer and thereby experiencing his hatred and twisted values may well generate moral outrage toward the torturer. But, by the same token, this moral outrage is parasitic on the ability to feel compassion for the torturer's victims and consequently on the ability to empathize with them. So, although in such cases empathy is not a sufficient condition of compassion, it may be part of a sufficient condition when combined with the original interpretation of the normalcy requirement. For example, one might argue that if Y knows that X is a torture victim *and* completely empathizes with X, *and* Y is a normal human being, then Y would be compassionate toward X. Thus, it is not implausible that the compassion of an Ideal Observer may be reducible to other attributes of Ideal Observer. If such a reduction were possible, Firth's worry that compassion would not add anything to the qualities of an ideal judge would be vindicated.

But whether this reduction thesis is true or not, adding compassion to the other attributes of the Ideal Observer can do no harm. If it were not reducible, it would make explicit one other consideration that we use in deciding moral issues. If compassion were reducible, it would be redundant. Either way it would strengthen the Ideal Observer Theory. Given this interpretation it would be much more difficult to say that an Ideal Observer could approve of morally objectionable acts or that different Ideal Observers could disagree.

A Noncognitive Ideal Observer Theory

The Ideal Observer Theory can be construed in noncognitive terms so that ethical statements are neither true nor false. Rather than stating facts, they would have other functions such as giving advice, making recommendations, condemning, and the like. Adopting a noncognitive construal of Ideal Observer Theory has certain advantages. In particular, it gives the practicality that many ethical theorists believe is the primary function of ethics discourse its due. Moreover, it makes unnecessary any defense of moral objectivity in the moral fact sense since there would be no moral facts.

This does not mean that ethics could not be objective in other senses. In one sense to say that ethics is objective is to claim that ethics can be impartial and unbiased.[17] Here objectivity involves the possibility of impartial reasoning—presenting reasons and arguments that show that a certain course of action, principle, decision, and the like is rationally justified. Objectivity in this sense not only contrasts with partiality and bias but also with irrationality and illogicality. There is no reason why noncognitive ethics could not have objectivity in this sense.

Consider now the noncognitive Ideal Observer Theory of William Frankena.[18] Frankena's theory differs from Firth's Ideal Observer Theory in the following ways: In Frankena's Ideal Observer Theory ethical statements are neither true nor false in a realistic sense. The properties Firth uses to define an Ideal Observer Frankena uses to define the moral point of view from which moral judgments are justified. Although Frankena was much less specific about the characteristics of the moral point of view than Firth was about the characteristics of the Ideal Observer, the two sets of properties are roughly similar and are capable of the same refinements.

Despite Frankena's sympathy with noncognitivism, he maintained that even the least extreme noncognitivists have too limited a view of justification and proof and presume a kind of basic relativism. Quoting with approval J. S. Mill, who pointed out that ethical justification should be understood in a broad sense in which considerations "are presented capable of determining the intellect either to give or withhold assent,"[19] Frankena went on to argue that even commands and expressions of emotion can be justified or unjustified depending on the background beliefs. For example, commands that cannot be obeyed and expressions of emotion such as anger that are based on false beliefs are irrational and justified.

Frankena argued that when someone gives a moral judgment the person implies that the claim is "objectively and rationally justified"; that is, it will stand up under scrutiny by the person making the claim and others "in light of the most careful thinking and the best knowledge, and that rival judgment will not stand up to such scrutiny."[20] Pointing out that Hume made a similar point, Frankena argued that in contrast to the language of "mere self-revelation," when we use moral language to express our sentiments in terms of approval, disapproval, evaluations, recommendations, advice, instructions, or prescriptions we "put them into the public arena for rational scrutiny and discussion, claiming that they would hold up under such scrutiny and discussion and that all of our audience will concur with us if they choose the same common point of view."[21]

Frankena applied this general approach to the justification of both judgments of intrinsic nonmoral value—that is, of things valuable in themselves—and judgments of moral values such as right, wrong, and obligation. With respect to the justification of judgments of intrinsic non-moral values, Frankena maintained that although they cannot be proven in any strict sense of the term, they can be justified by taking the non-moral evaluative point of view and seeing that judgments we make consider "the thing in question wholly on the basis of its intrinsic character, not its consequences or conditions."[22] When we take this point of view we are well informed, clear-headed, impartial, willing to universalize, and in general calm and cool. Frankena argued,

> If one considers an item in this reflective way and comes out in favor of it, one is rationally justified in judging it to be intrinsically good, even if one cannot prove one's judgment. In doing so, one claims that everyone else who does likewise will concur; and one's judgment is really justified if this claim is correct, which of course one can never know for certain. If others who also claim to be calm and cool do not concur, one must reconsider to see if both sides are really taking the evaluative point of view, considering only intrinsic features, clearly understanding one another, and so on. More one cannot do and, if disagreement persists, one may still claim to be right (i.e., that others will concur eventually if . . .); but one must be open-minded and tolerant.[23]

Moral judgments are in turn justified by taking the moral point of view rather than the point of view of "self-love or aesthetic judgments, nor the more general point of view involved in judgments of intrinsic value."[24] Frankena said that in taking the moral point of view we "must be free, impartial, willing to universalize, conceptually clear, and informed about all possible relevant facts."[25] In judging from this point of view we are justified in claiming that our judgment is objectively valid unless someone who does likewise disagrees. Our judgment is justified if it stands up to sustained examination from others who take the moral point of view.

CONCLUSION

In the last chapter I argued that the although major objections to having a nonreligious objective ethics are mistaken, a defense of nonreligious objective ethics is incomplete without a plausible metaethics that provides an analysis of the meaning of ethical terms and a method of justifying ethical judgments. In this chapter I have presented such a metaethics: the Firthian Ideal Observer Theory, a naturalistic semantic analysis of ethical expressions. However, I have slightly modified the properties of a Firthian Ideal Observer and have shown how the Ideal Observer Theory can be developed in advantageous ways. The question remains, however, of whether other rational methods of ethical justification are also compatible with atheism. An account of one such method of ethical decision-making that is closely related to the Ideal Observer Theory will be provided in the next chapter.

NOTES

1. Roderick Firth, "Ethical Absolutism and the Ideal Observer," in *Readings in Ethical Theory*, 2d ed., ed. Wilfrid Sellars and John Hospers (Englewood Cliffs, N.J.: Prentice Hall, 1970), pp. 200–21.

2. Provided that in some cases that the person is not a member of the same social group, or living at the same time.

3. Presumably, nonmoral factual knowledge would include knowledge *about* moral theory, which would not involve knowledge of moral facts.

4. Michael Martin, *Atheism: A Philosophical Justification* (Philadelphia: Temple University Press, 1990), pp. 292–97.

5. See Richard Brandt, "The Definition of the Ideal Observer Theory in Ethics," *Philosophy and Phenomenological Research* 15 (1955): 407–13; Roderick Firth, "Reply to Professor Brandt," *Philosophy and Phenomenological Research* 15 (1955): 414–21; Richard Brandt, "Some Comments on Professor Firth's Reply," *Philosophy and Phenomenological Research* 15 (1955): 422–23; Jonathan Harrison, "Comments on Professor Firth's Ideal Observer Theory," *Philosophy and Phenomenological Research* 17 (1956): 257–58; Thomas Carson, *The Status of Morality* (Dordrecht, Holland: D. Reidel, 1984), pp. 57–58; Charles Taliaferro, "Relativising the Ideal Observer Theory," *Philosophy and Phenomenological Research* 49 (1988): 123–38.

6. Carson, *The Status of Morality*, pp. 68–70.

7. Firth, "Ethical Absolutism and the Ideal Observer," p. 214.

8. Ibid.

9. Cf. Carson, *The Status of Morality*, pp. 63–64, who calls this the direct experience version of Ideal Observer Theory.

10. Richard Brandt, *Ethical Theory* (Englewood Cliffs, N.J.: Prentice-Hall, 1959), p. 249.

11. Although some maintain that certain emotions are essential to the Ideal Observer, Firth points out that it may be possible to define the Ideal Observer as having no emotions at all, either particular or general.

12. Carson, *The Status of Morality*, pp. 70–71.

13. This means that it makes sense to suppose that an Ideal Observer might be raised in a Hopi or Nazi culture and consequently that it makes sense to ask what the reaction of a Hopi or a Nazi Ideal Observer would be to some contemplated situation.

14. Taliaferro, "Relativising the Ideal Observer Theory," p. 129.

15. Thomas L. Carson, "Could Ideal Observers Disagree? A Reply to Taliferro," *Philosophy and Phenomenological Research* 50 (1989): 118–19.

16. However, he does not think moral wrongness can be known empirically. See Robert Merrihew Adams, *The Virtue of Faith* (New York: Oxford University Press, 1987), p. 142, n. 3.

17. This is one common dictionary definition of the terms. See also R. M. Hare, *Moral Thinking* (Oxford: Clarendon Press, 1981), p. 211; Peter Byrne, *The Philosophical and Theological Foundations of Ethics*, 2d ed. (New York: St. Martin's, 1999), pp. 8–9.

18. William Frankena, *Ethics*, 2d ed. (Englewood Cliffs, N.J.: Prentice-Hall, 1973), pp. 105–14.

19. J. S. Mill, *Utilitarianism*, chap. 1, quoted in Frankena, *Ethics,* p. 107.

20. Frankena, *Ethics*, p. 108.

21. Ibid.

22. Ibid., p. 111.

23. Ibid.

24. Ibid., p. 112.

25. Ibid.

4

WIDE
REFLECTIVE
EQUILIBRIUM

INTRODUCTION

In the last chapter I argued that a method of justifying ethical judgments that is compatible with atheism flows from the Ideal Observer
Theory. However, this is not the only such method. A decision procedure
in ethics widely accepted by contemporary philosophers is the method of
Wide Reflective Equilibrium. First developed by Nelson Goodman as a
general approach to justification[1] and then by John Rawls in the context
of ethics,[2] it has been adopted by David Brink[3] and Norman Daniels[4]
among others. Its compatibility with atheism has also meant that atheistic
philosophers such as Kai Nielsen have advocated it explicitly.[5] Indeed,
this theory provides a plausible account of moral reasoning without any
belief in God and is a plausible procedure for atheistic thinkers to adopt.
In this chapter I will explicate this method and show how it is related to
the Ideal Observer Theory. I will also show that the arguments maintaining that Wide Reflective Equilibrium is incompatible with moral
realism are unsound.

WIDE REFLECTIVE EQUILIBRIUM EXPOUNDED

Wide reflective equilibrium in ethical decision making is based on a coherentist epistemology. According to this theory of knowledge a belief B is justified if it is part of a coherent system of beliefs, and the degree of justification of B varies directly with the degree of coherence of the set of beliefs of which B is a member. This coherence is not merely a matter of logical consistency. Rather, the coherence of a belief system is based on the comprehensiveness of the system and the logical, probabilistic, and explanatory connections among its elements.[6] This coherentist approach is applicable not only to the justification of moral judgments but to the justification of scientific judgments as well. Indeed, one advantage of this approach is that it provides a uniform approach to justification that exposes the similarities between moral and scientific justification. This analogy between the scientific justification and moral justification suggests in turn that morality can be objective in the sense of being impartial and unbiased. Since science at its best uses objective reasoning in this sense and science and morality use similar methods of justification, morality at its best uses objective, impartial, and unbiased reasoning.

The general idea of Wide Reflective Equilibrium is that the justification of moral judgments lies not in some foundational moral principles or appeals to intuition but in being shown to be coherent with other beliefs, both moral and nonmoral. In other words, the object of this decision procedure is to bring one's beliefs into a balance in which there are no incoherencies. This involves a mutual adjustment between one's particular moral judgments—for instance, Jones did not do wrong in stealing the money—and one's more general moral principles such as stealing is always wrong; and between particular factual claims—for instance, Jones stole the money—and one's background theories. Similar adjustments have to be made in scientific reasoning whenever there is a conflict between or among a perceptual judgment, the theory that is being tested and background theories.

The difference between what Rawls has called Narrow Reflective Equilibrium and Wide Reflective Equilibrium lies in the scope of the elements brought into equilibrium. In Narrow Reflective Equilibrium the mutual adjustment is *only* between different levels of particular moral judgments and general theories. In Wide Reflective Equilibrium the adjustment is not only between different levels of moral discourse but also between background assumptions about an ideal society, theories of human nature, and the well-supported findings of social science and history. For example, suppose that some well-supported moral theory M in conjunction with well-established background assumption A entails a particular moral conclusion C. And now suppose that C conflicts with one's considered judgment that ~C. Following Wide Reflective Equilibrium, after impartial and well-informed reflection in the light of the evidence, one will decide that C is false.

When there is an obvious incoherence between the elements of the belief system, some adjustment must be made in order to preserve coherence. One way is to modify moral theory M. Another tactic is to change the empirical theory E, still another strategy is to alter the background assumptions A, and a third is to choose instead to give up one's considered judgment ~C. Which one of these moves is the appropriate one to make will depend on several factors, including which change preserves the greatest overall coherence.

It is important to understand that the particular moral judgments involved that are to be brought into harmony with the rest of one's beliefs are *considered* moral judgments. These are judgments that have an *initial* credibility, which is to say that they are prima facie justified. As Brink has put it,

> [M]oral beliefs formed under conditions generally conducive to the formation of true beliefs will be more reliable than beliefs not formed under these conditions. A belief based on available (nonmoral) evidence and thus well informed, that results from good inference patterns, that is not distorted by obvious forms of prejudice, or self-interest, that is held with some confidence, and that is relatively stable over time is formed under conditions conducive to truth. These conditions of general cognitive reliability confer some reliability on moral beliefs so formed. A yet more reliable class of moral beliefs is picked out by the addition of certain morally motivated conditions. . . . Because of the importance of impartiality in making moral decisions and the connection between morality and human goods and harm, we are likely to obtain a reliable class of moral beliefs by focusing on beliefs that have been formed not only under conditions of general cognitive reliability but also on the basis of an impartial and imaginative consideration of the interest of the relevant parties. We might call belief formed under such conditions *considered moral beliefs*.[7]

Like initially credible moral judgments, observational judgments are initially credible if they are made under certain conditions that are conducive to reliability: for example, if they are being made under standard conditions such as proper lighting and freedom from observer bias. There is an analogy between the function of considered moral judgments in ethical reasoning and the function of initially credible observational judgments in scientific reasoning. Both are used to test other beliefs, both general and specific. Both can be rationally rejected in terms of overall coherence. Both are normally based on years of learning and are expressions of good judgment. Both can become refined and improved through practice. This close analogy between considered judgments and perceptual judgments shows the strength of the method of Wide Reflective Equilibrium. Since the justification of perceptual judgments in science is taken for granted as rational procedure, so should the analogous process of justifying moral judgments.

Moreover, just as the basis of perceptual judgments need not be explicitly formulated so the basis of considered moral judgments need not be. Indeed, making them is often based on a skill which has been acquired through moral training which itself involves the consideration of many concrete cases and situations so that the rationale of considered judgments cannot be fully articulated by explicit moral rules or principles. Nevertheless, it is still possible that considered moral judgments could be brought into harmony with moral principles and factual theories just as it is possible that perceptual judgments can be brought into harmony with factual theories and background assumptions.

Although considered judgments must be brought into harmony with moral principles, doing so is not a mechanical process. There are alternative sets of moral principles that have various degrees of fit with the considered moral judgments. But the best fitting set is not necessarily the one to be chosen. Philosophical arguments derived from the background theories can be put forth to evaluate these sets. Suppose a set emerges as being best supported by these arguments. Then moral deliberation can move between the set of considered judgments, the favored set of moral principles, and background assumptions—revising some or all—until reflective equilibrium is achieved.

One important question to ask is how we can be assured that the background theories provide independent support for the moral principles. If the considered judgments used to support the background theories were the *same* as the considered judgments supported by the moral principles, there would be no independent support of the moral principles from the background theories. In order to meet this problem Norman Daniels has argued that it should be required that the background assumptions cohere with a set of considered moral judgments. However, this set must be independent of the set of considered judgments that the moral principles are used to support. Daniels puts it in this way where (a) stands for the considered judgments used, (b) for the moral principles, and (c) for the background theories:

> We should require the theories in (c) not to be just a reformulation of the set of considered moral judgments (a) in which we seek to "fit" the principles in (b). The background theories should have a scope reaching beyond the range of the judgments in (a).[8]

This requirement is analogous to the requirement in science that for background theories B to provide support independent of the direct evidence E_1 for theory T, B must be based at least in part on evidence that is distinct from E_1. Daniels shows how John Rawls's theory of justice can be understood in these terms. Just as in scientific theorizing different levels of theory independently support one another since they are supported by different observations, so in Rawls's theory different levels of theory mutually support one another since the theoretical levels are supported by different considered moral judgments. Thus, general social theory and the theory of moral development support and are supported by background theories such as the theory of persons, of procedural justice, of the role of morality in society, and of the ideal of a well-ordered society. The background theories support one another and Rawls's theory of contract, which in turn supports his famous principles of justice. However, the principles of justice are supported by considered judgments. Moreover, different considered judgments support Rawls's contract theory and the background theories.[9]

WIDE REFLECTIVE EQUILIBRIUM
AND THE IDEAL OBSERVER THEORY

What is the relation between Wide Reflective Equilibrium and the Ideal
Observer Theory? The Firthian Ideal Observer Theory is an analysis of
what ethical expressions mean as well as a method of justification. However, Wide Reflective Equilibrium does not purport to be an analysis of
the meaning of ethical expressions but rather an account of how ethical
justification should proceed. It is compatible with many different
accounts of the meaning of ethical expressions. But then could not atheists embrace the Ideal Observer Theory as an analysis of ethical expressions and Wide Reflective Equilibrium as an account of moral justification? As we have seen, Firth's Ideal Observer Theory itself entails a
method of justification. But could not the Ideal Observer Theory as a
method of justification and Wide Reflective Equilibrium be compatible?

There are interesting similarities between the two methods that suggest that they are not only compatible but stand in a close relation to one
another. The first thing that springs to mind suggesting this close relation
is that the characteristics of considered judgments—an essential aspect of
Wide Reflective Equilibrium—bear interesting similarities to the requirements of the reactions of an Ideal Observer. As Brink has argued, a considered moral judgment is one that is based on available (nonmoral) evidence and thus is well informed, that results from good inference patterns,
that is not distorted by obvious forms of prejudice or self-interest, that is
held with some confidence, that is relatively stable over time, and that is
based on impartial and imaginative consideration of the interested relevant parties. In their idealized forms most of these properties are the characteristics of an Ideal Observer. For example, whereas Brink only
requires considered judgments to be free from "obvious" forms of prejudice and self-interest, a Firthian Ideal Observer is completely free from
prejudice and self-interest. Whereas a Firthian Ideal Observer must be
omniscient with respect to nonmoral facts, a considered judgment is
simply based on the available nonmoral evidence. One might say that
those people who make considered judgments are quasi or semi Ideal
Observers—people with the characteristics of Ideal Observers but not in
their extreme forms. However, since human beings can in any event only

approximate to the characteristics of an Ideal Observer, making considered judgments might well be understood to be what an Ideal Observer realistically involves and human beings who make considered judgments might be called the real world analogues of Ideal Observers.

As was noted in the last chapter, the Ideal Observer Theory method of justification does not require complete fulfillment of the characteristic of Ideal Observer but only an approximation to the characteristics. Thus, so far the Ideal Observer Theory method of justification and Wide Reflective Equilibrium not only seem compatible but also seem quite closely related. However, there is more to Wide Reflective Equilibrium than making considered moral judgments. The judgments must cohere with well-supported moral principles and with well-supported philosophical and social scientific theories. What is not completely clear is whether these aspects of Wide Reflective Equilibrium go beyond the Ideal Observer Theory method of justification or whether they are implicit in an Ideal Observer analysis.

Many aspects of Wide Reflective Equilibrium seem to be implicit in Ideal Observer Theory. For example, an Ideal Observer would have complete social scientific knowledge and this knowledge would surely be consistent with what an Ideal Observer approves of. In fact, one might suppose that an Ideal Observer would achieve Wide Reflective Equilibrium effortlessly and instantaneously. Furthermore, it seems plausible to suppose that an Ideal Observer would have feelings of approval or disapproval of particular actions only while in a state of Wide Reflective Equilibrium.

On the other hand, one might be inclined to argue that in some respects the Wide Reflective Equilibrium method of justification seems to go beyond the Ideal Observer Theory. For example, an Ideal Observer has nonmoral factual knowledge but not necessarily the philosophical, logical, and theoretical knowledge that is necessary to achieve Wide Reflective Equilibrium. But if one eschews a narrow understanding of nonmoral factual knowledge, as I suggested in the last chapter, an Ideal Observer could have knowledge of this kind. Another apparent difference between the Ideal Observer Theory and Wide Reflective Equilibrium is that, according to Firth, it is not necessary for an Ideal Observer to have knowledge of moral facts. Now such knowledge does seem to be necessary for someone trying to achieve Wide Reflective Equilibrium. Considered judgments are brought into equilibrium with general moral principles that have independent support from philosophical and social scientific theories. Does this not entail knowledge of moral facts, for example, the moral facts specified by the moral principles? No, not necessarily. Someone who is attempting to achieve Wide Reflective Equilibrium need not suppose at this stage of deliberation that these moral principles are true. These principles are only supposed to be well-supported hypotheses that must be tested against considered judgments and background theories before they are accepted as true.

How then should we understand the relation between Ideal Observer Theory as a method of justification and Wide Reflective Equilibrium? I suggest that Wide Reflective Equilibrium be considered as a plausible explication of the Ideal Observer Theory as a method of justification. One plausible way filling in and elaborating Ideal Observer Theory as a realistic method of justification is working out the details of the Wide Reflective Equilibrium. So the method of Wide Reflective Equilibrium is not only compatible with Ideal Observer Theory as a method of justification but explicates it. The characteristics of Ideal Observer have real world analogues in the characteristics of the people who make considered judgments. Other aspects of Wide Reflective Equilibrium indicate how an Ideal Observer would proceed in coming to have a feeling of approval or disapproval toward some action. To be sure, although Wide Reflective Equilibrium and Ideal Observer Theory as a method of justification seem closely related this does not mean that they do not mutually entail each other. A person could consistently hold one theory and reject the other. However, this is true in other cases of explication. However, the method of Wide Reflective Equilibrium seems to me the best explication we have of an Ideal Observer Theory of ethical justification and should be the theory of choice for atheists.

WIDE REFLECTIVE EQUILIBRIUM AND MORAL REALISM

Some moral philosophers who are sympathetic to Wide Reflective Equilibrium as a decision method of ethics have argued that it is compatible with moral constructivism, not moral realism.[10] Moral realism seems more in accord with the common sense beliefs than moral constructivism and can be characterized as follows:

1. There are moral truths or facts.
2. These truths or facts are independent of the evidence for them.

Moral constructivism affirms (1) and denies (2), thus holding:

1. There are moral truths or facts.
2'. Moral truths or facts are constituted by the evidence for them.

It is important to see that both moral realism and moral constructivism assume there are moral facts. The two positions interpret moral facts differently. On a moral constructivism interpretation of Wide Reflective Equilibrium, the achievement of Wide Reflective Equilibrium is not an indication of independently existing moral truths but constitutes those truths. Since we are defending the objectivity, that is, the existence of moral facts, and moral facts are compatible with both moral constructivism and moral realism, this issue of moral realism versus moral constructivism is not directly relevant to our major concerns.

Nevertheless, it is useful to consider this issue briefly since several prominent advocates of Wide Reflective Equilibrium have advocated a moral constructivism interpretation. For example, Rawls in his later writings has argued for constructivism in ethics.[11] But, as Brink has shown, exactly what Rawls means by "constructivism" is not clear.[12] Some of what Rawls says indicates that he desires to maintain a metaphysical agnosticism and construes Wide Reflective Equilibrium in political and pragmatic terms. In this interpretation, Wide Reflective Equilibrium is used to achieve political agreement and should not be construed in metaphysical terms.[13] However, this interpretation sits uneasily with other of Rawls's claims that indicate he believes that his theory of justice is correct—not just pragmatically justified—as well as with antirealistic claims of Rawls such as this:

> The parties in the original position do not agree on what the moral facts are as if there were such facts. It is not that, being situated impartially, they have an undistorted view of a prior and independent moral order. Rather (for constructivism) there is no such moral order, and therefore no such facts apart from the procedure of constructivism as a whole, the facts are identified by the principles that result.[14]

Kai Nielsen, an atheistic philosopher and an advocate of Wide Reflective Equilibrium, asserts that philosophers who defend Wide Reflective Equilibrium are constructivists. Coherence of beliefs is not, according to Nielsen, a structure to be unearthed or discovered "but something to be forged—constructed—by a careful and resolute use of the method of reflective equilibrium." Moral realism, according to Nielsen, is a myth.[15] On the other hand, Nielsen is strongly influenced by Rawls's pragmatic construal of Wide Reflective Equilibrium that eschews epistemological and metaphysical commitments.[16] On this interpretation moral realism is not a myth. The independently existing truths of moral realism are simply not needed to achieve a pragmatically motivated Wide Reflective Equilibrium.

What reasons can be given to suppose that moral realism is incompatible with Wide Reflective Equilibrium either in the sense that independent moral truths do not exist or that even if they do, they are not needed? One reason that might be induced for supposing that moral realism is a myth is that a coherence theory of justification necessitates a coherence theory of truth. The trouble with this argument is, however, that a coherence theory of justification does not necessitate a coherence theory of truth. To suppose that it does require this begs the question against moral realism.[17] There is no reason to suppose that one could have a coherence theory of justification *and* a realistic theory of truth.

Another reason that might be given for the position that moral realism is a myth is that justification entails truth. To be sure, if it did, moral constructivism would be correct for there would be no logical gap between evidence for a belief and the truth of the belief. The evidence for beliefs would indeed constitute moral truths. However, this view of justification overstates the connection between justification and truth.[18] This is shown by many examples from science and everyday life where someone is justified in believing that p is true and yet p is false. However, in a moral realism interpretation this gap is acknowledged. On this interpretation Wide Reflective Equilibrium merely provides fallible *evidence for* truth.

Still another reason that could be given for moral constructivism is that moral realism with its separation of evidence from truth opens the door to skepticism, whereas moral constructivism closes the door and prevents skeptical worries. However, the fact that the evidence for a moral truth does not constitute that truth is compatible with having good grounds for believing that the truth exists independently of the evidence. Moreover, the worry about moral skepticism cannot be overcome so easily. Although skeptics may be mistaken they have a point: There is a gap between evidence and truth and moral constructivism cannot eliminate it by redefining truth.

Two reasons might be given to eschew metaphysics and understand Wide Reflective Equilibrium in purely pragmatic terms. First, the context of ethical deliberation is often set in political contexts in which a working consensus is crucial. Second, in this context metaphysics is unhelpful. However, metaphysical considerations can hardly be avoided while using Wide Reflective Equilibrium. A mere working consensus is morally inadequate unless the consensus is based on justified moral judgments and Wide Reflective Equilibrium provides this justification. To be sure, such justification might bring about a working consensus. But any consensus without this justification would only have the virtue of expediency. Moreover, if moral realism is correct, then justified moral judgments achieved by Wide Reflective Equilibrium are indicative of moral truth.

In short, although objectivity in the sense of moral facts is compatible with moral constructivism on a Wide Reflective Equilibrium approach there is no reason why moral facts could not be given a realistic construal.

CONCLUSION

The last chapter presented the Ideal Observer Theory account of how ethical judgments should be justified but the question remained of how the method of Wide Reflective Equilibrium, a type of coherentist justification of ethical claims, relates to Ideal Observer Theory. In Wide Reflective Equilibrium ethical claims are justified if they are brought into equilibrium with considered moral judgments as well as background theories of human nature and society. Wide Reflective Equilibrium is closely related to the Ideal Observer Theory in that what an Ideal Observer approves would be in reflexive equilibrium and many of the properties of an Ideal Observer have nonideal analogs in the make-up of considered judgments. Indeed, the method of Wide Reflective Equilibrium can be considered as a plausible explication of Ideal Observer Theory when it is considered as a method of ethical justification. Although Wide Reflective Equilibrium can be developed in either a constructivist or a realistic manner, the reasons given to prefer a constructivist development are not persuasive.

However, our task is still not complete. There have been many objections to and criticisms raised against both Ideal Observer Theory and Wide Reflective Equilibrium. These remain to be answered.

NOTES

1. Nelson Goodman, *Fact, Fiction, and Forecast*, 2d ed. (Indianapolis: Bobbs Merrill, 1965), pp. 63–64.

2. John Rawls, *A Theory of Justice* (Cambridge, Mass.: Harvard University Press, 1971), pp. 19–21, 48–51, 577–87.

3. David Brink, *Moral Realism and the Foundations of Ethics* (Cambridge: Cambridge University Press, 1989), chap. 5.

4. Norman Daniels, "Wide Reflective Equilibrium and Theory Acceptance in Ethics," *Journal of Philosophy* 76 (1979): 256–82.

5. Kai Nielsen, *Naturalism without Foundations* (Amherst, N.Y.: Prometheus Books, 1996), part 2.

6. Brink, *Moral Realism*, p. 103.

7. Ibid., p. 131.

8. Norman Daniels, "Two Approaches to Theory in Acceptance in Ethics," in *Morality, Reason and Truth*, ed. D. Copp and D. Zimmerman (Totowa, N.J.: Rowman and Allanheld, 1985), p. 122.

9. Norman Daniels, "Reflective Equilibrium and Archimedean Points," *Canadian Journal of Philosophy* 10 (1980): 88.

10. Brink, *Moral Realism*, chap. 2.

11. See John Rawls, "Kantian Constructivism in Moral Theory," *Journal of Philosophy* 77 (1980): 515–72; John Rawls, "Just as Fairness: Political Not Metaphysical," *Philosophy and Public Affairs* 14 (1985): 223–51.

12. Brink, *Moral Realism*, Appendix 4.

13. See Rawls, "Just as Fairness," p. 230.

14. Rawls, "Kantian Constructivism," p. 568.

15. Nielsen, *Naturalism without Foundations*, p. 17.

16. Ibid., chap. 5.

17. Brink, *Moral Realism*, p. 140.

18. Ibid.

5

THE IDEAL OBSERVER THEORY AND WIDE REFLECTIVE EQUILIBRIUM DEFENDED

INTRODUCTION

I have presented the Ideal Observer Theory as a plausible candidate for both an analysis of the meaning of ethical expressions and a method of justification. I have also put forward the method of Wide Reflective Equilibrium as a plausible explication of the Ideal Observer Theory method of justification. However, a number of criticisms have been raised against both theories. Objections to the Ideal Observer Theory try to undermine the nonreligious basis of the analysis. Moreover, criticism that grants its nonreligious status attempts to show that the Ideal Observer analysis is faulty in that it cannot provide a basis for moral obligation, or it is circular, or it confuses "is" with "ought," or it does not provide an adequate moral ontology. Finally, objections based on the content of the analysis purport to show that the Ideal Observer Theory either makes morality subjective or relative and/or that it has morally objectionable consequences.

Objections have also been raised to Wide Reflective Equilibrium. First, it has been argued that there are important disanalogies between observational statements in science and considered judgments in morality that indicate that the Wide Reflective Equilibrium when used in science and morality is radically different. Second, it has been claimed that Wide Reflective Equilibrium is a form of moral subjectivism or intuitionism or conservatism.

In this chapter the criticisms to both the Ideal Observer Theory and Wide Reflective Equilibrium will be considered.

OBJECTIONS TO THE IDEAL OBSERVER THEORY

1. *The Ideal Observer Theory Presupposes a Theistic Concept of Morality*

Some religious apologists have argued that the Ideal Observer Theory is itself a theistic moral position. Clearly, if this were so, Ideal Observer Theory could not provide a basis for an *atheistic* morality. Why would anyone suppose this? One reason is that the Ideal Observer has some of the same properties as God. For example, Firth's Ideal Observer is all-knowing. So is God.[1] It might seem then that the Ideal Observer Theory is a religious metaethics in disguise.[2]

However, an Ideal Observer can have *some* of the same properties of a theistic God without the Ideal Observer Theory presupposing God. An Ideal Observer will not seem much like God if one takes note of the differences between God and an Ideal Observer. For example, an Ideal Observer is not a creator, not an all-powerful being, not a morally perfect person, not a disembodied entity. Moreover, the Ideal Observer is *hypothetical*—it does not exist.

2. *The Ideal Observer Analysis Is Faulty*

a. No Moral Obligation

Some critics of the Ideal Observer Theory have argued that since an Ideal Observer is a hypothetical being it cannot create obligations. Again, if this charge were true, it would seem that the Ideal Observer could not provide an account of moral obligation. According to this criticism only an actual, personal being can morally obligate someone.[3] However, the objection that an Ideal Observer does not obligate us confuses an analysis of "moral obligation" and the creation of a moral obligation. An Ideal Observer does not create obligations. Rather, the Ideal Observer analysis tells us what moral obligation *means*. The relevant question in the case of the semantic interpretation of a Firthian Ideal Observer Theory is whether this analysis captures the meaning of "moral obligation."

Perhaps one can make sense of this criticism interpreted in a different way. One might maintain that only an analysis of moral obligation in terms of an actual, personal being would be adequate. For theists this actual, personal being would be God. R. M. Adams has argued that even if an Ideal Observer has the property of being loving in addition to its other ideal properties, the hypothetical nature of an Ideal Observer would make the unable to account for *some* moral obligations.[4] Only a Divine Command Theory that postulates an actual loving God would be adequate to account for all moral obligations. To be sure, Adams argues that if there were an Ideal Observer, then it could not approve of cruelty for its own sake. But he argues that with respect to other moral issues the Ideal Observer Theory and the Divine Command Theory would diverge. Adams considers a case that he believes is intuitively morally wrong: Suppose I painlessly and without being undetected kill a person who wants to live. But, if I do not kill him, this person will not live happily and other people's happiness would be increased by this death. Adams maintains that a loving God's disapproval of this act is a contingent matter and, unlike the disapproval of cruelty for its own sake, it does not follow from the nature of a loving God or an Ideal Observer.

Adams's argument is weak.[5] First, he has not shown that an Ideal Observer would approve of this act. Given his knowledge, loving nature, impartiality, and power of empathy perhaps it would disapprove. Second, it is not clear why in Adams's account an actual God would disapprove of the act except in terms of arbitrary fiat. If so, this would hardly provide any advantage for the Divine Command Theory over the Ideal Observer Theory. Third, an Ideal Observer defender might argue that an Ideal Observer would neither approve nor disapprove of the act of killing and that either action is morally permitted.

b. Confusion of "Is" and "Ought"

Some critics of the Ideal Observer Theory maintain that this theory confuses "ought" with "is." This criticism is a special case of the argument that theories like Firth's commit the naturalistic fallacy in that they wrongly attempt to define ethical expressions such as "moral obligation" by naturalistic terms.[6] However, to suppose that this is a fallacy is simply to beg the question. Thus, the Firthian Ideal Observer presents an analysis of "ought" statements in terms of "is" statements about an Ideal Observer and anyone who simply assumes without argument that this cannot be done is assuming what must be proven. Moreover, on neither the nonsemantic interpretation of the Ideal Observer Theory nor on a Frankenaian Ideal Observer Theory is there an attempt to provide such an analysis. Consequently, with respect to these versions of the Ideal Observer Theory this critique is not question begging but simply irrelevant.

c. Circularity

Some critics have claimed that the Ideal Observer analysis is circular. In its most crude form this objection is that an Ideal Observer analysis defines something as morally wrong if it is thought to be morally wrong by an Ideal Observer. It is held that in so doing the term "morally wrong" has been reintroduced.[7] However, as Firth makes clear, this is not the way "morally wrong" is defined by the Ideal Observer Theory. Rather it is defined in terms of an Ideal Observer's feeling of moral disapproval under ideal conditions. Such disapproval can be understood in terms of the phenomenological properties of the feeling of disapproval under uncertain conditions and not in terms of the belief of moral wrongness. Moreover, the criticism assumes a semantic interpretation of the theory although the Ideal Observer Theory has nonsemantic and noncognitive forms.

Jonathan Harrison, an English philosopher, has developed a more sophisticated argument concerning the circularity of the Ideal Observer analysis.[8] He has posed the following dilemma: Either morally right is made part of the definition of an Ideal Observer or what an Ideal Observer always approves of is right by definition or it is not. If it is, the analysis is circular. If it is not, then how do we know that the Ideal Observer will always approve of what is right?

But this dilemma is illusory. With respect to the first horn of the dilemma, the semantic interpretation of the Ideal Observer Theory analysis purports to capture the meaning of ethical expressions in naturalistic terms. As Firth made clear the analysis would be circular if ethical terms were used in this analysis. But there is no reason to think that they would be since all the terms used—omniscience with respect to nonethical facts, omnipercipience, disinterestedness, dispassionateness, consistency, and normalcy in other respects—are apparently nonethical notions. To be sure, this seeming ethical neutrality may be deceptive but this would have to be shown.

As for the second horn of the dilemma, insofar as the Ideal Observer analysis captures the meaning of ethical expressions in naturalistic terms we can be assured that the Ideal Observer will always approve of what is right. As Firth pointed out, the reason for thinking the attributes of an Ideal Observer capture the meaning of ethical expressions is that in determining the characteristics of an Ideal Observer we appeal to the procedures we actually regard either implicitly or explicitly as rational in deciding ethical questions. To be sure, we may have overlooked some procedures and may have incompletely captured others, but these possible errors would have to be shown.

It is important to note that Harrison's critique turns on the semantic interpretation of Ideal Observer Theory; that is, that Ideal Observer Theory is an analysis of the meaning of ethical expressions. His objections are irrelevant to the nonsemantic interpretation of the Ideal Observer Theory and to the Frankenaian Ideal Observer Theory, for in these versions there is no attempt to analyze the meaning of ethical expressions.

Another attempt to show that the Ideal Observer analysis is circular is this: If one compares the feeling of disapproval of an act of betrayal with the sort of feeling of disapproval one has toward a corny joke, there is no way of understanding what the relevant disapproval is without understanding what morally wrong is. In other words, the only way to say what the difference is, is to say that in the case of betrayal one thinks that a wrong has been done and in the case of a joke one does not. But then moral wrongness must be presupposed to make sense of the analysis and the definition is circular.[9]

One problem with this criticism is that it seems to assume that the act of telling a corny joke is never morally wrong. However, told in some contexts such a joke can be harmful and morally offensive. In such a case an Ideal Observer, knowing the pain that such a joke causes and being able to experience the pain as if it were its own, would surely have a feeling of disapproval toward the act. But now take the case of a harmless corny joke. Although an ordinary person might have a feeling of disapproval toward it, there is no good reason to think that an Ideal Observer would have such a feeling. Being knowledgeable with respect to nonmoral facts, an Ideal Observer would know that the joke causes no harm and that some people think it mildly amusing. In addition, it is possible that moral data such as feelings have a phenomenological quality that distinguishes them from other kinds of data. If so, then even if an Ideal Observer had a feeling of disapproval toward a harmless corny joke, it might be phenomenologically distinct from the feeling of disapproval of betrayal.[10]

d. Analysis Is Unjustified

Although William Frankena accepted a noncognitive version of an Ideal Observer Theory, he rejected any naturalistic versions of it. Indeed, he argued that one who accepts a naturalistic definition of ethical terms has not solved the problem of justification. His reason was that although one might in so doing justify ethical judgments one would not have justified the definition of ethical terms. Frankena rejected the retort a naturalist might give that an Ideal Observer definition is justified by the fact that it expresses what we ordinarily mean. Frankena said that the only thing this would show is that "moral principles have become enshrined in our moral discourse; it would not show why we should continue to give adherence to [the naturalist's] principles."[11] He concluded that one's basic ethical norms cannot be justified by grounding them in the nature of things in any strict logical sense, since this can only be done if ethical terms can be defined in nonethical terms. But since such definitions turn out to be disguised ethical principles that cannot be deduced from the nature of things, such definitions do not depend logically on facts about human beings and the world.

One problem with Frankena's argument is that analytical naturalism—naturalism based on a semantic reduction of moral terms to naturalistic terms—is not the only kind. Naturalists believe that there are moral facts that are either identical with or constituted by natural facts;

they need not believe that semantic reduction of ethical terms is possible. Yet this is precisely what Frankena assumed. Consequently, even if his argument against naturalism were accepted, the existence of natural moral facts would not be refuted.

Moreover, Frankena seemed to assume a notion of moral truth that presumes some form of naturalism. Although he spoke of 'true' moral principles, judgments, or codes as if he were using the word "true" in some nonstandard sense, he did not indicate what the sense is. However, since he used "'true'" and "justified" interchangeably when he implied that a sufficient condition of a "'true' or justified" moral principle, judgment, or code is an ideal consensus, a plausible interpretation suggests itself. Perhaps Frankena was tacitly presupposing an absolute constructivist view of moral facts.[12] In this view, the evidence for a moral fact would consist of a belief based on idealized epistemic conditions. In particular, Frankena may have held that a moral claim states a moral fact if the belief that is based on the idealized conditions he set forth. His use of "'true'" indicates that he tacitly acknowledged he was not using the term in a realistic way; that is, in one the moral fact exists independently of evidence for it.

e. Inadequate Moral Ontology

Some critics have argued that the theory does not provide an adequate moral ontology and if this charge were true, it would affect seriously any attempt to base an objective atheistic morality on the Ideal Observer Theory. Moral ontology is related to moral facts and objectivity in the following way. To say that Ideal Observer Theory assumes an objective morality is to say that Ideal Observer Theory assumes moral facts. But the claim that Ideal Observer Theory has an inadequate ontology presumably is the claim that Ideal Observer Theory cannot assume moral facts and consequently cannot assume objectivity in the sense of moral facts. For example, Paul Copan has maintained,

> Again, the [Ideal Observer] theory, while compatible with atheistic moral realism at the epistemological level, fails to substantiate the requisite metaphysics of personhood and its intrinsic dignity or value. Such metaphysics is necessary for an objective ethics to get off the ground.[13]

How Copan arrived at this conclusion is a mystery. After pointing out certain similarities between the Ideal Observer and God and mentioning none of the important differences, he concludes that the Ideal Observer Theory is metaphysically inadequate whereas presumably, a God-based morality is not. Given the drift of his argument one would have expected him to conclude that the Ideal Observer Theory is a promising theory for theists and atheist alike.

It is not clear why Copan thinks that the Ideal Observer Theory cannot substantiate "the requisite metaphysics of personhood and its intrinsic dignity or value." After all, such values would be analyzed in terms of the feeling of approval of an Ideal Observer. Moreover, the properties of an Ideal Observer are natural properties. So, metaphysically speaking, the attribute of intrinsic dignity would be a natural property. To be sure, such an analysis may be unsuccessful but nothing Copan has said shows this.

Thomas Carson has raised a different objection to the objectivity of Ideal Observer Theory in the sense of moral facts. When it is interpreted realistically the Firthian Ideal Observer Theory presupposes that there are moral facts. However, Carson objects that he cannot detect moral facts in the sense needed by the theory and he remains skeptical of their existence. According to Carson, moral realists hold that moral facts consist of the relation of fittingness or appropriateness between objects, acts, and so on and attitudes toward them. This relation is unanalyzable and self-evident, he says. For example, suppose that Jones has a moral obligation to pay back the money he borrowed. In Carson's view, this moral fact consists of an unanalyzable relation holding between Jones borrowing the money and the feeling of approval of rational beings to Jones paying it back. This relation would hold for all rational beings independent of any contingent facts about the world.[14]

However, if there are no moral facts in this sense, this does not mean there are no moral facts in some other sense. Although Carson does not use this term, he seems to assume some form of internalism; that is, the a priori thesis that the recognition of moral facts either necessarily motivates or provides reasons for action no matter what the facts are.[15] On this theory motive and reasons for acts are built into—internal—to recognition of moral facts. However, there is good reason to suppose that internalism is incorrect because whether the recognition of a moral fact is motivational or provides a reason is contingent on what the moral fact is and on the psychological state of the agent. Indeed, moral facts are compatible with externalism—the view that whether moral facts motivate is contingent on the psychological state of the moral agent and other contextual factors.[16]

In particular, when the Ideal Observer Theory is interpreted as being compatible with the existence of moral facts it can be understood in terms of externalism. Thus, for example, suppose Jones borrows money. Not all beings that are rational will have a feeling of approval that Jones should pay back his loan. It will depend on how closely they have approximated to the characteristics of an Ideal Observer and also on the known particulars connected with the borrowing. However, this will depend on contingent facts about the case and about the rational beings. For example, a rational being who lacks certain pertinent information or who lacks strong powers of empathy might not approve of Jones paying back the loan although it is a moral fact that he should.

In addition, a Frankenaian argument can be constructed in which moral facts play no role. So this criticism is irrelevant if the Ideal Observer Theory is interpreted in Frankena's way.

3. Problems of Content

a. Subjective

Some critics of the Ideal Observer Theory suppose that the theory makes ethical judgments arbitrary and subjective. For example, one might argue that knowledge of one's moral obligation depends upon knowing the reaction of an Ideal Observer whose judgments one can only estimate through extrapolation by approximating to the ideal properties of an Ideal Observer. This makes right and wrong depend upon how we think an ideal nonexistent being would react were it to exist. But this makes morality subjective.[17]

However, as I pointed out in an earlier chapter, the actual moral judgments that follow from Ideal Observer Theory need not lack impartiality, can refer to moral facts, and can refer to nonpsychological states; that is, in three senses of the term they need not lack objectivity. The critic is correct that extrapolation is involved but there is no more reason to suppose that such extrapolation lacks objectivity than that extrapolation to the behavior of ideal entities in science does. There is no reason to think that the nonexistence of Ideal Observers makes extrapolation of their reactions particularly problematic. The existence or nonexistence of some entity is not clearly related to whether one can extrapolate its behavior from known evidence. For example, the behavior of objects in a perfect vacuum can be predicted very accurately on the basis of known evidence. In contrast, next year's weather patterns—a real phenomenon—are not accurately forecast by extrapolation from this year's pattern.

b. Morally Objectionable Consequences

One of the major criticisms of the Ideal Observer Theory is that an Ideal Observer might approve of outrageous moral acts. Harrison gives a criticism of this kind when he argues that to say that an action is right if an Ideal Observer has a feeling of approval toward the action is like saying that an object is yellow if it seems yellow to a standard observer. The problem, according to Harrison, is that this makes it a matter of accident if an action is right or wrong. It is a brute fact that bananas appear yellow to standard observers but they could just as well appear red. But it does not seem accidental that cruelty is wrong.[18] It is conceivable, Harrison says, that cruelty would arouse a feeling of approval in an Ideal Observer. If it did, one would be bound to say that cruelty is right.

Harrison's example is misleading. He makes it seem as if all cruelty is wrong and, consequently, that if the Ideal Observer had a feeling of approval toward an act of cruelty, this would be a mark against the Ideal Observer Theory. But some acts of cruelty may be morally justified in terms of their consequences. There would be no counterintuitive implication if the Ideal Observer had a feeling of approval toward such acts.

Let us now reformulate Harrison's objection and understand wanton cruelty as cruelty that is not justified in terms of its consequences. So understood, his criticism is that the Ideal Observer might approve of an act of wanton cruelty. Now it is true that Firth used an analogy to visual perception in his discussion about the Ideal Observer analysis. But he simply intended this to be illuminating. He did not expect the two analogies to be perfect. In particular, it does not follow that since the yellowness of bananas is accidental, the feeling of disapproval of the Ideal Observer to wanton cruelty is accidental. If it were the Ideal Observer could have a feeling of approval toward an act of wanton cruelty. Yet this is extremely unlikely. After all, the Ideal Observer is omnipercipient and thus can completely imagine the pain and suffering wanton cruelty felt by the victim, not to mention the people the victim is close to. Moreover, the Ideal Observer is disinterested and thus, if he approved of wanton cruelty he would be willing to exchange places with victim. Indeed, given his powers of empathy, it would be as if the Ideal Observer were identical with the victim and with those close to him. Moreover, since the Ideal Observer would have complete knowledge of the consequences of the act, the Ideal Observer would know that the act was an act of wanton cruelty. Looked at in this light it seems difficult to understand why Harrison is convinced that an Ideal Observer might feel approval toward an act of wanton cruelty. In addition, an Ideal Observer Theory can be modified by adding to the other ideal attributes of an Ideal Observer the attribute of having complete compassion for all sentient beings. So understood it is difficult to understand how an Ideal Observer would approve of an act of wanton cruelty.

Ethical philosopher Henry David Aiken raised two objections against Firth's theory that purport to show that the Ideal Observer analysis is compatible with objectionable moral judgments.[19] First, he claimed that such a view would allow immoral acts such as human mutilation and disregard for the most elementary acts of kindness, veracity, and loyalty. To support his objection he presented two hypothetical cases. One involves a scientist who, because of his singleminded, disinterested pursuit of knowledge, would approve of such mutilation if it were a necessary consequence of this pursuit. The second involves an artist who, because of her single-minded disinterested pursuit of art, would approve of such immoral acts if they were necessary for that pursuit. According to Aiken, excluding disinterested interests that have certain immoral consequences would eliminate this problem. However, in doing this one would be writing "particular moral principles into the very definition of disinterestedness." But then the concept of disinterestedness "loses whatever virtue it may have had as a critical standard to which appeal could be made in trying to decide, among other things, whether that principle is objectively to be preferred to all others, or whether, in certain circumstances, it should be subject to exception."[20]

As we have seen, Firth stressed that an Ideal Observer is omnipercipient. Thus, it is able to experience vividly the pain and suffering inflicted by acts such as mutilations. Moreover, since the Ideal Observer is completely impartial, the Ideal Observer would have a feeling of approval if the Ideal Observer were to exchange places with the victims and feel their suffering. The only way that an Ideal Observer *might* have a feeling of approval is that if the mutilation is necessary to achieve some incredibly important social purpose and this end's value really outweighed the injury to the victims. But it is hard to imagine (except in fantasy and science fiction stories) what such circumstances might be.

Aiken's example of the disinterested scientist who ruthlessly pursues his goal by mutilations thus makes little sense. If the scientist took on the attributes of an Ideal Observer, he would have a feeling of moral approval toward the act of mutilating even if he and his loved ones were the victims while at the same time experiencing the pain involved. In the art for art's case a similar point can be made. If the artist who ruthlessly pursues art for art's sake took on the attributes of an Ideal Observer, she would be willing to allow cruelty, lying, and disloyalty even if she were to trade places with people on the receiving end of these actions and at the same time vividly experiencing their pain. Again such approval makes no sense.

Aiken's second objection was that the Ideal Observer theory rejects as partial and biased the preference of devoted parents for the well-being of members of their own family over any other group. But such a preference is reasonable and moral.

The second criticism misses the mark for there is no reason to suppose that an Ideal Observer would disapprove of the parents' action. After all, although the parents' action is biased toward their children, an impartial person could well approve of this as a universalized policy. Although an Ideal Observer is impartial, this does *not* mean that an Ideal Observer would disapprove of all acts that are not impartial. Consider what the alternative seems to assume: Parents should look after other people's children as they do their own. It might be the case that if parents tried to do this, then children would not be as well cared for as when each parent concentrated on her own. Supposing this is so, not only would an Ideal Observer know this but also the Ideal Observer would be able to put itself in the place of children who are cared for only by their own parents and children who are cared for "impartially" and experience the difference. It seems likely that given this knowledge that an Ideal Observer would have a feeling of approval of a principle advocating that except under special conditions children's welfare should be primarily the responsibility of the children's own parents.

It should be noted that in both of Aiken's examples he assumes the original Firthian Ideal Observer Theory. But if we add to an Ideal Observer's characteristics the attribute of being completely compassionate, Aiken's counterexamples become even less plausible. For example, in the case of the zealous research scientist an Ideal Observer who is completely compassionate could hardly advocate mutilation.

Sometimes the criticism that an Ideal Observer analysis leads to outrageous moral judgments is combined with the criticism that Ideal Observers with different backgrounds or from different cultures would disagree with one another. For example, Richard Brandt argued that different Ideal Observers might have different feelings toward the same act and that the reactions of an Ideal Observer raised in another culture might be morally unacceptable to us. Brandt used evidence from his study of Hopi ethics to illustrate his point. According to Brandt, the Hopi maltreat animals in a way that is morally shocking to us. As far as he was able to discern, this attitude of moral indifference toward animal suffering is not the result of the Hopi having different *beliefs* concerning animal suffering from those of people in our culture. Brandt was not sure if the Hopi people have less *vivid* beliefs concerning animal suffering than we do. However, since the vividness of a belief is not subject to objective measurement Brandt said that the sanest conclusion to draw is that different groups sometimes have different attitudes based on the same beliefs but "difficulties of the investigation justify a healthily degree of skepticism about the conclusiveness of the inquiry."[21]

However, Brandt seems to have forgotten some of the salient attributes of a Firthian Ideal Observer. After all, an Ideal Observer is omnipercipient and thus can feel completely the pain and suffering produced by wanton cruelty to animals. Moreover, since the Ideal Observer is impartial it would be willing to exchange places with the animals. Indeed, it would be as if the Ideal Observer *were* the animal. In addition, since an IO would have complete knowledge of the consequences of the act, then the Ideal Observer would know that the act was an act of wanton cruelty with no redeeming features. Seen in this light it seems difficult to understand why Brandt was convinced that a Hopi Ideal Observer would not feel moral disapproval toward an act of wanton cruelty to animals.[22]

In addition, as previously noted, an Ideal Observer Theory can be developed in which an Ideal Observer has the attribute of complete compassion for all sentient beings. Given this construction it does not seem possible that an Ideal Observer who is a Hopi could have a feeling of approval of wanton cruelty toward animals.

Thomas Carson has also argued that different Firthian Ideal Observers might have different reactions to the same moral situation and that some of these would be morally unacceptable to us.[23] For example, he suggests that two Ideal Observers who are given different moral training when they are young could differ in what they morally approve of. Indeed, Carson has claimed that Firthian Ideal Observers can disagree about *every* possible moral question. In order to support this view he considered the strongest possible case for moral objectivism and unanimity of the reactions of Ideal Observers—the Nazis' attempted extermination of the Jews.

Carson imagined a person who was raised in Nazi Germany and who was taught to hold wildly false beliefs about Jews. This person comes to love and admire only fanatical Nazis, and displaces his pent-up resentment and anger on the Jews. However, in his later life he becomes an Ideal Observer. He now realizes that his old views about Jews were mistaken. But the damage is already done. Despite his new powers he irrationally hates Jews. Indeed, we can imagine, according to Carson, that this Ideal Observer's hatred of Jews is so great that his impartiality does not prevent him from being a Nazi. (Indeed, he would consent to being killed if it could be shown that he was a Jew.) Such an Ideal Observer, according to Carson, would not disapprove of the attempted extermination of the Jews.[24]

Carson maintains that his own Ideal Observer Theory is better able than the Firthian version to rule out the possibility that an Ideal Observer could approve of the Holocaust. This is because in his view (i) not only must an Ideal Observer be fully informed about all relevant matters at present, but must also be fully informed about all relevant matter at all times in his past life (this means that an Ideal Observer cannot have attitudes which depend on his having had false beliefs or incomplete information in the past); (ii) an Ideal Observer cannot have his attitudes influenced by people who are not Ideal Observers, that is by people who acquired their attitudes as the result of some cognitive failure or irrationality; (iii) an Ideal Observer's attitude cannot involve a displacement of emotion.

Now whether there are the clear differences between Firthian Ideal Observers and Carsonian Ideal Observers as Carson has alleged is certainly not obvious. In any case, in our interpretation of the Firthian Ideal

Observer Carson's three attributes were included. Carson has argued that because of his early indoctrination and acceptance of Nazi role models, the Nazi who becomes an Ideal Observer cannot help still hating all Jews and desiring their extermination. But one need not assume that Firthian Ideal Observers are only Ideal Observers in their adult life. Given this understanding it difficult to see how an Ideal Observer could be indoctrinated at an early age into accepting false Nazi views or how he could be influenced by Nazi role models. A young Ideal Observer would instantly recognize that the views his teachers and parents are attempting to indoctrinate him with are mistaken and would see through the Nazi role models that his peers so blindly imitate. Moreover, as I also suggested earlier, Carson's requirements can be incorporated into a Firthian Ideal Observer Theory. In addition, an Ideal Observer Theory can be developed in which an attribute of the Ideal Observer is compassion for all sentient beings. Given this construction of the Ideal Observer Theory it is difficult to see how even an Ideal Observer raised in Nazi Germany could have any sympathy for the extermination of the Jews.

c. Relative Reactions

In addition to the question of whether an Ideal Observer can approve of a morally unacceptable action there is the issue of whether Ideal Observers can have different reactions. For example, it has been argued that the characteristics of an Ideal Observer do not determine a unique set of feelings, hence that the Ideal Observer Theory leads to ethical relativism. For if different Ideal Observers can have different reactions to the same situation, then the same situation will be moral and immoral relative to different perspectives.

Suppose that two different Ideal Observers are raised in different societies and that one culture has a masculine code of honor whereas the other stresses harmonious relations and pacifism. These two Ideal Observers would presumably differ in their feelings of approval regarding the appropriate response to an insult.[25]

But, as Firth pointed out, although ethical statements are not systematically ambiguous they are often accidentally ambiguous. This could be true of a quasiethical term like "insult." It could well have a different meaning in an honor code context from its meaning in other contexts.

Consequently, an Ideal Observer's reaction to an insult would be different in different societies since the meaning of "insult" is different in the two cases. If so, this would not show that relativism in any important sense ensued from the Ideal Observer Theory.

Second, let us suppose that the meaning of "insult" is not accidentally ambiguous but that it means exactly the same in the two societies. Why should one suppose that two Ideal Observers would have different reactions? After all, an Ideal Observer would know that both masculine honor codes and pacifism are culturally and historically relative and also that his or her society's customary reactions are rejected by other cultures. Moreover, an Ideal Observer is impartial and extremely knowledgeable. This surely involves freedom from individual prejudices and biases as well as from cultural, class, and gender ones as well.

One should not suppose that just because ordinary people in two cultures have different beliefs about the morality of an insult, the Ideal Observers from these two different cultures would. For example, suppose that in the one culture the masculine honor code is based on certain gender myths and stereotypes. An Ideal Observer from this culture would not have these myths and stereotypes. Suppose that the advocacy of radical pacifism in the other culture is based on a certain historically incorrect interpretation of Jesus' teaching or on false views about human nature. An Ideal Observer from this culture would not hold this interpretation or these views of human nature.

Putting aside Carson's claim that Firthian Ideal Observers could disagree about every moral issue including the Holocaust because of differences in training and the influence of peers, parents, and loved ones, it still might be true that they could disagree about some moral issues for these reasons. Carson considers the case of two Ideal Observers, X and Y, raised to have different attitudes concerning lying. X is raised in such a way that X has a strict deontologist attitude concerning lying. X is punished harshly for lying unless it is necessary to save the life of an innocent person. X's peers, parents, and role models display scorn for dishonesty and show great respect for honesty even when it leads to extremely unfavorable consequences. Y was raised to have a more teleological attitude toward lying. Y was taught to suppose that the moral presumption against lying is weak and has many exceptions. Y was punished and reprimanded by Y's parents for lying but only when Y could not offer any kind of plausible justification in terms of good consequences. Carson maintains that given their vast knowledge, X and Y would know that they disagree because of their early training. But knowing this would not cause either to modify their attitudes toward lying unless they had reason to suppose that the moral principles in which they were indoctrinated were incorrect. However, Carson maintains that this cannot be known without begging the question and assuming that Ideal Observers could not disagree.

But if we allowed X and Y to be Ideal Observers from an early age, it seems very unlikely that they could be indoctrinated into a particular moral stance on lying. Whatever else indoctrination is, it involves getting people to accept certain views and attitudes without adequate backing and without fairly presenting alternative views. But Ideal Observers could not be indoctrinated since they would know the arguments on both sides and have the impartiality to weigh them fairly. They would know the strengths and weaknesses of deontology and teleology in morality. Given their unlimited impartiality they would be able to assess in a fair way the impact of the alternative approach to lying on society and the people concerned. In addition, as I have argued, it is compatible with Firth's theory that young Ideal Observers are not influenced by non–Ideal Observers. Given these requirements it is certainly not clear that different Ideal Observers would have different views about lying.

Nevertheless, Carson maintains that the reactions of Ideal Observers of different species would more widely diverge than would human Ideal Observers even if the Ideal Observer Theory were modified in the way he suggests. To illustrate his point Carson uses as an example Ideal Observers who are Martians. He argues that a human Ideal Observer might approve of X while a Martian Ideal Observer might disapprove of X and there would be no objective way to choose between them. Although the reason for their possible disagreement is not clearly specified by Carson,[26] one can have a fairly good idea of what he has in mind. Martians would not only have different training but might also have none of our natural tendencies or ways of viewing the world. Thus, suppose they were innately asexual, amoral, asocial, impervious to pain and fear, and intolerant of human weakness. Is it then not obvious that a human and a Martian Ideal Observer would disagree in many instances about what they approve or disapprove of?

No, it is not. It goes without saying that predicting the reactions of

Ideal Observers of other species is extremely speculative. However, given the properties of Ideal Observer it is far from obvious that Carson is correct. Since Martian Ideal Observers would have complete powers of empathy they would be able to look at and experience the world through human eyes. For example, they could experience sexual desire, the feeling of moral obligation, and pain and fear. Moreover, since Martian Ideal Observers would be completely impartial and impartiality involves being able to exchange places with humans, they would gauge their reactions to a moral decision concerning humans in terms of how humans viewed and experienced the world, not in terms of how Martians did. Human Ideal Observers would do the same thing with respect to Martians. Why would the differences between a human and a Martian Ideal Observer make any difference? Just because humans and Martians differed in their ethical reactions it does not follow that human and Martian Ideal Observers would.

However, it may be argued that despite their best intentions Martian Ideal Observers would be influenced by their innate desires and tendencies to disapprove of things that conflict with what human Ideal Observers approve of. For example, since by hypothesis Martian Ideal Observers would have no sexual desires it could be argued that they might disapprove of human sexual relations not aimed at procreation. But how could they disapprove if they were impartial and empathetic? In such a case, they would have to approve of sexual abstinence except for procreation even if they changed places with humans and experienced human sexual desire and completely understood the importance of sex in human life. This disapproval seems unlikely.

OBJECTIONS TO WIDE REFLECTIVE EQUILIBRIUM

1. Disanalogy between Considered Judgments and Observational Judgment

Some critics of Wide Reflective Equilibrium have questioned the analogy between considered moral judgments and observational judgments. It has been maintained that observational judgments made under certain idealized conditions are initially credible but that moral statements are not. It has also been said that one can give a causal account of why the observational judgments are reliable under standard conditions but not why moral judgments are.

However, it is not obviously true that no causal account can be given of the reliability of considered moral judgments. For example, we know that observational judgments made under conditions of good lighting tend to be more reliable than those made under poor lighting since we know from physiological studies that poor lighting adversely affects visual acuity. But surely we also know that moral judgments made under the condition of emotional calm will be more reliable than those made under emotional distress since we know from psychological studies that emotional distress, anxiety, and so on adversely affect the reliability of all judgments.

Although Norman Daniels has defended Wide Reflective Equilibrium, he has maintained that even sincerely held moral judgments that are not made under conditions conducive to mistakes can be biased by self-interest, self-deception, and cultural and historical influences.[27] But Daniels's claim is dubious if one takes the conditions that characterize considered judgments seriously, for these judgments are made under conditions of impartiality. Thus they would tend to exclude self-interest and cultural bias. They are also well informed. Thus they would tend to exclude self-deception.

Daniels suggests that it is a mistake to try to draw too close an analogy between moral judgments and observational reports and that a more appropriate parallel is between theoretical statements in science and moral statements. In particular, he says that arguments and reasons support moral judgments as they do theoretical statements in science. For example, whereas one defends a perceptual judgment that something is red by simply saying it seems red, one who defends a considered moral judgment that X is a moral obligation would ordinarily bring up theoretical reasons to support the claim and not just say that X seems like a moral obligation.

However, Daniels's suggestion is misleading. In the first place, it rests on the long abandoned dichotomy between observation and theoretical statements. Philosophers of science now recognize that statements can be both observational *and* theoretical. Moreover, reasons specifying the conditions under which an observational statement was made can serve as a defense of the kind of statement. For example, someone might say, "I saw a robin. My belief is justified since I saw what looks like a robin in good lighting; I was in an emotionally calm state, and I have 20/20 vision." Such reasons, it should be well noted, presume a number of well-supported theories concerning physiology and psychology. Similarly, reasons specifying the conditions under which a moral judgment was made could be used to defend it. Someone might say, "Jones has a moral obligation to return the money. I am justified in my belief since I approve of her returning the money after a careful examination of all the relevant facts in which I impartially and imaginatively considered the alternatives and their consequences." These reasons in turn presume a number of theories of psychology. To be sure, the perceptual theories may be better confirmed than the moral one. However, difference in degree hardly detracts from the analogy.

2. Subjective

One line of criticism against Wide Reflective Equilibrium asserts that it is a form of moral subjectivism. The English ethical philosopher R. M. Hare, for example, argues that Rawls advocates a type of subjectivism in the "narrowest and most old-fashioned sense."[28] According to Hare, Rawls is claiming that moral theories are tested by whether they are in agreement with people's moral judgments. Presumably, Hare is saying that with respect to Wide Reflective Equilibrium moral judgments must be biased, since they are tested by being in agreement with one's biased moral judgments. Small wonder, given this reading of Rawls, that Hare accuses Rawls of inconsistency in claiming that his moral principles are objective in the sense of unbiased.

However, this is an uncharitable interpretation at the very least of Wide Reflective Equilibrium and at worst it represents a complete misunderstanding of it, for Hare overlooks two vital points. First, he does not take seriously the meaning of "considered" in considered judgments. As we have seen, moral theories are not tested by one's biased moral judgments but by one's *considered* ones. This would rule out many moral judgments since they would not pass the test of being well-informed and based on impartial and imaginative consideration of the interests of the parties concerned. Once one fully understands what "considered" means, to call considered judgments "subjective" is an abuse of language.

Second, Hare seems to have confused Narrow Reflective Equilibrium and Wide Reflective Equilibrium. Moral theories must cohere not just with considered judgments but also with well-established theories of society and human nature that are established independently of the considered judgment used to support the moral theories. Once this aspect of Wide Reflective Equilibrium is recalled, Hare's interpretation of Wide Reflective Equilibrium as old-fashioned subjectivism is obviously false.

What is strange about Hare's interpretation is although he sees an analogy between considered moral judgments and observation statements,[29] he does not see what this entails. Observation statements are not taken seriously in science as providing a test of theories unless they are made under conditions conducive to reliability. The same is true of moral judgments. Moreover, observational statements are tested by their coherence with independently well-confirmed theories of perception just as considered judgments in morality are tested by how well they cohere with well-confirmed theories of moral development and with other social science theories. Testing moral theories by considered moral judgments (correctly understood) is no more subjective than testing scientific theories by observation statements (correctly understood) is.

A related objection of Hare's to the method of Wide Reflective Equilibrium is that it is a form of intuitionism and intuitionism is a form of "disguised subjectivism."[30] Wide Reflective Equilibrium has also been interpreted in this intuitistic way by Ronald Dworkin, David Lyons, and Richard Brandt.[31] However, Wide Reflective Equilibrium in general and considered moral judgments in particular are not based on intuition as this is usually understood. Intuitions are supposed to be self-justifying or self-evident. But although considered moral judgments are initially credible, this is not because they are self-justifying—even initially. They are *initially* credible because they are made under conditions that are conducive to reliability. Evidence and arguments support this. Consequently, the initial credibility of considered judgments is not self-justifying. Moreover, the ultimate credibility—in contrast to the initial credibility—of moral judgments is not self-justifying either, but a function of coherence with the system of belief to which it belongs.

Peter Byrne, an English philosopher of religion who maintains that Rawls's method of reflective equilibrium is "seriously misleading," proffers a similar critique of Wide Reflective Equilibrium. He characterizes reflective equilibrium as the attempt "to provide a theory of how our 'moral intuitions'. . . follow from as few number of principles as possible." He argues that talk of "moral intuitions implies that ground level moral judgments are guesses or hunches only achieving the status of judgment or knowledge when integrated into a theoretical structure." Byrne maintains that this is mistaken and that moral judgments "should be viewed more along the lines of perceptions. They are expressions of discernment."[32] But on the interpretation of Wide Reflective Equilibrium given here, considered judgments are *not* guesses or hunches and *are* analogous to perceptual judgments. When made by morally sensitive persons considered judgments could also be expressions of discernment.

Moreover it is not accurate to say, as Byrne does, that the object of reflective equilibrium is to provide a theory of how our considered judgments follow from as few principles as possible. Byrne seems to be confusing Wide Reflective Equilibrium and Narrow Reflective Equilibrium. As I have argued, the reflective equilibrium is not just between specific considered judgments and more abstract moral principle. Moral theories must cohere not just with considered judgments but also with well-established theories of society and human nature that are established independently of the considered judgments used to support the moral theories. Finally, Byrne's use of the term "follows from" wrongly suggests that the connection between moral principles and theories of society is deductive. But probabilistic and explanatory connections among the elements of the belief system are also relevant.

3. Morally Conservative

Another objection to Wide Reflective Equilibrium is that it is basically a conservative view that is committed to the moral *status quo*.[33] In particular, it is said that Wide Reflective Equilibrium allows for no external viewpoint from which one can assess prevailing basic moral commitments. As a result one is stuck with these commitments and the only changes that can be brought about are small, insignificant ones. But this is incorrect. Radical change can be brought about in one's system of beliefs in a variety of ways.

First, suppose the system is fairly coherent given a large number of *nonconsidered* moral judgments. However, in a Wide Reflective Equilibrium approach many particular nonconsidered moral beliefs would have to be rejected once they were evaluated in light of the evidence and imaginative and impartial considerations. This transition from nonconsidered judgments to considered ones could bring about large changes in the rest of the system if coherence is to be preserved. Second, no one's belief system is perfectly coherent. Bringing about a coherent system might also result in large-scale changes even if there were no mass transition from nonconsidered judgments to considered ones. Third, Wide Reflective Equilibrium involves bringing one's considered judgments and moral principles into reflective equilibrium with well-confirmed social scientific theories. This element could well bring large-scale changes in the belief systems of many who are not conversant with social science. Fourth, moral deliberation by means of Wide Reflective Equilibrium would involve seeing if one's considered moral judgments cohere not just with one's presently held moral views but with different views that could replace them. In order to do this, comparative evaluation is essential. This evaluation could show that radically different moral views would fit more coherently into one's system of belief than one's present view.

CONCLUSION

A complete defense of a nonreligious morality not only must present a plausible analysis of the meaning of ethical expressions and a credible method of justifying ethical claims, but must meet the objections that have been raised against this analysis and this method. My candidate for a plausible analysis is the Ideal Observer Theory and my candidate for a credible method is the method of Wide Reflective Equilibrium. In this chapter I have shown that the various objections that have been raised against these have not been successful. The Ideal Observer Theory does not presume a theistic concept of morality and the Ideal Observer Theory's hypothetical nature does not mean it cannot provide an analysis of moral obligation. The Ideal Observer Theory does not make morality subjective or relative and does not have morally objectionable consequences. In addition, it has yet to be demonstrated that the Ideal Observer Theory confuses "ought" with "is" or provides a circular analysis of ethical terms. Moreover, the arguments used to show that the Ideal Observer Theory does not provide an adequate moral ontology fail.

Nor are the objections raised against Wide Reflective Equilibrium successful. Wide Reflective Equilibrium is not a form of moral subjectivism, intuitionism, or conservatism. Further, there are important analogies between observational statements in science and considered judgments in morality that indicate that Wide Reflective Equilibrium is correctly used in both science and morality.

One more step is needed to complete my project. A thorough defense of nonreligious ethics should show what is wrong with its rival: religious ethics. In part 2 this task will be undertaken.

NOTES

1. Paul Copan, "Can Michael Martin Be a Moral Realist? Sic et Non," *Philosophia Christi*, Series 2, 1, no. 2, p. 51, n. 25.

2. In a debate with the British philosophical theist Peter Williams in the *Philosophers' Magazine* Williams said that my description of an Ideal Observer sounds like God. See Peter Williams "Is There a Personal God?" *Philosophers' Magazine* 8 (autumn 1999): 22–23.

3. Ibid.

4. R. M. Adams, "Moral Arguments for Theistic Beliefs," in *Rationality and Religious Belief*, ed. C. F. Delaney (Notre Dame, Ind.: University of Notre Dame Press, 1979), p. 117; see also Adams, "A Modified Divine Command Theory of Ethical Wrongness" and "Divine Command Metaethics as Necessary *A Posteriori*," reprinted in *Divine Command Theory of Morality*, ed. Paul Helm (New York: Oxford University Press, 1981), pp. 83–119.

5. Charles Taliaferro, "The Divine Command Theory of Ethics and the Ideal Observer," *Sophia* 22 (1983): 3–9.

6. For a detailed analysis of the is/ought thesis see David Brink, *Moral Realism and the Foundation of Ethics* (Cambridge: Cambridge University Press, 1989), chap. 6.

7. See http:/www-personal.umich.edu/~sdarwall/361me197.txt.

8. Jonathan Harrison, "Ethical Objectivity," *The Encyclopedia of Philosophy*, ed. Paul Edwards (New York: Macmillan, 1967), p. 74.

9. Ibid.

10. Whether moral data have distinctive phenomenological properties is a matter for psychological research.

11. William Frankena, *Ethics*, 2d ed. (Englewood Cliffs, N.J.: Prentice-Hall, 1973) p. 101.

12. Relativistic moral constructivism would hold that there are a number of sets of moral facts, each constituted by different bodies of evidence. For example, some constructivists believe that a moral claim p such as "the death penalty is wrong" states a moral fact for person P if the evidence for p constitutes the fact. Suppose that the evidence for p is that P believes that p is correct after serious well-informed reflection. Then that evidence would constitute p. In another relativist constructivist view, a moral claim p is a moral fact for a person P if the evidence for p is that most people in P's society would believe p after serious well-informed reflection. Then that evidence would constitute p. Absolute moral constructivism would hold that there is a distinct set of moral facts that would be constituted by a single body of evidence. Usually the evidence for a moral fact according to an absolute moral constructivism would consist of a belief based on idealized epistemic conditions. Such a belief would constitute the moral fact.

13. Copan, "Michael Martin," p. 51, n. 25.

14. Thomas Carson, *The Status of Morality* (Boston: D. Reidel, 1984), pp. 43–46.

15. Ibid., p. 27.

16. See Brink, *Moral Realism*, chap. 3.

17. Williams, "Is There a Personal God?" pp. 22–23.

18. Although Harrison uses the example of cruelty, not wanton cruelty, his case is strengthened by the addition. After all, some cruelty is morally justified in terms of the consequences. The meaning of wanton cruelty seems to rule this out.

19. See Henry David Aiken, *Reason and Conduct* (New York: Alfred A. Knopf, 1962), pp. 152–61.

20. Ibid., p. 155.

21. Richard Brandt, *Ethical Theory* (Englewood Cliffs, N.J.: Prentice-Hall, 1959), p. 286.

22. In his reply to Brandt, Firth points out the great difficulty of determining whether two persons really have all of the properties of Ideal Observers. For example, how can we tell if a person is completely impartial? See Roderick Firth, "Reply to Professor Brandt," *Philosophy and Phenomenological Research* 15 (1955): 414–16.

23. Carson, *The Status of Morality*.

24. Thomas L. Carson, "Could Ideal Observers Disagree? A Reply to Taliaferro," *Philosophy and Phenomenological Research* 50 (1989): pp. 115–24, 121–22.

25. See http:/www-personal.umich.edu/~sdarwall/361me197.txt.

26. See Charles Taliaferro, "Relativising the Ideal Observer Theory," *Philosophy and Phenomenological Research* 49 (1988): 135.

27. Norman Daniels, "Wide Reflective Equilibrium and Theory Acceptance in Ethics," *Journal of Philosophy* 76 (1979): 270.

28. R. M. Hare "Rawls's Theory of Justice," in *Reading Rawls*, ed. Norman Daniels (New York: Basic Books Inc., 1976), p. 82.

29. Ibid.

30. Ibid., p. 133.

31. Ronald Dworkin, "The Original Position," in Daniels, *Reading Rawls*, pp. 28–32; David Lyons, "Nature and Soundness of the Contract and Coherence Arguments," in *Reading Rawls*, p. 147; Richard Brandt, *A Theory of the Good and the Right* (New York: Oxford University Press, 1979), pp. 16–23.

32. Peter Byrne, *The Philosophical and Theological Foundations of Ethics*, 2d ed. (New York: St. Martin's, 1999), p. 34.

33. Cf. Brandt, *A Theory of the Good and the Right*, pp. 21–22, R. M. Hare, *Moral Thinking* (Oxford: Oxford University Press, 1981), pp. 75–76; D. Copp, "Considered Judgments and Moral Justification," in *Morality, Reason and Truth*, ed. D. Copp and D. Zimmerman (Totowa, N.J.: Rowman and Allanheld, 1984), pp. 141–68.

PART TWO

THE CHRISTIAN FOUNDATION OF MORALITY

6

INTRODUCTION TO THE FOUNDATIONS OF CHRISTIAN ETHICS

In part 1 of this book I defended a nonreligious foundation of ethics. However, someone might accept my defense and yet maintain that a religious foundation of ethics is also possible. One might maintain that a nonreligious and a religious foundation of ethics are compatible. Perhaps they are in theory, but I believe that in fact the religious foundation of morality is seriously flawed. So, in order to complete my project of defending nonreligious morality, a further step is necessary: I need to show the problems with religious-based morality in order to show its inferiority to nonreligious-based morality.

In part 2 of this book I will critically evaluate the religious foundation of morality; that is, morality based on God. In this context I will use the expression "a religious foundation of moral morality" in a broad sense to refer to religious metaethics plus the more theoretical aspects of a religious normative ethics. However, since the most dominant and articulated religious normative ethical system in our society is Christian ethics it will be appropriate to concentrate on the metaethics and more theoretical basis of Christian ethics as opposed to the metaethics and theoretical basis of other religious ethics.

However, most of the points that will be made about Christian metaethics apply with equal validity to Jewish and Muslim metaethics.

Thus, for example, insofar as Jewish metaethics and Muslim metaethics are based on the Divine Command Theory, criticisms of Christianity's use of that theory would apply to them. In contrast, however, criticisms to follow of notions such as the imitation of Christ have little relevance to the theoretical aspects of Jewish and Muslim normative ethics.

In this chapter some preliminary matters will be investigated. In particular, I will evaluate how problems connected with the presumption of God and the major doctrines of Christian ethics affect the foundations of Christian ethics. In the remaining chapters in part 2 these problems will be put to one side and I will concentrate on other issues. In chapters 7 and 8 I will show that the Divine Command Theory is untenable. Although the Divine Command Theory is not, strictly speaking, entailed by Christian theism—one can consistently be a Christian theist and reject it—it is commonly associated with it. If one believes that God is all-powerful and the creator of the universe, it is natural to assume that he created moral truths and that their existence depends on his will. Thus, in order to preserve God's unlimited power it seems plausible to many theists that God is the creator of moral truths. It is for this reason that the Divine Command Theory is the metaethics of choice among theistic thinkers. If God were not the creator of moral truths, this would seem to limit God's power. I will also show, in chapter 9, that a fundamental command of Christian ethics—that one should imitate Christ—is problematic, while in chapter 10 I will indicate how Christian ethics lead to moral skepticism.

Unlike a nonreligious foundation of morality, which is compatible with belief in God, a Christian foundation of morality is not compatible with atheism. This is not to deny, of course, that Christian ethics can be based on metaethical and historical assumptions that do not presuppose the existence of God or the truth of major doctrines of Christianity. However, in this case it would be misleading to speak on a *Christian* foundation of morality. Atheists reject the Christian foundations of morality because they reject Christianity. Indeed, Christianity can be considered a background theory, which provides support and meaning to Christian ethics. Since atheists reject this background theory they reject the ethics on which it is based unless Christian ethics can be given a nonreligious foundation.

The assumptions of the nonexistence of God and the falsehood of the major doctrines of Christianity have been defended in other publications.

Nevertheless, it is appropriate here to remind the reader why atheists are justified in holding these assumptions by briefly surveying the reasons that atheists have used to support them.

First, there are no good reasons for the belief that a theistic God exists. Second, there are good reasons for believing a theistic God does not exist. Finally, there are good reasons to suppose that the major doctrines of Christianity—the resurrection, incarnation, virgin birth, second coming— are unlikely. Let us briefly consider these reasons in turn.

THERE IS NO GOOD REASON FOR BELIEVING A THEISTIC GOD EXISTS[1]

1. The Cosmological (First Cause) Argument fails since at most it proves a first cause. However, a first cause is compatible with deism, polytheism, a finite god, and an impersonal force. In addition, with respect to the beginning of the universe (including time and space), given recent well-respected cosmological theories such as Stephen Hawking's, there is reason to suppose that the universe had no cause. Independent of these theories it is difficult to make sense of a cause of time and space since causality itself is a temporal and spatial notion.

2. The Teleological (Design) Argument also fails since it at most proves the existence of a designer or designers and this is compatible with deism, polytheism, or a finite god. The latest version of the Teleological Argument—the Fine-Tuning Argument—maintains that there are an extremely large number of possible values for the physical constants in the universe and only a very narrow range of possible values are compatible with human life; consequently, it is extremely improbable that human life occurred by chance. However, this Fine-Tuning Argument is valid only if one makes the unjustified assumption that all possible values are equally probable. None of our current probability theories—classical, frequency, propensity—can be nonproblematically applied to the beginning of the universe. Moreover, if human life in the universe is caused by design, why is it so rare and why did it arrive so late? As far as we know, human life exists now on only one insignificant planet and did not exist at all for about 10 billion years.

3. The Ontological Argument represents an attempt to show that

God—a Perfect Being or a Necessary Being or a Being such that no greater being can be conceived—exists by definition. It has taken many different forms but all have proved to be unsound after examination. Moreover, even if the argument is sound, it would fall short of proving the existence of the theistic god, for the god of this argument need not be a person or reveal himself through miracles and scripture.

4. The Argument from Miracles also fails to prove theism since at most it would prove a supernatural miracle worker or workers. Moreover, it assumes that there is evidence of miracles; that is, events that can never be explained by scientific theories. But we do not know of any such events. Alleged miracles such as the "cures" at Lourdes need strong evidence to be believed and this is lacking.

5. Religious experience provides no reason for belief in the theistic God since there is no good reason to suppose that any religious experiences are veridical. Indeed, we know that some of them are not since they conflict with others. In particular, there is no reason to suppose that religious experiences of a theistic God are veridical and that conflicting nontheistic religious experiences are not.

6. Pragmatic arguments such as Pascal's wager fail since they give us no reason to believe in the theistic God rather than in other kinds. Moreover, they fail to acknowledge that God may take a dim view of betting on his existence. In any case, such arguments at most show that it is useful to believe in God—not that the belief is true or probable.

7. Alvin Plantinga has argued that theists' belief in God is a properly basic belief. Like simple perceptual and simple mathematical beliefs, it is rationally held yet not inferentially based on more basic beliefs. However, this analysis not only allows conflicting religious beliefs to be properly basic but also provides no clear non–question begging criteria for excluding astrological and magical beliefs as properly basic.

THERE ARE GOOD REASONS TO SUPPOSE THAT A THEISTIC GOD DOES NOT EXIST

1. One good reason to disbelieve in God is the existence of the large amount of evil in the world. How can a perfectly good and all-powerful being allow so much evil? The simplest and most plausible explanation

of this evil is that God does not exist. One of the most common defenses against this argument is to argue that evil is the result of the misuse of our free will. However, this Free Will Defense is seriously flawed.[2] Moreover, the Free Will Defense gives no account of natural evil; that is, the evil that results from natural disasters, diseases, and the like. In addition, none of the usual explanations of natural evil seem to work.[3]

2. Still another reason for disbelieving in God is the large number of disbelievers in the world.[4] This Argument from Nonbelief is especially telling against evangelical Christianity,[5] although it has some force against other religions, for example, Orthodox Judaism.[6] Supposing evangelical Christianity to be true, it is difficult to understand why there are nearly 1 billion nonbelievers in the world. Why would a merciful God, a God who wants all humans to be saved, not provide clear and unambiguous information about his word to humans when having this information is necessary for salvation? Yet, as we know, countless millions of people down through history have not been exposed to the teaching of the Bible and those that have been are often exposed in superficial and cursory ways, ones not conducive to acceptance. Even today there are millions of people who, through no fault of their own, either remain completely ignorant of the Christian message or because of a serious lack in their Christian education reject it. One would expect that if God were rational, he would have arranged things in such a way that there would more believers.

3. Still another reason to reject belief in God is that such a belief is incoherent. One tacit assumption theists make when arguing for the impossibility of an atheistic foundation of morality and for the necessity of a theistic one is that a theistic ontological foundation of something is logically possible. But unless the concept of God is shown to be coherent, theism cannot possibly be thought to be an ontological foundation of morality or anything else.

I have argued in detail elsewhere that the various attributes of God are incoherent with one another and that they are sometimes internally incoherent[7] and even more recently, Theodore Drange surveyed other arguments of a similar kind.[8] Moreover, Douglas Walton has revived Carneades' argument that God's moral nature is incoherent.[9] To my knowledge neither my arguments nor those presented by Drange and Walton have been refuted. Until they are, claims about the necessity of theistic morality are without merit.

In addition, there are serious objections to the major doctrines of Christianity. Such doctrines are based on miraculous historical events—the resurrection, the virgin birth, and the incarnation. Because miracle claims are initially incredible, belief in them requires very strong evidence.[10] However, this evidence is unavailable. Until it is produced, the initial incredibility of these claims is not rebutted.

The difficulties of theism in general and Christianity in particular represent one reason why nonreligious foundations of ethics are superior to religious foundations of ethics: Atheism does not make the questionable assumptions that form the metaphysical and historical background of Christian theism. In the following chapters of part 2 I will for the most part put to one side the problems of Christian ethics that involve the presumption of God's existence and the major doctrines of Christianity and concentrate on other problems. For example, even if Christian ethics by definition was not committed to religious notions, and a nonreligious foundation were theoretically possible, atheists could maintain that the content of Christian ethics is morally problematic. So Christian ethics might be false even if a nonreligious foundation of Christian morality is possible.

NOTES

1. See more details in Michael Martin, *Atheism: A Philosophical Justification* (Philadelphia: Temple University Press, 1990), part 1.

2. See ibid., chap. 15.

3. See ibid., chap. 16.

4. See Theodore Drange, *Evil and Nonbelief* (Amherst, N.Y.: Prometheus, 1998).

5. Evangelical Christianity is the view that (1) God is a merciful and all-loving God, compassionate and caring toward humanity; (2) the Bible and only the Bible is the source of God's word; (3) God wants all humans to be saved; and (4) a necessary condition for being saved is becoming aware of the word of God and accepting it.

6. In Orthodox Judaism the question is why are there so many descendants of the Israelites who since the time of Moses have rejected one or more of the following: (1) There exists a being who rules the entire universe; (2) This Being has a chosen people, namely, the Israelites; and (3) He gave them a set of laws, the Torah, he wants them to follow and which he wants their descendants to follow.

7. Martin, *Atheism*, chap. 12.

8. Theodore M. Drange, "Incompatible-Property Arguments: A Survey," *Philo* 1 (fall–winter 1998): 49–60.

9. Douglas Walton, "Can an Ancient Argument of Carneades on Cardinal Virtues and Divine Attributes Be Used to Disprove the Existence of God?" *Philo* 2 (fall–winter 1999): 6–21.

10. Michael Martin, *The Case against Christianity* (Philadelphia: Temple University Press, 1991). See also Michael Martin, "Why the Resurrection Is Initially Improbable" *Philo* 1 (1998): 63–74.

7

THE
DIVINE
COMMAND
THEORY

As Christian ethics is usually articulated it is based on false beliefs: a belief in God and a belief in the major doctrines of Christianity. But the question remains whether Christian ethics is implausible on independent grounds. The most widely accepted metaethics in Christian thought is the Divine Command Theory. This theory purports to provide the semantical and epistemological foundation of Christian morality. In this chapter I will evaluate this theory without assuming either that God does not exist or that the major doctrines of Christianity are false. I will show that this theory has several formulations and all of them have serious problems.

Although I will not assume that God does or does not exist in my criticism, the Divine Command Theory can be used either to support or to undermine theism. On the one hand, if Christian theism is true and certain assumptions are made about God's power and creative scope, then the Divine Command Theory follows. So if the Divine Command Theory were implausible, this would tend to undermine Christian theism. Or alternatively, if the Divine Command Theory were plausible and the assumptions were acceptable, then Christian theism would be inductively supported.

But what is the Divine Command Theory? According to this theory moral truths do not exist independently of God's will but are created by an act of his will. In other words, a human action is morally obligatory because God commands it; God does not command it because it is morally obligatory. Thus, morality is not discovered by God but is created by him. The Divine Command Theory thus makes moral knowledge directly dependent on theological knowledge in that without knowing what God commands, one could not claim to know what one's moral duties were. In the past Ockham, Augustine, Duns Scotus, and Calvin have advocated this theory,[1] among others, and in our time it has been held by Brunner, Buber, Barth, Niebuhr, and Bultmann.[2]

Furthermore, the Divine Command Theory is often cited by its advocates as being superior to secular metaethical systems. Indeed, it is on the basis of this theory that theists sometimes maintain that if there were no God, then moral anarchy would follow. However, as we have seen in part 1 of this book, moral anarchy is not a necessary consequence of secular morality. One often-cited advantage of the Divine Command Theory over secular theories, then, is that according to it moral truths are objective and absolute. But, as we have seen in part 1, nonreligious metaethics, for example, the Ideal Observer Theory, maintains that moral truths are objective and absolute. Moreover, as I will argue later in this chapter, the objectivity of morality becomes questionable in the light of the problems of the Divine Command Theory.

VARIETIES OF THE EXTREME DIVINE COMMAND THEORY

In its most extreme form the Divine Command Theory maintains that God's command that some action be done constitutes the complete reason why this action is morally required. In weaker versions, God's command is simply a necessary part of the complete reason. The remainder might be, for example, that God is the creator of the universe and its creatures; hence, God's creatures have an obligation to obey their creator's command just as children have an obligation to obey their parents' commands.

One way to understand the most extreme version of the theory is as an analysis of the meaning of moral terms. On this construal, advocates of the theory are claiming that expressions such as "morally required," and "morally permitted" are to be defined in terms of theological expressions such as "God commands." Thus, this semantic version of the theory maintains that

1. It is morally required that p = God commands that p.[3]

Analyses of related ethical terms would follow similar lines, for example:

2. It is morally permitted that p = It is not the case that God commands that ~p.
3. It is morally forbidden that p = God commands that ~p.

It should be noted that in order to capture the intent of the theory, the righthand side of definitions (1), (2), and (3) must be understood as conceptually prior to the lefthand side. That is to say, the moral term is explained by the theological term and not the reverse. Thus, the analyses provided in (1), (2), and (3) reduce moral terms to theological terms; they do not reduce theological terms to moral terms.

In contrast to what I will henceforth call the Actual Semantic Divine Command Theory, consider the Semantic Hypothetical Divine Command Theory. In this interpretation moral obligation is defined in terms of what God *would* command *if* God existed. Hence, there is no assumption that God does exist. The basic analyses of the theory can be stated in this way:

1'. It is morally required that p = If there were a God, God would command that p.
2'. It is morally permitted that p = It is not the case that if there were a God, God would command that ~p.
3'. It is morally forbidden that p = If there were a God, God would command that ~p.

To contrast this theological hypothetical analysis, let us briefly consider another analysis of ethical terms. As was noted in chapter 3, according to the Ideal Observer Theory, the meaning of "moral obligation" is analyzed in terms of the feelings of approval of a hypothetical ideal observer, a person who is fully informed, unbiased, impartial, completely rational, and completely empathetic.[4] Thus:

1". It is morally required that p = If there were an Ideal Observer, the Ideal Observer would contemplate that p with a feeling of approval.

Analyses of related terms would follow similar lines:

2". It is morally permitted that p = It is not the case that if there were an Ideal Observer, the Ideal Observer would contemplate that p with a feeling of disapproval.

3". It is morally forbidden that p = If there were an Ideal Observer, the Ideal Observer would contemplate that p with a feeling of disapproval.

Although there are important similarities between this hypothetical analysis and the Hypothetical Semantic Divine Command Theory, there are also crucial differences. True, both theories attempt to analyze what certain ethical terms mean, the analyses of both are in terms of what some hypothetical being would do, and the hypothetical beings have some similar properties. For example, God is all-knowing and the Ideal Observer is as knowledgeable as is compatible with logical coherence. The differences, however, are significant. The Hypothetical Semantic Divine Command Theory defines moral expressions in terms of what God would command whereas the Ideal Observer Theory defines them in terms of what an Ideal Observer would have a feeling of approval or disapproval toward. Moreover, the Ideal Observer lacks certain properties that God is supposed to have. For example, God is necessarily all-powerful but the Ideal Observer could not be in some interpretations and need not be in others. Furthermore, depending on how one defines God, the Ideal Observer may have certain characteristics that God lacks. For example, the Ideal Observer has complete powers of empathy and, consequently, can experience any human emotion or feeling. It is not clear if this is true of God.[5]

In contrast to the actual and hypothetical semantic Divine Command Theory analysis, Phillip Quinn has presented an Actual Nonsemantic Divine Command Theory.[6] Its core is presented in three propositions:[7]

T_1. It is necessary that for all p it is morally required that p if and only if God commands that p.

T_2. It is necessary that for all p it is morally permitted that p if and only if it is not the case that God commands that ~p.

T_3. It is necessary that for all p it is morally forbidden that p if and only if God commands that ~p.

It should be noted that Quinn's version of the Divine Command Theory does not depend on an analysis of the meaning of ethical terms: although T_1, T_2, T_3 are supposedly necessary truths, they are not necessary because of the meaning of the terms involved. For example, the necessity involved in T_1 is that in any possible world in which it is morally required that p, God commands that p and in any possible world in which it is God's command that p, it is morally required that p. One need not suppose that "moral obligation" is definable in terms of what God commands.

A Hypothetical Nonsemantical Divine Command Theory and a Nonsemantical Ideal Observer Theory could be developed as well.[8]

EVALUATION OF THE EXTREME DIVINE COMMAND THEORY

The Semantic Problem

One important objection to the Actual Semantic Divine Command Theory is semantic: It seems mistaken to suppose that this analysis captures what people usually mean by "moral obligation," "morally permitted," and "morally forbidden." Thus, for example, some maintain that ethical expressions are not definable in terms of theological ones. For instance, according to British rationalist and theist Richard Price (1723–91), rightness and wrongness are as much objective properties of acts and situations as are the properties of mass and hardness. He argued that human understanding is competent to know such properties without knowing what God commands.[9]

Moreover, it seems unlikely that definitions 1, 2, and 3 above capture what nonbelievers and agnostics have meant by these terms. One reason is that definitions 1, 2, and 3 entail moral anarchy—the view that everything is morally permitted—if God does not exist. For example, if definition 1 is correct and God does not exist, then nothing is morally required since God would not command anything. In general, however, nonbelievers have rejected moral anarchy although they are aware of the anarchistic implications of definitions 1, 2, and 3. So it seems very unlikely that they would embrace these definitions.

Interestingly enough, nonbelievers can consistently embrace the Hypothetical Divine Command Theory without accepting moral anarchy for they can accept definitions 1', 2', and 3' and yet not believe that everything is permitted. For even if God did not exist, they could maintain that certain actions would still be forbidden because *if* God existed, he would command that certain actions be forbidden.[10]

One way of getting around the semantic problem of the Actual Divine Command Theory is to argue that the theory does not purport to capture the meaning of "morally obligatory," and so on in the discourse of nonbelievers and agnostics or even all Christians or Jews. Thus, it could be claimed merely that the analysis captures the meaning of these terms for most Christians and Jews. But this more restricted thesis also has problems.

Suppose an atheist says that it is morally obligatory that p and a typical theist—a person, let us assume, who would believe that ethical terms mean what the Divine Command Theory maintains they mean—says that p is morally forbidden. These two people certainly seem to be contradicting each other. But in the present account they would not be—indeed, they could not be—in conflict, since "morally obligatory" would mean something different to each of the two people. The theist would be saying that God commanded that ~p. But the atheist would certainly not be saying that God commanded that p. Thus, the restricted thesis being considered entails that these two people are not contradicting each other, appearances notwithstanding. Further, if an atheist asserts that it is morally forbidden that p and a typical theist asserts that it is morally forbidden that p, they appear to be agreeing. But they cannot be on this interpretation.

The apparent ability of nonbelievers and theists to agree and to contradict one another in moral matters suggests that the present attempt to restrict the scope of the theory has implausible implications. Thus, without further evidence we are justified in rejecting the view that most Christians and Jews mean by "morally obligatory," "morally permitted," and "morally forbidden" what definitions (1), (2), and (3) claim they do.

The Nonsemantic Divine Command Theory does not have the same problems, but it can be accused of failing to capture what religious people mean when they say that morality is dependent on God. T_1 simply says that "It is morally required that p" and "God commands that p" are necessarily true or false together. But it does not follow from this that something is morally obligatory *because* God commands it.

Consider the following possibility that seems perfectly compatible with T_1: God exists in every possible world; he is necessarily morally perfect in the sense that he would command what is morally required in all possible worlds because he is morally required to do so; there is a standard of what is morally independent of God's command. Although T_1 would be true, morality would not be dependent on God's command in the sense that some religious believers maintain. Rather, God's command could depend on what is morally required. God who by hypothesis is morally perfect would command what is morally required in all possible worlds on the basis of this independent standard.[11]

Clearly, then, some further assumption is needed in order to capture the idea that God's commands determine what is morally required. And Quinn does, in fact, make one, namely that "God is free to command anything he chooses to command."[12] This in effect assumes that God has no essential moral properties that would constrain his choice. Indeed, given T_1, T_2, and T_3 it is difficult to see what other assumption Quinn could make that captures the idea that God's commands determine what is morally required, morally permissible, and morally forbidden. The assumption that God has certain essential moral properties would be consistent with God's choice being based on some independent moral standard.

Given that God has no essential moral properties, it follows that:

1. For every x, it is logically possible that God could have commanded x (where x is a variable ranging over every possible set of actions).

But (1), combined with T_1, T_2, T_3, entails,

2. There are possible worlds in which God commands cruelty for its own sake and this command is morally required.[13]

Moral Problems

This brings us to the most infamous problem of the Divine Command Theory, namely that it has morally outrageous consequences. This is seen most clearly in the Actual Semantic Divine Command version. By definition, if God commands cruelty for its own sake, this is morally required. By definition, if God commands people not to be kind to each other, then being kind to each other is morally forbidden.[14] In the Hypothetical Divine Command Theory, the same problem arises. By definition, if there were a God and he commanded cruelty for its own sake, then the practice of cruelty for its own sake would be morally obligatory.

The Nonsemantic Divine Command Theory has the same problem, although not so obviously or directly as the semantic variants. To many morally sensitive people the idea that there are possible worlds in which God commands cruelty for its own sake and that this command is morally required—an implication of the Nonsemantic Actual Divine Command Theory of Quinn—constitutes a reductio ad absurdum of this version.

THE EPISTEMOLOGICAL PROBLEM

Since the Divine Command Theory supposes that morality is based on God's commands, the question arises of how one knows what God's commands are. There are three issues to consider here. First of all, there are several apparent conflicting religious sources of God's commands—the Bible, the Koran, the Book of Mormon. How does one choose the correct source? Second, even within the same source, e.g., the Bible, there seem to be conflicting moral commands. Third, there are different interpretations of the same command, e.g., thou shall not kill, but I will save discussion of this problem for a later chapter.

THE CONCEPTUAL PROBLEM

This discussion has so far been assuming that the notion of a command of a transcendent God makes sense, but this may not be so. The notion of a command is ambiguous in that it is sometimes considered a certain kind of speech act and is sometimes understood to be the content of this speech act. For example, the content of the command to close the door is conveyed by an imperative sentence "Close the door!" and is the result of a speech act involving an utterance of the words "Close the door!" on a certain occasion. This ambiguity holds in religious contexts too. Thus, the content of the command to not kill is conveyed by the imperative sentence "Thou shall not kill!" and is presumably the result of a speech act involving the utterance of the words "Thou shall not kill!" But this creates a certain problem.

If one interprets God as a nonspatial, nontemporal being without a body, what sense can one make of his performing a speech act? Such a being would seem incapable of an act that assumes, if not a body, at least some spatial and temporal point of origin. The only sense one can make of a *divine* command is to understand God in a nontranscendent way, as a being operating within space and time. But even this concession may not be enough, for it is unclear how a being within time and space could fail to have a body or how such a being could issue commands. The existence of a voice issuing commands seems to presume some physical vocal apparatus; golden letters written in the sky would seem to presuppose some physical writing appendage. However, this understanding of God assumes an anthropomorphism rejected by sophisticated theologians. Moreover, since this anthropomorphic God is a being operating within time and space, it is subject to empirical investigation. Unfortunately, the available evidence no more supports the hypothesis of its existence than it supports the hypothesis that Santa Claus exists.

Advocates of the Divine Command Theory are, thus, presented with a dilemma. If God is transcendent, the notion of a divine command seems difficult to understand. If God is construed in anthropomorphic terms, then the concept of a divine command makes sense but the hypothesis that God exists becomes very improbable.

One can attempt to overcome the problem by supposing that God uses the physical body of humans to issue commands; that God, the transcendental being, speaks through the mouth of Christ or Moses or Reverend Sun-Myung Moon. But this only pushes the problem back one step for it is not clear how a transcendent being, a being without a body, a being outside of time and space can speak through a being in time and space.

In ordinary life we understand perfectly well how one person can speak through another. By speech or writing the first individual conveys information or desire to the second who then conveys it to others. In this case, the second person is explicitly authorized or is understood by convention to be speaking for the first person. The process involves a causal chain operating between bodies; in particular, one person giving information, directions, or the like to another by voice or deed. But this clear familiar picture does not apply to God. For God to convey information or instructions to Jesus, Moses, or Reverend Moon by voice or deed would require a body he does not have.

The only other possibility would be for God to convey commands to human beings via something analogous to telepathy or thought transference. Then presumably there would be no need for God to perform some speech act. There is still a serious problem, however, for God is outside space and in some accounts outside time. It is difficult enough to understand what it would mean to say that thought exists outside of space and time. It is incomprehensible how thoughts or desires could be transferred or conveyed to human beings in space and time. Transfer and conveyance suggest a temporal process occurring between two points in space; even instantaneous transference, assuming this even makes sense, involves at least two spatial points. But, in the case of transfer of information from a transcendent God to his spokespersons, there is no spatial point of origin. One might as well speak of a marriage involving only one person or a parent who never had any children.

A MODIFIED DIVINE COMMAND THEORY

If the Divine Command Theory in its most extreme form does not work, might a modified version work? Now some advocates of the Modified Divine Command Theory believe that although the command of God is not a sufficient condition for moral obligation, it is a necessary condition. This would mean that necessarily if an action is morally obligatory, then God commands it. But there does not seem to be any reason to believe this. Even if God exists in this world, why could there not be possible worlds in which he does not exist? And why in some of these worlds could not human beings have a moral obligation not to practice cruelty for its own sake? Many nonbelievers would maintain that our actual world is such a world. Thus,

N. Necessarily, if it is morally obligatory that p, then God commands that p

has no support.

In addition to the problems already raised, the Modified Divine Command Theory has all the conceptual problems of its more radical version. If it is unintelligible how a transcendent God can issue commands, it is no less unintelligible how a transcendent God can issue commands and can create human beings who are supposed to obey them. It is difficult to see how giving commands and creating are acts that a nontemporal and nonspatial being could perform.[15]

Putting these problems aside, it might be argued that under certain conditions the divine command of God is a sufficient condition of moral obligation. In this view the mere fact that God commands that p does not entail that p is morally required. Suppose, for example, we add to the claim that God commands such and such that he is the creator of human beings. According to this modified version, children have a moral obligation to obey their parents. Insofar as we are to God as children are to their parents, human beings have an obligation to obey God just as children have an obligation to obey their parents. Thus, according to the Modified Divine Command view, the claim that God commands that p combined with the assumption that God created humans entails that humans should obey that p.[16]

However, it is far from clear that the modified view is correct, for it is uncertain under what circumstances God the Creator's commands bring about a moral obligation to follow the commands. Consider a Modified Nonactual Divine Command Theory. Stated schematically, the principle that would specify a sufficient condition of moral obligation would be this:

M. Necessarily if God commands that p under conditions C, then it is morally obligatory that p.

Conditions C would be those conditions found in a religious context that are analogous to the ones found in the context of ordinary life that create an obligation for children to follow the commands of their parents.

One obvious condition is that children only have an obligation to follow the commands of their parents if they are capable of doing so. Similarly for the children of God. Humans have an obligation to follow the commands of God only if they are capable of doing so. Stated more formally the general principle at work seems to be this:

P. If X created Y and Y is capable of following commands and X commands that p, then Y has the moral obligation to do that p.

Given P and the alleged fact that God issues the command that p is morally required and that God created humans and that humans are capable of obedience, it follows that p is morally required.

One problem in the application of P is that parents can issue conflicting commands. If they do, their children will not be capable of following all their commands. A similar problem could occur in religious contexts. If it did, God's children would have no obligation to follow the commands of God since they would be incapable of doing so. As it happens, in some instances the alleged commands of God do seem to be in conflict. Consider a famous example presented by Richard Brandt:

> Consider the Ten Commandments. One of them reads: "Remember the Sabbath day, to keep it holy. . . . In it thou shalt not do any work." Another reads: "Honour thy father and thy mother." These rules, which we assume may be taken as ethical statements (for example, "It is always wrong not to honour your father and mother.") are doubtless rather vague. There is one point, though, on which they are not vague: It seems that there is something we are always to do. These facts lead to difficulties. Suppose my father calls me on the phone on Sunday morning, tells me that a storm has blown off a piece of his roof the previous evening, and invites me to come and help him repair it before there is another rain. I seem to not be "honouring" my father if I refuse; I am breaking the rule about the Sabbath if I comply.[17]

Another problem with P is that it makes it obligatory to perform apparently immoral acts if a parent commands them. Surely if a parent commands a child to kill an innocent person for the parent's pleasure, the child has no obligation to do this. In a similar way, if God commanded one of his creatures to perform an immoral act for God's pleasure, the creature would have no moral obligation to do so. Yet, according to P, they would.[18]

It seems implausible in the extreme to believe that humans have an obligation to follow immoral commands even if God did create humans. Religious believers can attempt to overcome this problem by denying that these commands are immoral, appearances notwithstanding, or by denying that they are really the commands of God. The first attempted solution is implausible. Suppose that God commanded cruelty for its own sake. How could it be denied that this command is immoral? Surely humans would have no moral obligation to obey even though God created humans. The second solution assumes that there is a plausible way of distinguishing the apparent commands of God from those that are genuine. But, as we have seen, no way is readily available.

It may be argued that P simply needs to be modified. Consider:

P'. If X created Y and Y is capable of following commands and X commands x and x is not immoral, then Y has the moral obligation to do x.

But even this may not be enough, for children can legitimately refuse to follow a parent's command that is not immoral if it conflicts with some stronger obligation, and the same holds true for religious contexts. Thus, although the alleged command of God to refrain from stealing is not immoral, it should be disobeyed if, for example, stealing would save a life.

Clearly P' will have to be weakened further. Consider:

P". If X created Y and Y is capable of following commands and X commands x and x is not immoral and Y has no stronger obligation, then Y has the moral obligation to do x.

But even this may not be enough. Imagine that Smith's parents command him to paint their kitchen. Suppose Smith has no stronger obligations but that his parents have ill-used him all his life and, in general, have been cruel toward him. Does Smith really have an obligation to obey his parents? It is doubtful that he does.

The relevance of this example to the religious context is fairly clear. If we follow the analogy to one's parents through, it would entail that whether or not humans should feel obligated to follow God's commands should depend on how God has treated them. Here the problem of evil is relevant. This problem is traditionally posed as follows: Why believe that God exists given the existence of evil? For if God is all-good, he would want to prevent evil, and if God is all-powerful he could prevent evil, so why is there evil? One solution to the problem is to suppose that God is not all-good—at least not in our sense of "good." But, then, humans may just as legitimately refuse to follow the command of God as a child can refuse to follow the command of a parent who has ill-treated him or her.

Perhaps the most that can be said is this:

P'''. If X created Y and Y is capable of following commands and X commands x and x is not immoral and Y has no stronger obligation and X has not ill-used Y, then Y has the moral obligation to do x.

It is unclear, however, if even this principle is acceptable. For example, why should a child follow his parents' command to paint their kitchen, even if he has no stronger obligation and the parents have treated the child well, if they can afford to hire someone to paint it or if the kitchen has recently been painted or if there are other children who are eager to help the parents? It is at least debatable in these circumstances that the child is morally obligated to follow his parents' commands.

Is there an analogue to this in the religious context? Suppose God commands Smith to start a church in order to save the world. Does Smith have a moral obligation to obey if there are other people better able to do so and more willing to help? Does Smith have an obligation to obey even though he can see no need for such a church and God does not explain to him why there is a need? If we take the child-parent, human-God analogy seriously, it is not clear that he does. Of course, religious believers might say that Smith has a moral obligation since God has singled him out and God moves in mysterious ways. But parents can single out a child for some tasks and the parent's choice can appear mysterious to the child. The child has a right to know why he or she is chosen rather than a sibling who seems more qualified and more eager and also why the task needs to be done. Thus, if one follows through the analogy between parent and God to its ultimate conclusion, there is reason to suppose that even P''' fails. The only way that P''' (or P'' or P') would hold would be if one supposed that children have a blind obligation to obey their parents. They do not. If we take the analogy seriously, neither do God's children.

So far we have been unable to find a satisfactory formulation of condition C in M above. Thus, the obligation that children owe their parents and, by analogy, the obligation that humans owe God because he created them remains elusive. But let us suppose that a more subtle formulation of this obligation is satisfactory. A serious problem still remains.

In order to apply any of the above principles (or presumably a more subtle modification of them) it is necessary to have knowledge of one's moral obligations independently of them. For example, in order to apply P''' one must know both that the action under consideration is not immoral and that one has no stronger obligation. Thus, even if P''' is correct, it could not be applied without independent moral knowledge of what is immoral and of the other moral obligations one has. But the Divine Command Theory is supposed to tell us what is immoral and what our obligations are. Thus, the Modified Divine Command Theory does not seem capable of providing a sufficient condition for moral obligation without independent moral knowledge.

Another attempt to develop a Modified Divine Command Theory maintains that what is morally forbidden is identical with what is contrary to what a loving God commands. (Presumably, similar accounts could be given of moral obligation and moral permissibility.) Let us consider the nonsemantic version developed by R. M. Adams,[19] itself a modification of a version he put forward earlier.[20] Adams argues that properties like water and H_2O are necessarily identical although the identity cannot be known a priori; it is an empirical fact. In a similar way, the property of contrariety to a command of a loving God is, according to Adams, necessarily identical with the property of moral wrongness although this is not something one can know a priori; it is known a posteriori.[21]

One advantage this theory has over the other modified Divine Command Theory is that a loving God would not presumably command cruelty for its own sake. Thus, the theory would not have some of the outrageous moral implications discussed here. According to Adams, the theory has other advantages as well. He argues that his theory accords well with certain general characteristics that any plausible account of moral wrongness must have. For example, as the concept of wrongness functions in our thinking, the moral wrongness of an action is a property that an action has independent of what people think. Moral wrongness as identical with what is contrary to what God commands has this characteristic.

Nevertheless, there are several problems with Adams's theory. First, the advantages of his version of the Divine Command Theory are also shared by metaethical theories that do not assume the existence of a loving

God. One interesting alternative metaethical theory that differs from Adams's in one crucial respect is a hypothetical version of his Divine Command Theory. Instead of determining what is morally wrong in terms of the commands of an actual loving God one determines what is morally wrong in terms of the commands of a hypothetical loving God.[22]

Adams tries to meet this objection. Admitting that some ethical conclusions can be derived from the concept of a loving God—for example, a loving God would not command cruelty for its own sake—he argues that the hypothetical version fails to answer many other ethical questions.[23] He says that the concept of a loving God permits conflicting interpretations of what such a God would command and thus creates moral dilemmas and gives us no way of reconciling them. For example, a loving God would proscribe the killing of a person to increase the happiness of other people. But if the person will live the rest of his or her life in misery, then God's love might require the person's painless death. However, according to Adams, in relying on the actual commands of God such uncertainty is eliminated.

However, Adams is mistaken in supposing that if God reveals himself to human beings moral uncertainty is eliminated. First of all, if Adams is talking about historical revelations such as the Ten Commandments, these are themselves subject to different interpretations and can come into conflict. Moreover, they do not help to reconcile conflicts like the one specified above. However, Adams argues that he does not necessarily have historical revelation in mind and that his view of revelation is compatible with appeals to conscience and the Quaker view that God is revealed through "an Inner Light."[24] But appeals to conscience are often of no help, for conscience is frequently silent or else it issues inconsistent directions.[25] The upshot is that Adams has supplied no good reason why his version of Divine Command Theory has advantages over a hypothetical version.

In addition, Adams's theory inherits many of the problems of the other divine command theories. The conceptual problem remains of how a transcendent being, one that is nonspatial and on some accounts nontemporal, could make commands. We also have the problem of how a nonspatial and nontemporal being could be loving since a loving being entails loving action and loving action involves a body. Furthermore, Adams explicitly relates moral wrong to what God commands rather than to what God wills. This, he correctly argues, assumes a theory of revelation. He suggests several theories of revelation but he does not even attempt to answer the questions that can be raised against such theories. Finally, Adams admits that his theory has the apparently paradoxical implication that no action would be ethically wrong if there were no loving God. He attempts to dispel the apparent paradox by maintaining that if there were no God, people would still use the word "wrong." People would still call certain things "wrong." They might even call the same things "wrong" as we do. Indeed, he says that people might even express the same psychological state by saying "Cruelty is wrong" as we express by using these words. Unfortunately, none of this dispels the paradox. For, in his view, it would be true that if God did not exist, nothing would be wrong. Although, if God did not exist, people might correctly say in some sense "Cruelty is morally wrong," cruelty would not really be wrong. Any theory with this paradoxical implication is prima facie unacceptable. This, combined with other problems with the theory, gives us good grounds for rejecting it.

CONCLUSION

The variants of the Divine Command Theory examined here have serious problems that indicate the inferiority of Divine Command Theory to the nonreligious metaethical positions examined in earlier chapters. One of the most obvious disadvantages of Divine Command Theory is that there are no moral facts if God does not exist. In contrast, the nonreligious metaethics allows moral facts whether God exists or not. Since theism does not entail Divine Command Theory, the latter's problems do not entail that theism is false. Nevertheless, as previously noted, the theory does follow from theism when it is combined with certain assumptions about the nature of God—assumptions that many theists accept. Consequently, the failure of the Divine Command Theory entails that either theism is false or these assumptions are mistaken.

What implications does Divine Command Theory have for the objectivity of theistic ethics? First, it is difficult to see how theistic ethics can be objective if certain versions of the Divine Command Theory are accepted. Consider objectivity in the sense of being justified by impartial reasons and arguments. On the Extreme Divine Command Theory ethical claims are based on the arbitrary commands of God. This seems like the opposite of objectivity. Second, even some of the modified versions of Divine Command Theory provide no objective justification of ethical claims since they rely on alleged divine revelations about what God commands. But there are unreconcilable conflicts between the alleged divine revelations of different religious traditions and unreconcilable conflicting interpretations of the same alleged divine revelation in the same tradition. Third, consider objectivity in the sense of the existence of moral facts. All versions of Divine Command Theory assume that the creation of moral facts by divine commands makes sense. But the conceptual problem outlined above shows that it does not.

NOTES

1. For example, see Paul Helm, introduction to *Divine Commands and Morality*, ed. Paul Helm (Oxford: Oxford University Press, 1981), pp. 2–5 for a brief historical discussion of the theory.

2. See Kai Nielsen, *Ethics without God* (Amherst, N.Y.: Prometheus Books, 1973), p. 1.

3. According to Helm, Ockham held a view similar to this. See Helm, introduction, p. 3.

4. For a contemporary statement of this theory see Roderick Firth, "Ethical Absolutism and the Ideal Observer," *Philosophy and Phenomenological Research* 12 (1955): 317–45. See also Richard Brandt, *Ethical Theory* (Englewood Cliffs, N.J.: Prentice Hall, 1959), pp. 173–76. For a comparison of the Ideal Observer Theory and the Divine Command Theory see Charles Taliaferro, "The Divine Command Theory of Ethics and the Ideal Observer," *Sophia* 22 (1983): 3–8.

5. For example, I have elsewhere argued that it is logically impossible in one standard conception of God for God to experience the emotions of hate or greed or envy since God is morally perfect. See Martin, *Atheism: A Philosophical Justification* (Philadelphia: Temple University Press, 1990), chap. 12. However, this conception of God is not the only one that theologians have accepted. On this standard conception of God it is assumed that God necessarily would not experience hate, greed, envy, and so on, because these are morally forbidden emotional states. But, as we shall see, in many versions of the Divine Command Theory it is doubtful that God has any essentially moral nature. In these versions

of the Divine Command Theory, God could make any emotional state morally permissible.

6. Phillip L. Quinn, *Divine Commands and Moral Requirements* (Oxford: Clarendon Press, 1978).

7. Ibid., p. 30.

8. I propose a nonsemantic version of Ideal Observer Theory in chapter 3.

9. See, Richard Price, *Review of the Principle Questions in Morals*, partly reprinted in Richard B. Brandt, *Value and Obligation* (New York: Harcourt, Brace and World, Inc., 1961), pp. 330–41.

10. The question might be raised of how, if they did not believe that God exists, nonbelievers could know what God would command. One answer is that an atheist would try to approximate to the properties of God that are relevant for making commands about what is morally permitted and morally forbidden. For example, suppose it is logically necessary that if God exists, he is infinitely merciful and loving. Nonbelievers would attempt to determine what God would command if he were to exist by being as merciful and loving as they could be.

However, this suggestion has a problem. In some versions of the Divine Command Theory God does not have any essential or necessary moral nature. Although he may be infinitely merciful or loving in this world, he is not in all possible worlds. What God commands is based on arbitrary fiat. Thus, approximating to the essential properties of God would not enable an atheist to determine what God would command if he were to exist. Since God has no essential moral properties, it would seem that what God would command would be unpredictable in principle. God himself could not even know what he would command in other possible worlds. Thus, although nonbelievers could embrace the Hypothetical Divine Command Theory without commitment to moral anarchy, they could not know what God would command if God were to exist. The Divine Command Theory in hypothetical form would be useless in determining what should be done.

The Ideal Observer Theory does not have this problem since the Ideal Observer does have essential properties—unbiasedness, impartiality, unlimited powers of empathy, and being completely informed. An atheist can approximate to these properties and see whether, when contemplating the act in question, he or she has a feeling of approval or disapproval.

11. See Thomas B. Talbott, "Quinn on Divine Commands and Moral Requirements," *International Journal for the Philosophy of Religion* (1982): 194–98. See also John Chandler, "Is the Divine Command Theory Defensible?" *Religious Studies* 20 (1984): 443–52.

12. Quinn, *Divine Commands and Moral Requirements*, p. 31.

13. See Talbott, "Quinn on Divine Commands," pp. 201–202.

14. This problem was first raised in Plato's *Euthyphro*. The question posed was whether a pious or holy thing was beloved by the gods because it was pious or holy or whether it was pious or holy because it was beloved by the gods. The latter thesis suggests that anything can be pious or holy if it is beloved by the gods. See Helm, "Introduction," p. 2.

15. For a criticism of aspects of Brody's theory not considered here see Robert Young, "Theism and Morality," in Helm, *Divine Commands and Morality*, pp. 156–60.

16. A theory along these lines is developed by Baruch A. Brody in "Morality and Religion Reconsidered," in Helm, *Divine Commands and Morality*, pp. 141–53.

17. Richard B. Brandt, *Ethical Theory* (Englewood Cliffs, N.J.: Prentice-Hall, Inc., 1959), p. 17.

18. The Old Testament is full of various alleged commands of God that seem morally dubious. A few famous examples are death for unchastity (Deut. 22:20, 21); death for straying near the tabernacle (Num. 1:51); death for blasphemy (Lev. 24:16).

19. Robert Merrihew Adams, "Divine Command Metaethics as Necessary *a posteriori*," *Journal of Religious Ethics* 7 (1979): 71–79. Reprinted in Helm, *Divine Commands and Morality*, pp. 109–19.

20. Robert Merrihew Adams, "A Modified Divine Command Theory of Ethical Wrongness," in Helm, *Divine Commands and Morality*, pp. 83–108.

21. However, he does not think moral wrongness can be known empirically. See Robert Merrihew Adams, *The Virtue of Faith* (New York: Oxford University Press, 1987), p. 142, n. 3.

22. Avi Sagi and Daniel Statman, *Religion and Morality* (Amsterdam: Rodopi, 1994), pp. 36–37.

23. Robert Merrihew Adams, "Moral Arguments for Theistic Beliefs," in *Rationality and Religious Belief*, ed. Cornelius Delaney (Notre Dame, Ind.: Notre Dame University Press, 1979), p. 122.

24. Ibid., p. 116.

25. Cf. Sagi and Statman, *Religion and Morality,* p. 38.

8

TWO DEFENSES OF THE DIVINE COMMAND THEORY

As the last chapter made clear, there are several problems with the Divine Command Theory, perhaps the most troubling of which is that the theory seems to entail absurd moral consequences. Suppose, for example, that God commands the torture of children. According to this theory this action would be morally obligatory. Yet the torturing of children is a morally outrageous act. On the other hand, if it denied that God would issue such a command, it would seem that God's commands are determined by some independent standard of morality. In other words, if God's commands are based on his will, they can be morally outrageous. If they are not, then they are independent of God and the Divine Command Theory is false.

In this chapter two strategies employed by defenders of the Divine Command Theory to block this difficulty will be considered. The two approaches are rooted in rather different Christian traditions. The Blunting the Absurdity Response strategy falls clearly in the Divine Voluntarism tradition of John Duns Scotus and William of Ockham. In this tradition the divine will rather than divine or human reason is the ultimate standard of morality. Consequently, an act is immoral simply because God wills it to be so. This strategy stresses the absolute power of God's will and attempts to show that the moral outrageousness of the Divine Command Theory is only apparent or else that it is real but acceptable.[1] What I call the Essential Moral Attribute Response falls squarely in the Augustinian tradition of theology according to which God has an essential moral nature that limits the power of his will.[2] The Essential Moral Attribute Response maintains that although morality depends upon God for its existence, it is not arbitrary because God's will is restrained by his essential moral nature. That nature provides an unchanging and absolute moral standard.

ESSENTIAL MORAL ATTRIBUTE RESPONSE

To begin with, the Essential Moral Attribute Response argues that if God exists he has essential moral attributes that prevent him from issuing commands such as to torture babies. It also maintains that God's necessary moral attributes set the standard of morality and without them there would be no morality.

For the sake of the argument let us accept the view that God is a being that is essentially good. It does not follow why should we accept the thesis that morality would be impossible without God. In general, the following is an invalid argument:

1. Property P is part of the essential nature of X.
2. If X did not exist, property P would not be a property of anything.

For example, the property of being benevolent is part of the essential nature of being a saint. But it does not follow that if saints do not exist, the property of being benevolent would not be a property of anything. So the view of God assumed by the Essential Moral Attribute Response does not entail that moral goodness would be impossible without God.

Of course, one might try to support the thesis that morality is impossible without God by arguing that if God is essentially good, it follows that properties such as benevolence and justice are good by virtue of being necessary properties of God. But it is irrelevant to the *moral* nature of benevolence and justice that they are essential to God's nature. In fact, in general this is an invalid inference:

1. X is P.
2. X is an essential part of Y.
3. Y is essentially P.
---
4. Hence, X is P because X is an essential attribute of Y.

For example, let X be compassion, P be good, and Y be sainthood. The conclusion that compassion is good because it is an essential attribute of sainthood does not follow. Granted, compassion is good, but this is not because it is an essential attribute of being a saint.

So far I have questioned the assumption that God's essentially moral nature entails the thesis that morality is impossible without God. But are there reasons for supposing that morality is possible without God? If "possible" refers to *logical possibility*, there seems to be a very simple reason to suppose morality is possible without God. Something is logically possible when it is not logically impossible. However, the following claim is not logically impossible:

1. There are moral facts and God does not exist.

Now it might be argued that (1) is a logically impossible claim since God's existence is itself logically necessary.[3] However, this counterargument presumes the soundness of some version of the Ontological Argument. But this argument is widely discredited.[4] Without the soundness of this argument I see no reason to suppose that (1) is logically impossible.

There are two more reasons for rejecting the impossibility of moral facts without God. The first is that in order to show that atheistic morality is necessarily impossible, theists must show that all attempts to ground morality on a nontheistic basis fails. To my knowledge, however, the attempts of Roderick Firth, Richard Boyd, Peter Railton, and David Brink to defend moral realism without a religious foundation[5] have not been refuted.[6]

In addition, if it were true that morality is dependent on God it would follow that if God did not exist, then the basic belief that the gratuitous torture of babies is morally wrong would be mistaken. But this is absurd. Israel philosophers Avi Sagi and Daniel Statman[7] have pointed out that the Divine Command Theory has (depending on its formulation) two basic problems. On the one hand, if Divine Command Theory is formulated in terms of the will of God, it has the Problem of Moral Arbitrariness. Morality is arbitrarily determined by God's commands. Consequently, gratuitous torture of babies is morally obligatory if God commands it. This is absurd. On the other hand, if Divine Command Theory avoids the Problem of Moral Arbitrariness by arguing that God is necessarily kind and loving, then there is the Karamazov Problem. If there were no God, then anything is morally permitted—including the gratuitous torture of babies. However, this is equally absurd.

Sagi and Statman appeal to the requirement that all metaethics theories including Divine Command Theory must be compatible with our basic moral beliefs. However, both formulations of Divine Command Theory conflict with our basic moral beliefs. According to Sagi and Statman basic ethical statements regarding the wrongness of actions such as wanton cruelty and the murder of innocent people are analytic in a broad sense of the term. It is just as inconceivable that gratuitous torture of babies is not morally wrong in some possible world than it is that an object is green and red all over at the same time in some possible world. However, one need not suppose, as Avi and Statman do, that such ethical statements are analytic in a broad sense to suppose that the claim is absurd that wanton cruelty is not wrong. Such a claim would conflict with our most well-supported moral judgments. It has the same absurd epistemic status as the claim that the earth is flat. It is not necessarily false but it is manifestly false nonetheless.

One reason why theists resist allowing morality to be independent of God is that they assume this would compromise God's omnipotence. It is assumed that if morality is not based on God, then God's power is lessened. In the case of logic, however, many theists take a different attitude. Instead of supposing that logic is dependent on God, they make perfectly good sense of godless worlds in which logical principles such as the law of noncontradiction hold. Why cannot they also make perfectly good sense of godless worlds in which objective moral principles hold? In neither case is God's power affected. He can do everything it is logically possible for him to do but it is logically impossible for him to make both P and ~P true. Similarly, since he is essentially good, it is logically impossible for him to command the gratuitous torture of infants. The principles of logic are not dependent on God and neither are the moral principles. The existence of independent standards is quite compatible with the admission that God's nature is essentially logical and essentially moral and, consequently, that God could act neither illogically nor immorally.

Another obstacle to embracing the view that morality is independent of God is the assumption that if this were so, God would have to consult an independent standard of morality whenever he acted. This seems paradoxical. However, this assumption is incorrect. Insofar as God is essentially good this standard is instantiated in his nature and he is good effortlessly and spontaneously. No continuing consultation is necessary. But this no more shows that morality is dependent on God than the effortless and spontaneous goodness of some saints shows that morality is dependent on them.

Although an advocate of Essential Moral Attribute Response may not explicitly raise any epistemological issues in defending Divine Command Theory, an epistemological problem is close to the surface. Supposing that God is essentially good, how can we know what God commands? One might suggest that we can know what an essentially good God would command without recourse to religious sources such as divine revelation. However it seems unlikely that all knowledge about God's commands could be known without revelation. If God exists, he would need to convey particular and specific directions to humans that cannot be deduced from his essential goodness. Since there are seemingly unreconcilable conflicting commands in different religions and seemingly unreconcilable conflicting interpretations of the same command in the same religion, how can we know which alleged command or interpretation is correct?

BLUNTING THE ABSURDITY RESPONSE

Two recent applications of the Blunting the Absurdity Response are to be found in the writings of Phillip Quinn and Paul Rooney.[8] Quinn argues that his formulation of the Divine Command Theory does not have absurd implications because our moral intuitions "fail to produce agreement about controversial issues, as recent actual cases involving abortion, euthanasia and similar problems show quite clearly."[9] He seems to be saying that unreliable and controversial moral intuitions have been adduced to show that cruelty for its own sake is wrong. Consequently, such intuitions cannot be used against the Divine Command Theory. However, considered judgments, not intuitions, are involved in the case of commanding cruelty for its own sake. Moreover, these judgments are hardly controversial.

Quinn adds that moral intuitions are especially unreliable when one is called on "to go beyond actual moral problems into the realm of the merely possible."[10] Since the case of God commanding cruelty for its own sake is a possibility, not an actuality, he seems to be saying that our considered judgments—what he calls intuitions—would be especially unreliable. But, in fact, possible cases are usually less difficult to cope with than actual ones since actual cases involve disputes about the facts that in possible cases can be decided by fiat. Moreover, in possible cases one can simplify the situation to its essentials.[11]

In the case at issue—God's commanding cruelty for its own sake— one can make all the necessary simplifying assumptions. For example, there is no problem of whether God really is commanding cruelty for some indirect human benefit. He is not. There is no complication that the apparent pain involved in the cruel act is illusory. It is not. And so on. The complications involved in actual cases can all be eliminated by stipulation.

Quinn goes so far as to say that reliance on moral intuitions in order to refute the Divine Command Theory is merely moral dogmatism. He says there is "no reason why a divine command theorist should subscribe to a view which licenses moral dogmatism on the part of his critics."[12] This position seems to assume that the critics are relying on a controversial moral intuition. But, as I have already shown, the belief that cruelty for its own sake is morally wrong is scarcely controversial. Moreover, it is based not on intuitions but on uncontroversial considered judgments.

Furthermore, Quinn himself seems to rely on considered judgments about cruelty. He says that some possible world with the

> greatest over-all similarity to the actual world in which God commands what we call "gratuitous cruelty" might yet be very unlike the actual world, so dissimilar that intuition is an unreliable guide to what is required and what forbidden there. It might be, for example, that in such worlds what we call "gratuitous cruelty" provides cathartic release for its perpetrators without causing pain to its victims.[13]

This example seems to assume that people's moral judgments about "cruelty" would be in agreement if certain background circumstances were changed and made explicit. That is, he assumes that if we knew that what we called "gratuitous cruelty" involved cathartic release for people who committed it and did not cause harm to those whom it was committed against, then our moral judgments would be in agreement that gratuitous cruelty would not be morally wrong. If Quinn relies on considered moral judgments in this way in this case, surely the critics of the Divine Command Theory can do so in other cases. The critics must just be sure that the background circumstances on which their judgments are based are made explicit.

It should be noted that Quinn's example does not tell at all against the argument that there is a *genuine* case of gratuitous cruelty, not one merely (wrongly) called "gratuitous cruelty." In Quinn's example, it is clear that there is no gratuitous cruelty. First, the "cruelty" is not gratuitous since there is a beneficial side effect. Second, it is unclear why one even speaks of "cruelty" in this case since the victims are not in pain. In the example adduced here, however, there is no beneficial side effect and people are in pain. It is significant that Quinn had to change the example in order to make his point.

For his part, Rooney accepts the view that God's commands are arbitrary in some senses of the term and thinks that if God commanded humans to torture children "for fun" we would have a moral obligation to do so. However, he endeavors to soften the apparent absurdity of this implication and tries to make the arbitrariness acceptable.

In order to understand the full impact of the position at issue we must understand the expression "One has a moral obligation to torture children for fun." Presumably what is at issue is the infliction of severe pain on children for no reason other than that one enjoys doing it. However, the phrase "for fun" does not present the problem in its starkest and purest terms. First of all, to say that one has a moral obligation to torture children for fun is ambiguous. It could be understood hypothetically: If one has fun torturing infants, then one has a moral obligation to do it. So interpreted it would have no implication for someone who did not have fun engaging in torture. Since presumably only a few sadists would get pleasure from such an activity and most people would think that torturing children is anything but fun, the impact on this command might be rather restricted. However, the obligation can be understood in a different way. The obligation might be that everyone has an obligation to torture children *and* have fun while doing it. This would be an unreasonable obligation in that it would be one that people could not fulfill.

In addition to the ambiguity, insofar as the phrase "for fun" seems to refer to the motive of the action, it diverts attention from the justification of the action. Torture of children, although done "for fun," could conceivably be morally justified if there was an overriding moral reason for doing it. For example, suppose torturing a child were necessary to prevent a mad bomber from blowing up New York City. If someone tortured this child for fun, the action would still be morally justified. I suggest that the phrase "torture for fun" be dropped and that we speak instead of "gratuitous torture," that is, torture when there is no overriding justification such as the saving of human life, obtaining vital information, and the like. So interpreted let us understand the alleged moral obligation created by God's command to be that everyone is morally obligated to gratuitously torture children. Whether they have fun doing so would be irrelevant.[14] And let us see if anything Rooney says blunts the moral outrageousness of the gratuitous torturing of children.

THE UTILITARIAN ANALOGIES
AND CONFUSIONS

To try to overcome the apparent absurdity of his view Rooney uses an argument from analogy derived from utilitarian moral theory. He points out that on utilitarian grounds torture is sometimes morally justified:

> [I]t is not self-evidently true that torture is wrong in all circumstances. It could certainly be justified with a degree of plausibility on utilitarian grounds, if it were undertaken for the common good and likely to effectively achieve it. If information necessary for the very survival of one's immediate society, or society as a whole society, could only be obtained by torturing one's enemy then there would be a utilitarian case in favour of torture, nor would it be of much relevance that the victim was innocent.[15]

However, this point is irrelevant to the case at issue. Few people would deny that under extreme circumstance torture is morally permitted, even morally required. The question is whether the *gratuitous* torture of children is ever morally justified. Rooney also introduces the following example. He considers a surgeon who operates on a child to save the child's life although no anesthetic is available:

Suppose that the surgeon takes pleasure in inflicting pain in these circumstances, and acts with that pleasure as the end he has in view: if we wish now to condemn on moral grounds what occurs then this can only be because "what occurs" includes the intention of the agent. We condemn him for his bad intention or his wrongful motive. But if that is our only reason for condemning him then it is clear that in this case, a case deliberately intended by Swinburne and others to be, on accounts of its extreme nature an example of something always and undeniably wrong, that the unchanging moral status of the action is only to be admitted after due consideration of the end of the action or the intention of the agent. The action *in itself* can be thought of as morally indifferent: what one intends to convey by *action in itself* may be only observable, let it be supposed, in which case the surgeon's state of mind forms no part of it.[16]

This example is still not one of torture, let alone gratuitous torture, and Rooney's comments on it are, moreover, confused. The doctor is saving the child's life and of necessity is causing the child great pain. On utilitarian grounds the doctor's action is morally correct. Thus, the action in itself is hardly morally indifferent as Rooney says. The peculiarity of the example is that the doctor's motive is apparently to cause the child pain and not to save his life. Just how the doctor could have such a motive and proceed with the operation is not explained. One would have thought that given the doctor's goal of causing pain other means would have made more sense. In any case, although the doctor's motive is reprehensible, this does not affect the moral correctness of the action. Indeed, the doctor's motive is irrelevant to assessing whether the action is morally obligatory.

What Rooney needs is an example of child torture that is not a necessary means to some more important moral goal which is not obviously morally impermissible. This he has not supplied. By means of a smoke screen of irrelevant examples and a confusion of the motive for the action with the morality of the action itself, that omission is hidden.

NECESSARY AND INSTINCTIVE BELIEFS

Rooney also tries to make his position acceptable by arguing that moral convictions such as that the torture of children is morally wrong are not logically necessary or even necessary for human life, but are based on contingent instinctive beliefs. He admits that his position "seems irrational" and is "scarcely imaginable." If God commanded torture, this would "seriously violate our fundamental instinctive beliefs." It would be "unacceptable" if we were required to violate the "non rational but essential human aspect of personality at His command (because such actions would be strictly speaking non human)."[17] But this does not induce Rooney to question the Divine Command Theory. He argues:

> What follows, if God's rational nature is to be preserved, is that we must assume God would not command torture or permit torture for pleasure without first bringing about some fundamental change in our nature, or that if He did command or permit it, while our nature remained as it is now, then He had some good reason which is beyond our power to grasp. We are not entitled to rule out a priori any such divine command or permission however.[18]

Rooney does not say what changes in our nature he has in mind. Some changes would block the absurdity of his position only by eliminating torture or gratuitous torture. Suppose, for example, that God could make people who did not feel pain. Then there could be no *torture* since torture by definition entails the infliction of pain. Or suppose that God could make human beings in such a way that torture was always necessary for human flourishing. Then there could be no *gratuitous* torture since gratuitous torture would entail torture that is not necessary for some important moral goal. Or suppose that God could create people without moral sensitivity. Then no one would be morally repulsed by gratuitous torture although it might be going on all around them. Still this would not show that the gratuitous torture of children was morally permissible, let alone morally obligatory.

Rooney also considers the possibility that God might command torture without bringing about any change in our nature. But he assures us that, if this happened, God would have good reason for doing so that was beyond our grasp. Does he mean that God would have good *moral* reason that, if known, would justify the torture? If so, then we still do not have a case of gratuitous torture that is morally obligatory. And if some other type of reason is intended, then we have a case of God issuing a morally outrageous command. Nothing Rooney has said makes this acceptable.

DIVINE MEANS AND ENDS

A strategy similar to this last is to say that according to the traditional view what is intrinsically wrong is always relative to what God has created as ends for human beings. Thus, Rooney says that "intrinsic wrongness is itself defined in relation to the divinely ordered end for man. . . . *[G]iven* human nature as it is, nothing can make right certain actions which always impede or prevent proper development and flourishing. Again, the divine voluntarist can accept this, for he merely seeks to point out that omnipotent God could have ordained some other end for man" (emphasis in original).[19]

There are, however, two problems with this idea. First, since God is all-powerful he could make anything a means to any end so long as the means chosen is not logically in conflict with the end chosen. God could have achieved human proper development and flourishing in an indefinite number of ways. God could have made torture a means to the end of human flourishing however this is characterized, so long as this were not in conflict with this end. But there is no obvious necessity in his doing so. Given that he had other means, why should he use this end?

Second, even if Rooney is correct that a means cannot be considered in isolation, his discussion of divine ends merely pushes the difficulty back. In the divine voluntarist's view any end God chooses for humans is by definition good. But this is just as morally absurd as is the idea that the gratuitous torture of children is morally obligatory. Suppose that God decided that the proper development and flourishing of human beings is abject misery. Human development would then be characterized in terms of an increase of degrading pain and humiliating suffering. Let us assume that the torture of children was indeed a logically necessary means for achieving this end. It would certainly not follow that either the end or the means was morally good. Indeed, far from this strategy blunting the absurdity of Rooney's position, it brings it into bold relief.

THE ALLEGED ARBITRARINESS
OF ALL MORALITIES

The last strategy that Rooney uses to try to overcome the absurdity of his position is to argue that the basis of any moral system is arbitrary. Consequently, the Divine Command Theory is in no worse shape than an atheistic morality since the basis of such a morality must also be arbitrary. He argues thusly:

> If an objector to divine command theory continues to be dissatisfied with the account of morality according to which God's pleasure, so to speak, is made to be the foundations of morality—perhaps arguing that there is nothing particular moral about this—then he should be reminded that, whatever morality is based upon, the ultimate criterion of the good must be something that is non moral. As Brown observes, in order to avoid an infinite regress "it follows that the very possibility of morality depends upon the possibility of having an ethical criterion which is not adopted by passing a moral judgment on it." In the absence of a Divine Creator, it would not appear to be implausible to base morality upon the happiness of human beings—which would amount to no more than basing it on what people like. Indeed, some atheistic moralities are precisely of this kind. Then if the core belief of traditional Christianity is correct, if Almighty God exists, such objectors ought to be prepared to accept an account which accords His pleasures the place given to man's pleasures in corresponding atheistic accounts.[20]

The first problem with this argument is that one of the main premises is wrong—namely that, barring an infinite regress, the ultimate criterion of morality must be nonmoral. In fact, there are at least two other possibilities that are not considered by Rooney. One is that some moral claims may be basic and foundational; that is, not justified by another criterion either moral or nonmoral. Intuitionism is an example of such a view. Although there are problems with this position, many of the objections to it are misplaced.[21] Moreover, it is not an absurd view as is Rooney's for it does not have morally outrageous implications. A second possibility is to ground moral claims in a coherence theory of justification as both John Rawls and David Brink have done.[22] The second problem with Rooney's argument is that it assumes that an infinite regress of moral justifications is vicious. But such justifications need not be so.[23] And a third problem with Rooney's view is that even a secular justification of morality in terms of human happiness does not have the same morally absurd implications as his own view. Although one consequence of utilitarianism may be that children under certain extreme conditions should be tortured, the theory forbids the gratuitous torture of children—something that Rooney's view would allow.

CONCLUSION

The Essential Moral Attribute Response does indeed avoid one unacceptable implication of the Divine Command Theory: In this view God could not command such acts as the gratuitous torture of children. It does so by rejecting a voluntarism view of the divine and arguing that God's moral attributes are essential. But the Essential Moral Attribute Response does not establish that morality is dependent on God. Nor does it establish that God's moral attributes are moral simply because they are necessary attributes of God. Moreover, no good reasons have been offered to suppose that morality is impossible without God.

The use of Blunting the Absurdity Response by Quinn and Rooney to soften the absurdity of making the gratuitous torture of children morally required if commanded by God is in its turn unsuccessful. Quinn fails to acknowledge the uncontroversial status of the considered judgment of the immorality of cruelty for its own sake. Rooney systematically confuses the question of whether gratuitous torture is morally acceptable with the question of whether torture is acceptable if it is done for overriding reasons. Although he admits that God's commanding torture would violate our fundamental instinctual beliefs, he does not say what fundamental changes in our nature would make torture acceptable. His argument that the intrinsic evil of torture is relative to certain divinely chosen ends also fails since questions can be raised about the evil of these ends. Finally, his attempt to argue that the basis of all moral systems is arbitrary is unsuccessful.

But the examination of the Essential Moral Attribute Response and the Blunting the Absurdity Response again indicates the inferiority of the Divine Command Theory of morality to the nonreligious metaethics developed in earlier chapters. For example, this latter stance allows for objectivity in the sense of moral facts whether or not God exists. In contrast, both the Essential Moral Attribute Response and the Blunting the Absurdity Response entail that there are no moral facts if God does not exist. Moreover, Rooney's and Quinn's unsuccessful defense of the Blunting the Absurdity Response indicates that their interpretations of Divine Command Theory lack objectivity in the sense of impartiality. First, there is the moral problem of the arbitrary nature of divine commands and second there is the epistemological problem of unreconcilable conflicting commands and unreconcilable conflicting interpretations of the same command. Although the defense of the Essential Moral Attribute Response does not have all of the problems of the Blunting the Absurdity Response with respect to objectivity in the sense of impartiality, it still has some. There is no impartial way of reconciling conflicting revelations in different religious traditions and conflicting interpretations of the same revelation in the same tradition.

NOTES

1. See Paul Rooney, *Divine Command Morality* (Aldershot, England: Avebury, 1996) and Phillip L. Quinn, *Divine Commands and Moral Requirements* (Oxford: Clarendon, 1978), pp. 58–60.

2. This approach was adopted by Greg Bahnsen, John Frame, and more recently by Paul Copan. See Greg Bahnsen, *Theonomy in Christian Ethics* (Phillipburg, N.J.: Presbyterian and Reformed Publishing Co., 1977), p. 284, and John Frame's position in the Martin-Frame Internet Debate (http://www.infidels.org/library/modern/michael_martin/martin-frame/). See also Paul Copan, "Can Michael Martin Be a Moral Realist? Sic et Non," *Philosophia Christi* Series 2, 1, no. 2 (1999): 45–71.

3. John Frame used this argument in our Internet debate. http://www.infidels.org/library/modern/michael_martin/martin-frame/

4. See Michael Martin, *Atheism: A Philosophical Justification* (Philadelphia: Temple University Press, 1990), chap. 2.

5. See, for example, Roderick Firth, "Ethical Absolutism and the Ideal Observer," in *Readings in Ethical Theory*, 2d ed., ed. Wilfrid Sellars and John Hospers (Englewood Cliffs, N.J.: Prentice-Hall, 1970); Richard Boyd, "How to Be a Moral Realist" and Peter Railton, "Moral Realism," in *Moral Discourse and*

Practice, ed. Stephen Darwall, Allan Gibbard, and Peter Railton (Oxford: Oxford University Press, 1997); David O. Brink, *Moral Realism and the Foundations of Ethics* (Cambridge: Cambridge University Press, 1989), pp. 37–39, 197–203.

6. Copan, "Michael Martin," and my rebuttal, Michael Martin, "A Response to Paul Copan's Critique of Atheistic Objective Morality," *Philosophia Christi* Series 2, 1, no. 2 (1999): 127.

7. Avi Sagi and Daniel Statman, *Religion and Morality* (Amsterdam: Rodopi, 1995), pp. 55–61.

8. Quinn, *Divine Commands*, and Rooney, *Divine Command Morality*.

9. Quinn, *Divine Commands*, p. 58.

10. Ibid.

11. This is why possible cases are often used to make a clear moral point. See Thomas B. Talbott, "Quinn on Divine Commands and Moral Requirements," *International Journal for the Philosophy of Religion* 13 (1982): 205.

12. Quinn, *Divine Commands*, p. 60.

13. Ibid.

14. The statement "One has a moral obligation to gratuitously torture children," lacks precision. One can give it more clarity by arbitrarily supposing that God by his command creates the following alleged moral obligation:

GT. There is moral obligation to gratuitously cause excruciating physical pain to every person from birth to age 16 for ten hours a day.

To be sure GT can be given even harsher formulations but nothing in my argument turns on what particular formulation one adopts.

15. Rooney, *Divine Command Morality*, pp. 107–108.

16. Ibid.

17. Ibid.

18. Ibid.

19. Ibid., p. 109.

20. Ibid., p. 111.

21. See Brink, *Moral Realism*, Appendix 3.

22. John Rawls, *A Theory of Justice* (Cambridge, Mass.: Harvard University Press, 1971); Brink, *Moral Realism*, chap. 5.

23. Brink, *Moral Realism*, Appendix 1.

9

CHRISTIAN ETHICS AND THE IMITATION OF CHRIST

CHRISTIAN NORMATIVE ETHICS AND THE DIVINE COMMAND THEORY

In chapters 7 and 8 the Divine Command Theory, the metaethics of choice among most Christian ethicists, was evaluated and found wanting. In this chapter I will consider a theoretical issue of Christian normative ethics. In particular, a fundamental commandment of Christian ethics will be examined: the commandment to imitate Jesus. Many Christians claim that to imitate Jesus is the ethical goal of their faith and that the implicit rule to imitate him is the basic maxim of Christian ethics. They maintain that whatever Jesus may have said, it is the example set by his actions that give substance to Christian morality and provide its fundamental guidelines. They argue that as Christians they should strive to do what Jesus did.

In this chapter I will argue that what following the command to imitate Jesus involves is unclear and that following this command is infeasible and morally inappropriate. In my discussion I will consider the views of two representative thinkers who advocated the imitation of Jesus: Philip Quinn, a contemporary Christian philosopher, and Thomas à Kempis, a fifteenth-century German monk.

IMITATING JESUS

Let us suppose, then, that the basal decree of Christian morality is this: Imitate Jesus! To be sure, Christians will grant that they cannot in principle completely follow the command to imitate Jesus. After all, Jesus as God-incarnate was morally perfect and human beings cannot be perfect. Still they will assume that although completely following the command to imitate Jesus is impossible, it is a goal worth striving for and approximating as much as possible. Moreover, even some atheists may harbor the thought that when it is divorced from its theological trappings, following the command to imitate Jesus is a goal nonbelievers might well strive to attain.

Let us consider the feasibility, clarity, and moral appropriateness of the command to imitate Jesus.

THE FEASIBILITY OF THE COMMAND TO IMITATE JESUS

In order to imitate somebody's life one must have accurate knowledge about it. In the case of Jesus this is precisely what we lack. Indeed, there is a vast scholarly literature detailing our immense ignorance concerning his life. Modern critical methods of biblical scholarship have called into question the historical accuracy of the New Testament concerning Jesus.[1] For example, W. Trilling has argued that "not a single date of his life" can be established with certainty[2] and J. Kahl has maintained that the only thing that is known about him is that he "existed at a date and place which can be established approximately."[3] Other scholars have argued that the quest for the historical Jesus is hopeless.[4]

In addition to this quite justified general skepticism concerning the details of Jesus' life, there are reasons for being skeptical about the historical accuracy of the ethical pronouncements in the Gospels which form the justification of his ethical behavior. As I have argued at length elsewhere, early Christian writers say nothing about Jesus' ethical pronouncements.[5] Indeed, even when it would be to their advantage to do so Paul and other early Christian writers do not refer to the ethical teachings of Jesus as they are stated in the Gospels.

The apparent ignorance of these early Christian writers about the ethical teachings of Jesus raises serious questions about whether he really did teach what the Gospels say he did and whether he did perform the moral actions he is said to have done. How could it be that *none* of these early writers invoked Jesus' views and ethical example when it would have been to their advantage to do so? One obvious explanation is that the teachings of Jesus are a later addition and were not part of the original Christian doctrine. If this explanation is accepted, there is no good reason to suppose that so-called Christian ethics is what Jesus taught or that Jesus' alleged ethical behavior is in fact the way he acted. However, most Christians seem to ignore this problem and take the synoptic Gospels as the basis for imitating Jesus.

Although he advocates the imitation of Jesus' life, in a recent paper Christian philosopher Philip Quinn seems to admit that the New Testament picture of Jesus is not completely accurate. He suggests that at "some points" gospel narratives assert what "might" have happened and not what necessarily did or did not happen.[6] However, this suggestion raises more questions than it answers. For one thing Quinn provides no indication of how numerous these "points" are. For example, suppose they are very numerous, making up, say 70 percent of the narratives. Then, one could hardly suppose that narratives about Jesus are reliable or that imitating the Jesus portrayed in these narratives would be imitating the real Jesus.

Moreover, Quinn does not say what he means by "might have happened." One obvious interpretation is that he means, "it is logically possible that it happened." Another is that "it might have happened" means "it is not initially improbable that it happened in light of our background knowledge." Now, many things crucial to an acceptance of the Christian faith might have happened in either of these senses. The problem is that we have no good reason to suppose they did. For example, in the logically impossible sense Jesus might have walked through walls in his postresurrection appearances, but we have no good reason to believe that he did and in terms of our background knowledge we have good reason to suppose that he did not. Thus, the claim that something *might* have happened entails nothing about what is rational to believe concerning what *actually* happened. But then the claim provides no grounds for imitating the real Jesus rather than a mythical one.

There is another problem with the feasibility of following the command to imitate Jesus that has nothing to do with the difficulty of knowing what Jesus did. Let us suppose that the Gospels present an accurate picture of what he said and the way he acted. Since Jesus is supposed to be morally perfect, most Christians do not expect to imitate him completely: His behavior is simply an ideal to be approximated. However, this does not seem to have been Jesus' own view. Although Jesus did not explicitly formulate as a separate rule that we must regulate our thoughts, feelings, and language as well as our actions, such a commandment seems to play an important role in his ethical thinking. He said, "You have heard that it was said to the men of old, 'You shall not kill; and whoever kills shall be liable to judgment.' But I say to you that everyone who is angry with his brother shall be liable to judgment; whoever insults his brother shall be liable to the council and whoever says: 'You fool!' shall be liable to the hell of fire" (Matt. 5:21–22). He opposed swearing of various kinds (Matt. 5:34–36). He also said, "You have heard that it was said 'You shall not commit adultery.' But I say to you everyone who looks at a women lustfully has already committed adultery with her in his heart" (Matt. 5:27–28). Jesus demanded that his disciples follow these commands to the letter. Indeed, he wanted moral perfection in his followers: He said that one must be perfect "as your heavenly Father is perfect" (Matt. 5:48). This Christian perfectionism raises special issues that will be discussed in the next chapter. However, for now it can be said that this demand for perfection entails that the command to imitate Jesus cannot be followed the way that Jesus wished.

THE UNCLARITY IN THE COMMAND TO IMITATE JESUS

For the sake of argument let us suppose that the New Testament narratives about Jesus are fairly accurate and that Jesus did not demand perfection. Then other problems arise. How are Christians supposed to imitate Jesus? Quinn seems to mean by doing what Jesus did.

Which actions of Jesus should Christians imitate? Quinn wants Christians to conform their own lives to Jesus' as closely as circumstances allow. This qualification would presumably exclude such actions such as walking on water and bringing the dead back to life since circumstances do not allow actions that are beyond human capacity. But would it include dying as a martyr at a relatively young age, becoming celibate, and forming a group of disciples? These things are in our power to do and there certainly are opportunities to perform these actions. Is the suggestion that such opportunities should be sought out? For example, should Christians seek missionary work among groups of people who are very likely to murder them? If this strategy were successful it would be self-defeating, depleting the number of missionaries and slowing the spread of Christianity. Should Christians try to become missionaries for religious groups that demand complete celibacy? Were all people to follow this advice it would be the end of the human race. Should every Christian aim to form a new religious group and gather disciples? Then there would only be leaders and no disciples. Or is it being suggested that there are circumstances that *could* arise in which becoming a martyr, forsaking family ties, and gathering disciples would be appropriate actions? Then, being willing to act should these circumstances arise is all that is required in order to imitate Jesus. If one accepts the former interpretation, very few people in history have imitated Jesus. Moreover, there are not enough circumstances to accommodate the need: for example, of 1.6 billion Christians few could find opportunities for martyrdom. If one accepts the latter interpretation, since no guide is provided as to what the appropriate circumstances would be, the typical Christian will have no idea if he or she is imitating Jesus.

THE MORAL APPROPRIATENESS OF THE COMMAND TO IMITATE JESUS

More important still, if one takes the Gospel's narratives as our guides, several aspects of Jesus' behavior turn out to be dubious models of ideal conduct. Should Christians imitate these as well? For example, it is quite clear that Jesus believed that people who do not embrace his teachings will be and should be severely punished. Thus, he said to his disciples, "And if anyone will not receive you or listen to your words, shake off the dust from your feet as you leave that house or town. Truly, I say to you, it shall be more tolerable on the day of judgment for the land of Sodom and Gomorrah than for that town" (Matt. 10:14–15). Moreover, although Jesus preached forgiveness, he maintained that "whoever blasphemes against the Holy Spirit never has forgiveness and is guilty of an eternal sin" (Mark 3:29). Indeed, it is clear that Jesus sanctioned the eternal punishment of the fires of hell for those who sin (Matt. 25:41, 46). "You serpents, you brood of vipers, how are you to escape being sentenced to hell?" (Matt. 23:33) What would imitating Jesus involve in the light of such passages? Would it involve being punitive and unforgiving at least in some circumstances? If so, which ones?

In some places the synoptic Gospels teach universal salvation. For example, in Luke it is proclaimed that "all flesh shall see the salvation of God" (3:6). However, in other passages Jesus is shown as conceiving of his mission as narrowly sectarian, namely, that of saving the Jews. Thus he said to his disciples: "Go nowhere among the Gentiles and enter no town of the Samaritans, but go rather to the lost sheep of the house of Israel" (Matt. 10:5–6). Clearly believing that he was the *Jewish* messiah, he said: "Think not that I have come to abolish the law and the prophets; I come not to abolish them but to fulfill them" (Matt. 5:17). Indeed, he said to a Canaanite woman whose daughter was possessed by a demon and who begged for his help, "I was sent only to the lost sheep of the house of Israel." Only after the woman pleaded with him and made a brilliant reply to his justification for his refusal to help did he heal the daughter (Matt. 15:22–28). It seems clear, then, that without the mother's perseverance and quick wit Jesus would not have healed the Canaanite's daughter although a Jewish woman's daughter would have been.

Christian apologists might argue that these seemingly conflicting passages can be reconciled by a passage from Paul: "I am not ashamed of the gospel: it is the power of God for the salvation of everyone who has faith: the Jew first and also to the Greek" (Rom. 1:16). The quote from Matthew where Jesus is interested in only saving the Jews reflects, it said, an earlier period of time when Jesus was preaching only to Jews. But other passages where he teaches universal salvation reflect his later expanded conception of his mission. In reply it can be argued that Paul's words hardly explain Jesus' harsh command: "Go nowhere among the Gentiles and enter no town of the Samaritans, but go rather to the lost sheep of the house of Israel." Moreover, it is not clear why Jesus would want to or need to save the Jews first. Why should a completely just savior of humanity want to save some religious group first? Jesus should have no favorites. Why would the Son of God need to start salvation with any one religious group and then expand his efforts? The Son of God could have had thousands of disciples saving Jews and Gentiles at the same time. He was not limited to twelve.[7]

Although he preached nonresistance to evil Jesus did not always practice it. He used force and drove out "those who sold and those who bought in the temple, and he overturned the tables of the money changers and the seats of those who sold pigeons" (Mark 11:15). He made no effort to win over the wrongdoers by love. Now Christian apologists may argue that Jesus' action was an example of righteous anger that was justified in a context in which love was not effective. However, Jesus did not advocate nonresistance and love on pragmatic grounds. He did not say that love and nonresistance to evil should be practiced only when it is effective and when it is not effective violence and force should be used.

In other cases, Jesus' actions are far less than compassionate and gentle. Not only did he fail to speak against the inhumane treatment of animals, but in one case his actual treatment of them was far from kind: He expelled demons from a man and drove them into a herd of swine that thereupon rushed into the sea and drowned (Luke 8:28–33). It has been noted that Jesus could have expelled the demons without causing the animals to suffer.[8] The story of the fig tree is also hard to reconcile with Jesus' teachings and our idealized picture of him. On entering Bethany he was hungry and seeing a fig tree in the distance, he went to it to find something to eat. Since it was not the season for figs the tree had no fruit. Jesus then cursed the tree and later it was noticed by Peter that the tree had withered (Mark 11:12–14, 20–21).

Imitating Jesus on the basis of such narratives would often be to act in violent and mean-spirited ways. And Jesus' practice has an additional problem in that he does not exemplify important intellectual virtues.

Both Jesus' words and his actions indicate that he does not value reason and learning. Basing his entire ministry on faith, he said, "unless you turn and become like children, you will never enter the kingdom of heaven" (Matt. 18:3). As we know, children usually believe uncritically whatever they are told. Jesus seldom gave reasons for his teachings. When he did they were usually of one of two kinds: He either claimed that the kingdom of heaven was at hand or that if you believed what he said you would be rewarded in heaven whereas if you did not, you would be punished in hell. No rational justification was ever given for these claims. In short, Jesus' actions suggest that he believed that reasoning and rational criticism are wrong and that faith, both in the absence of evidence and even in opposition to the evidence, is correct. Imitating Jesus, would seem, then, to involve the forsaking of reason.

Finally, Jesus explicitly addressed few of the moral concerns of our society today. For example, he said nothing directly about the morality or immorality of abortion, the death penalty, war, slavery, contraception, or racial and sexual discrimination. Unfortunately, it is not clear what one can deduce about these topics from his sayings and his practice. His doctrine of not resisting evil suggests that he would be against all war, yet his violent action in driving the money-changers from the temple suggests that he might consider violence in a holy cause to be justified. His "love thy neighbor" commandment suggests that he would be opposed to the death penalty, yet his threats of hellfire for sinners suggest that at times he might deem death or worse to be an appropriate punishment. In imitating him should Christians also be silent on these issues or say conflicting things?

Jesus made no explicit pronouncements about the moral questions connected with socialism, democracy, and tyranny. To be sure, he did address one issue connected with government: paying taxes. In advocating paying taxes to the government, however, he gave advice that is compatible with almost any form of government. Moreover, when understood as having no exceptions, it is questionable policy. Other things being equal, citizens have a moral obligation to withhold taxes from an evil government.

In addition, what one can infer from some things Jesus says seems to be in conflict with other things he says. Consider his attitude toward poverty. His advocacy of selling everything and giving it to the poor (Luke: 18:22) may suggest that he was opposed to poverty and wanted it eliminated. Yet when a woman who poured on his head expensive ointment that could have been sold and the money given to the poor was rebuked for this by his disciples, Jesus defended her saying that you always have the poor with you (Matt. 26:11). Christian apologists argue that, when taken in context, there is no conflict between the two passages since Jesus was praising the woman for preparing his body for burial. However, it is not clear if this really reconciles the conflict. After all, the woman could have sold the expensive oil, given some of the proceeds to the poor, and purchased less expensive oil for anointing Jesus.

Moreover, the extreme nature of Jesus' views on poverty can hardly be taken seriously and are not in general taken so by the vast majority of Christians. He advocated material poverty by maintaining that a rich man cannot enter the kingdom of heaven (Matt. 19:23–24), and, as in Luke's version of the beatitudes, that the poor are blessed and that theirs is the kingdom of heaven (Luke 6:20). To be sure, citing servants of the poor such as Mother Teresa and William Booth of the Salvation Army, and also the fact that Christian churches do a large amount of social services work, some apologists argue that Christians do take seriously Jesus' pronouncements on poverty. But this hardly proves the point, since the vast majority of well-off Christians do not give all of their money to the poor and would think anyone who suggested that they should insane. Yet such Christians do not seem to be imitating Jesus. In addition, it is not clear that they should imitate Jesus since it not obvious that giving all one's money to the poor is the best way to eliminate poverty. Poverty is a complex problem with political, economic, psychological, and geographical aspects. Jesus' view seems not only unrealistic but also simplistic.

In some cases, Jesus' silence on the morality of a practice can only be interpreted as tacit approval. For example, although slavery was common in his own world, there is no evidence that he attacked it.[9] As Morton Smith has noted,

> There were innumerable slaves of the emperor and of the Roman state; the Jerusalem Temple owned slaves; the High Priest owned slaves (one of them lost an ear in Jesus' arrest); all of the rich and almost all of the middle class owned slaves. So far as we are told, Jesus never attacked this practice. He took the state of affairs for granted and shaped his parables accordingly. As Jesus presents things, the main problem for the slaves is not to get free, but to win their master's praise. There seem to have been slave revolts in Palestine and Jordan in Jesus' youth. (Josephus, *Bellum*, 2:55-65); a miracle-working leader of such a revolt would have attracted a large following. If Jesus had denounced slavery or promised liberation, we should almost certainly have heard of his doing it. We hear nothing, so the most likely supposition is that he said nothing.[10]

Furthermore, if Jesus had been opposed to slavery, it is likely that his earlier followers would have followed his teaching. However, Paul (1 Cor. 7:21, 24) and other earlier Christians writers did not speak out against slavery.[11]

Now some Christian apologists try to defend Jesus' silence about slavery and Paul's failure to speak out against it by saying that it made no difference to Jesus whether humans were free or slaves. The crucial question was the salvation of a person's soul. Christians wanted to reform the heart and not the social order. This, however, is precisely what is wrong with Jesus' stance: He accepted the social status quo of earthly slavery and preached salvation in the world to come. In so doing he provided a rationalization for slavery for centuries. In defense of Jesus, it might be objected that if he had preached against slavery he would have neglected the more pressing task of soul saving. But why? Could not Jesus have saved souls and also helped free slaves? With respect to Paul's statement it might be objected that he said if you can gain your freedom, avail yourself of the opportunity to do so (1 Cor. 7:21). But there is nothing in Paul's statement that condemns slavery as an evil. Yet it is an evil practice that should be condemned. The same is true of Paul's letter to Philemon in which he returns a runaway slave to his owner. What Paul does not say is that slavery is wrong. Indeed, the letter recognizes the owner's right to own slaves and hopes he will continue to own the slave forever. The letter asks the owner, as a favor, to treat this slave as a brother.[12]

In addition there is good reason to suppose that Jesus was a hypocrite.[13] To cite just two examples: Jesus cited the Old Testament commandment "Honor your father and mother" (Matt. 15:4, 19:19; Mark 7:10, 10:19; Luke 18:20), yet was curt and even rude to his mother (Luke 2:1; John 2:4, 19:26). Jesus spoke out against anger (Matt. 5:22) and yet displayed his own anger (Mark 3:5, 11:12–19; Matt. 11:22–24, 21:12–15, 19; Luke 10:13–15, 19:45–47, John 2:13–17).[14]

So it would seem to follow that if we imitated Jesus, we would be punitive, unforgiving, violent, mean-spirited, hypocritical, and inconsistent; and we would tacitly approve of slavery, forsake reason, and have no opinions on the central moral issues of the day.

AGAPE AND SUFFERING

Oddly enough, in his discussion of the imitation of Jesus, Quinn says nothing about agape. One would have thought that whatever else imitating Jesus involved it would include manifesting Christian love. However, there may be good reasons why Quinn did take this tack. For one thing the unclarity of the "love thy neighbor" commandment allows it to be interpreted in different ways,[15] some of which have unacceptable implications. In addition, some interpretations are so unclear that it is impossible to discern what the commandment entails while others are so close to secular systems of ethics that it is difficult to understand the difference. Thus, the advice to imitate Jesus by manifesting agape would either be too unclear to follow, morally objectionable, or not significantly different from the advice to follow certain secular ethical systems.

Let us interpret agape in part as engaging in beneficial social activities that help the poor, sick, and downtrodden for purely selfless motives. Further, let us interpret imitating Jesus at least to include agape in this social activist sense. Although Christian thinkers like Quinn do not specify what imitating Jesus involves, Quinn at least is clear that it will most likely involve great suffering and being despised. But surely in this present interpretation this is an exaggeration. After all, some Christians were venerated for their good works even in their own lifetimes. Moreover, doing good will tend to lead to that person's suffering and being despised *only* in certain circumstances. For example, in our day someone who creates a shelter for the homeless will likely receive the admiration of the homeless and at least some other members of the community. Most members of the community will not usually despise such a person and her good works. Rather the typical response will be that of indifference and apathy. The danger is not that the shelter-builder will be made to suffer for her good deeds, but that she and her good works will tend to be ignored. On the other hand, civil rights workers in rural Mississippi in the 1960s were likely to be subjected to abuse and violence. Public indifference was not their main problem.

THOMAS À KEMPIS'S
OF THE IMITATION OF CHRIST

A discussion of imitating Jesus would not be complete without a brief consideration of *Of the Imitation of Christ* (1426), a devotional treatise probably written by Thomas à Kempis (1380?–1471), a German monk and mystic.[16] This book on the interior life and ways of practicing virtue is not so much philosophical or theological as it is practical. Although originally intended as a handbook for monks, its "tender concentration on the figure of Christ made attractive its doctrine of resignation—the surrender of all worldly concerns to the service and imitation of Christ" gave it a much wider audience.[17] Indeed, it is claimed that *Of the Imitation of Christ* has been translated into more languages than any book except the Bible.

The first part of Kempis's treatise is concerned with the spiritual and moral reform of the individual, the second part is devoted to preparation for the inner contemplative life, the third part gives a further account of ascetic practices with some passages that "hint at the kind of mystical experience awaiting those who truly love Christ,"[18] and the fourth part is a manual for those who take Holy Communion. Let us examine the first two parts of Kempis's book in more detail and consider in what sense following the practical advice in this treatise involves imitating Jesus.

To be sure, some of the moral advice Kempis gives in part 1 can be clearly derived from aspects of the New Testament picture of Jesus. For example, Kempis advises being humble (p. 14), and resisting the temptation of carnal pleasure (p. 20). However, other aspects of Kempis's moral advice seem only based on a loose analogy to Jesus' life. For example, Kempis says that one should never be entirely idle but should either be reading or writing or praying or meditating or endeavoring something for the public good while bodily exercise should be used with discretion (pp. 40–41). But although it is not implausible to suppose that Jesus was opposed to idleness and there is reason to suppose that he prayed and meditated, there is no reason to suppose he read or wrote in his spare time. Whether he did anything for the public good all depends on what one means. For example, although he allegedly healed some sick people miraculously and fed the five hundred, this sort of work for the public good is probably not what Kempis had in mind.[19] Moreover, there is no evidence that Jesus used bodily exercise to fill his idle time. And there are other aspects of Kempis's advice that also seem far removed from the New Testament picture of Jesus. For example, Kempis says that one should not converse much with young people or strangers (p. 32).

When we come to part 2 of Kempis's treatise, the ascetic themes of the inward life and forsaking of worldly comforts become prominent. Kempis urges the faithful "to despise outward things and give yourself to things inward and you shall perceive the kingdom of God to come to you"

(p. 63). He advocates that true Christians "esteem all comfort vain, which come to you from any creature" (p. 71). However, there is another theme that is equally prominent but more obscure: Kempis darkly suggests that following Jesus will be hard and involves suffering that is somehow analogous to Jesus' Passion (pp. 85–91).

Now it is difficult to relate the first two themes to Jesus' life and teaching. Although Jesus believed that the Kingdom of God was near and that people should give up all worldly goods, it is unlikely that he believed that this kingdom would come through inward mediation and ascetic denial. I have argued earlier that the claim that following Jesus always involves suffering caused by being persecuted and despised by other human beings is exaggerated. Let us call this the *external interpretation* of the suffering involved in following Jesus. However, on Kempis's interpretation of salvation, the suffering involved in following Jesus seems to be based on the psychological pain of the mastering of one's desires for worldly goods. Let us call this *internal interpretation*. However, in this interpretation imitating Christ has little to do with conforming to Jesus' life except in a metaphorical way. On the external interpretation Jesus suffered on the cross and in following Jesus Christians must suffer by taking up the cross, that is, by being persecuted and despised. In the internal interpretation Jesus suffered on the cross and in following Jesus Christians must suffer by taking up the cross, that is, by experiencing the pain involved in the inner mastery of their worldly desires.

Besides the irrelevance of much of Kempis's treatise to imitating Jesus' life, there is the inappropriateness of his moral advice. Kempis is correct that Jesus advocated humility. Insofar as Jesus meant simply that one should not be proud or arrogant, it is excellent advice. However, Kempis gives humility a more radical interpretation and Jesus seems to have intended it in a stronger way as well. For Jesus humility involved serving people in lowly ways, not caring about prestige, not demanding honors or recognition, not judging others, giving alms and praying in secret.[20] For Kempis it involved taking no pleasure in your natural gifts or talents, not being proud of your good works, setting yourself lower than all men (p. 21), and demeaning yourself (p. 27). But taken to these extremes this advice seems questionable. It is important to know one's own strengths and weaknesses and to act accordingly.[21] Sometimes this will involve putting oneself forward, sometimes not. Sometimes taking a lowly position would serve no useful purpose, and would be morally undesirable; sometimes to act superior would be a pretense and cause great harm. If, for example, the pilot of an airplane has a sudden heart attack, and you are an experienced pilot, and without your taking over the plane will crash, is it not your moral obligation to put your knowledge into operation even if this involves an overt display of superiority? In this circumstance being humble and insisting on some lowly role would seem to be insanity.

Like Jesus, Kempis is silent on the social issues of his day as well as the issues that might concern us today. For example, he does not speak out against social injustice and oppression. Although in passing he mentions doing something for the public good, in general Kempis seems much more concerned with loving Christ than loving suffering humanity. Again agape is strangely absent from his account.

Some of Kempis's other moral advice, such as that one should not converse much with young people and strangers, is at the very least arbitrary and at worst biased and self-defeating. No reason is given for such exclusion and one can only suspect that it is based on prejudice. Surely, if this advice were followed, it would have the effect of unjustly ostracizing such groups. Moreover, it is self-defeating for Christians since young people and strangers may be prime candidates for conversion. Furthermore, Kempis's asceticism has little to recommend it. Taken seriously it would eliminate romantic love, the joys of sex, and the furthering of technology aimed at improving the standard of living.

Although Kempis's advice may be appropriate for a fifteenth-century monk, it is fortunate that his millions of readers down through the centuries did not take up the cross and follow the monkish inner life of self-denial that he urged.

CONCLUSION

Interpreting the command to imitate Jesus as the basic command of Christian ethics shows the problematic nature of this ethics. The command to imitate Jesus is not only infeasible since so little of Jesus' life is known that imitation is impossible, it is an unclear and morally questionable command. Even if his life were known, Jesus' demand for perfection in actually following the command to imitate him renders it pragmatically questionable. In any case, it is not clear which aspects of Jesus' life one should imitate and, in any event, many aspects of Jesus' life are morally questionable and should not be imitated. Moreover, imitating Jesus' life would involve remaining silent instead of speaking out on important social injustices since this is what Jesus did. The advice in Kempis's famous treatise has similar problems and, in addition, tends to be irrelevant to the imitation of Jesus. All of these difficulties indicate that following the command to imitate Jesus can hardly be based on impartial and logical reasons and that Christian ethics construed in this way lacks objectivity.

NOTES

1. See, for example, Robert Morgan and John Barton, *Biblical Interpretation* (Oxford: Oxford University Press, 1988).

2. W. Trilling, *Fragen zur Geschichtlichkeit Jesu*, 3d ed. (Düsseldorf, 1969). Quoted by G. A. Wells, *Did Jesus Exist?* rev. ed. (London: Pemberton, 1986), p. 1.

3. J. Kahl, *The Misery of Christianity*, trans. N. D. Smith (New York: Penguin Books, 1971), p. 103. Quoted by Wells, *Did Jesus Exist?* p. 2.

4. Albert Schweitzer in *The Quest for the Historical Jesus: A Critical Study of Its Progress from Reimarus to Wrede,* trans. W. Montgomery (New York: Macmillan Publishing Co., 1968) argues that the Jesus most people associate with the Gospels is a myth. After the first appearance of Schweitzer's work in 1910 many scholars despaired of writing a historical biography of Jesus. See, for example, the surveys by F. G. Dowing, *The Church and Jesus* (London, 1968), and H. McArthur, ed., *In Search of the Historical Jesus* (London, 1970) cited by Wells, *Did Jesus Exist?* p. 1.

5. See Michael Martin, *The Case against Christianity* (Philadelphia: Temple University Press, 1990), chap. 2.

6. Philip L. Quinn, "The Meaning of Life According to Christianity," in *The Meaning of Life*, ed. E. D. Klemke (New York: Oxford University Press, 2000), p. 58.

7. I owe this point to Donald Morgan (personal communication).

8. Bertrand Russell, "Why I Am Not a Christian," in *Philosophy and Contemporary Issues*, ed. John R. Burr and Milton Goldinger (New York: Macmillan, 1984), p. 123.

9. Indeed, as Adolf Grünbaum has pointed out from the time of St. Paul to the middle of the nineteenth century the Catholic Church taught that slavery was

morally acceptable. It was not until 1890 that Pope Leo XIII finally condemned it and he did so only after the laws of every civilized country had eliminated it. See Adolf Grünbaum, "The Poverty of Theistic Morality," http://www.infidels. org/library/modern/adolf_grunbaum/poverty.html. This essay was originally published in *Science, Mind and Art: Essays on Science and the Humanistic Understanding in Art. Epistemology, Religion, and Ethics in Honor of Robert S. Cohen.* Boston Studies in the Philosophy of Science, vol. 165 (Dordrecht, The Netherlands: Kluwer Academic Publisher, 1995), pp. 203–42.

10. See Morton Smith, "Biblical Arguments for Slavery," *Free Inquiry* 7 (spring 1987): 30.

11. Ibid.; see also Edward A. Westermarck, "Christianity and Slavery," in *A Second Anthology of Atheism and Rationalism,* ed. Gordon Stein (Amherst, N.Y.: Prometheus Books, 1987), pp. 427–37. Unfortunately, Jesus' apparent tacit approval of slavery is obscured in the Authorized and Revised Versions of the New Testament by a translation of the Greek word for slave *doulos* as "servant." For example, in the Revised Standard Version Jesus says that a servant is like his master (Matt. 10:25). A more accurate translation would be that a slave is like his master.

12. See Morton Smith, "On Slavery: Biblical v. Modern Morality," in *Biblical v. Secular Ethics,* ed. R. Joseph Hoffmann and Gerald A. Larue (Amherst, N.Y.: Prometheus, 1988), p. 75. In other New Testament letters probably not written by Paul one finds the same thing. In Colossians the writer urges slaves to be obedient to their masters (3:22–25) as does the writer of 1 Timothy while at the same time urging the masters to be kind to slaves. The institution of slavery is simply accepted.

13. See Donald Morgan, "Jesus Was a Hypocrite," http://www.infidels.org/ library/modern/donald_morgan/jesus_was_hypocrite.html.

14. For more details see ibid.

15. Martin, *The Case against Christianity*, pp. 171–91.

16. Thomas à Kempis, *Of the Imitation of Christ* (New Kessington, Pa.: Whitaker House, 1981). Page references to this book will be placed in the body of the text.

17. Ninian Smart, "Thomas à Kempis," in *The Encyclopedia of Philosophy*, ed. Paul Edwards (New York: Macmillan, 1967), vol. 8, p. 104.

18. Ibid.

19. Christian apologists will no doubt point to all the public service, for example, poverty relief, hospitals for the needy, that has been done in Jesus' name. But the question is of what actions of *Jesus* are these good work imitations?

20. Martin, *The Case against Christianity*, p. 165.

21. See Richard Robinson, *An Atheist's Values* (Oxford: Basil Blackwell, 1964), pp. 153–55.

— 10 —

CHRISTIAN THEISM AND MORAL SKEPTICISM

INTRODUCTION

A seldom-mentioned problem of Christian morality has yet to be examined. Christian apologists have often claimed that atheism leads to moral skepticism. This claim is without basis, but, as we will see in this chapter, Christian ethics itself leads to four different kinds of moral skepticism. Different types of doubt lead to different types of moral skepticism. The four types to be discussed here are moral nihilism, moral epistemological skepticism, amoral skepticism, and pragmatic moral skepticism.

MORAL NIHILISM

How does Christian theism lead to moral skepticism? As I have said, although the Divine Command Theory of morality is not entailed by Christian theism, this is the metaethical theory of choice for most Christian theists. So to all practical intents and purposes Christian ethics can be considered based on the Divine Command Theory. In one common interpretation of this theory, "X is morally wrong = X is disapproved of by God" and "X is right = X is approved of by God." Similar definitions hold for "X is morally obligatory" and "X is morally forbidden." It follows that if God does not exist, nothing is right or wrong. This position is known as moral nihilism.

Moral nihilism takes two forms. Weak Moral Nihilism is the view that there is no good reason to suppose that there are moral truths. Thus, for example, there is no good reason to suppose the statement "Torture is wrong" is either true or false. In contrast, Strong Moral Nihilism is the view there is good reason to suppose that there are no moral truths.

Skepticism about the truth of Christian theism when combined with the Divine Command Theory of morality leads to one or the other forms of moral nihilism. Since, as we saw in chapter 6, there is excellent reason to doubt the truth of theism,[1] the following argument for Weak Moral Nihilism can be constructed:

1. If there is no good reason to believe that God exists, then Weak Moral Nihilism is true.
2. There is no good reason to believe that God exists.
3. Hence, Weak Moral Nihilism is true.

Premise (1) follows from the Divine Command Theory and the meaning of Weak Moral Nihilism. Premise (2) is based on the refutations of the arguments for God surveyed in chapter 6. Therefore, (3) follows from (1) and (2).

In chapter 6 I also argued that there is good reason to suppose that God does not exist.[2] Assuming the Divine Command Theory, the following argument for Strong Moral Nihilism can be constructed:

1'. If there is good reason to believe that God does not exist, then Strong Moral Nihilism is true.
2'. There is good reason to believe that God does not exist.
3'. Hence, Strong Moral Nihilism is true.

Premise (1') follows from the Divine Command Theory and the meaning of Strong Moral Nihilism. Premise (2') is based on the arguments considered in chapter 7. Premise (3') follows from (1') and (2').

In short, unless atheistic arguments are refuted, theism when combined with the Divine Command Theory results in either Weak Moral Nihilism or Strong Moral Nihilism.[3]

MORAL EPISTEMOLOGICAL SKEPTICISM

A second type of moral skepticism is epistemological rather than nihilistic. According to this position, moral statements are either true or false. The problem is that we can have no knowledge of their truth or falsehood. In order to see that Christian theism leads to moral epistemological skepticism it is only necessary to suppose, as many Christians do, that Christian morality is based on God's approval and disapproval, and to acknowledge that it is difficult, if not impossible, to tell what God approves or disapproves of. Consider first that the alleged sources of God's revelation conflict with one another.[4] In the Western tradition alone there are the Bible, the Koran, the Book of Mormon, and the teachings of Reverend Moon and many other religious figures. Clearly it is impossible to follow the alleged commands issued by all these various books. How then should one decide between conflicting sources?

One suggestion is to appeal to historical evidence, but such recourse is to no avail. In particular, the historical evidence adduced to support claims about miraculous events is weak and yet this evidence is crucial. For example, in the Christian tradition the evidence used to support the resurrection, the virgin birth and the incarnation is flimsy. Another idea would be to appeal to moral considerations to decide between the conflicting traditions. But this cannot be done without admitting that morality is independent of religion. For example, it will not do to argue that the New Testament rather than the Koran is the true revealed word of God on the grounds that its message is morally superior to that of the Koran. This argument presumes that we have some way of judging the superiority of the moral teachings of a tradition without knowing if God reveals his moral teachings in this tradition. However, in the present view this is precisely what cannot be done.

Moreover, let us suppose that some religious tradition, for example, the Christian tradition, is singled out as the one and only one in which the word of God is revealed. The question remains of how this tradition is to be interpreted. The uncertainties involved generate epistemological skepticism.

1. As I noted earlier, the Christian position on many issues is unclear.

2. On other issues believers have interpreted the Bible in conflicting ways. Thus, there are differences among Christians over the morality of the death penalty, war, abortion, premarital sex, homosexuality, private

property, social drinking, and gambling among other things. Most of these differences are based on different interpretations of Christian revelation. To suppose that there is a rational way to reconcile these controversies by appealing to revelation stretches credibility to the breaking point.

Consider the death penalty. The Old Testament explicitly requires it for homosexuality, bestiality, blasphemy, cursing one's parents, witchcraft, working on the Sabbath, and non-chastity. Since these requirements were not revoked in the New Testament, they should, according to Greg Bahnsen, be made part of the criminal law of all nations.[5] On the other hand, John Howard Yoder, professor of theology at Notre Dame, has said it "should not be necessary to argue that Christ's teaching and his work lead Christians to challenge the rightness of taking life under any circumstances."[6] Who should a Christian believe?

3. The basic principles of Christian morality are vague and in many cases it is not possible to tell what they entail. Consider the "Love thy neighbor as thyself" commandment. As we have seen, different scholars interpret this commandment very differently. Even in particular applications its implications are often vague and unclear. The Golden Rule seems equally vague and unclear in its implications.

4. Since the Old and New Testaments have inconsistent ethical views on certain issues and Christians base their ethical views on these books, this precludes moral knowledge and generates moral skepticism connected with these issues.[7]

a. According to Luke 6:27 and 6:35 one should love one's enemies. But elsewhere in the New Testament Jesus maintains that those who are not for him are against him (Matt. 12:30) and those who are against him will be sent to hell (Matt. 13:41–42, 49–50). These passages can be made consistent only by introducing the implausible assumption that loving one's enemies is compatible with sending them to eternal damnation. Other passages in the Old Testament, for example, Exodus 32:25–28, suggest that one should slaughter those who are not on God's side, which hardly seems compatible with loving one's enemies.

b. Jesus seemed to imply that one should not call other people insulting names (Col. 3:8) and in particular forbade us to call a person fool and threatened hell's fire for those who did (Matt. 5:22, 23:17). Yet Jesus himself called people fools (Matt. 23:17), dogs, swine, (Matt. 7:6), vipers, snakes (Matt. 12:34, 23:33), and many other names.

c. Jesus told his followers that lying is evil (Matt. 15:19, Mark 7:22) and the Old Testament condemns it (Prov. 6:17, 19). Yet there are many passages in the Old Testament in which God causes humans to believe lies or endorses lying. For example, in 2 Thessalonians 2:11–12 God causes people to believe a lie and to be damned for their false beliefs and in Ezekiel 14:9 God deceives the prophets.

d. In the Old Testament part of the Ten Commandments says that one should honor one's father and mother. Jesus endorses this principle in Matthew 15:4, 19:19, Mark 7:10, 10:19, and Luke 18:20, yet in Luke 14:26 he says that being his disciple involves hating one's father and mother. Indeed, in several passages Jesus does not exhibit particularly respectful behavior toward his mother. He speaks harshly to her (John 2:4), scolds her when he is only twelve (Luke 2:49), and addresses her merely as "woman" (John 2:4, 19:26).

In summary, the lack of a rational basis for choosing a source of God's commands and for interpreting a source once it is chosen brings about moral epistemological skepticism.

AMORALIST SKEPTICISM

A third type of moral skepticism has to do with action rather than belief. Suppose that someone believes that she has a moral obligation to do X, but has no motivation or reason to do X. Such a person has been called an amoral skeptic.[8]

Now according to the view called motivational internalism there could not be such an amoralist since the position is incoherent. Thus a motivational internalist would claim that it is conceptual truth that if someone believes that she has a moral obligation to do X, she has the motivation to do X. Such a person would say that if she does not have the motivation, then she really does not believe that she has an obligation. To be sure, she might *say* she has a moral obligation. However, if she does, she will merely be using the term "moral obligation" in what has been called the inverted-commas sense: not to express her own view but to state the views of others with whom she does not agree.

A defender of Christian morality might argue in the same way. He or she might say that it is conceptually incoherent to suppose that a Christian could believe that Jesus approves of X and yet have no motivation to do X. To be sure, a Christian might *say* that "Jesus approves of X" and yet have no motivation to do X. But such a theist would be using "Christ approved of X" in the inverted-commas sense; she or he would not really believe that Christ approves of X.

However, this attempt to block moralist skepticism is unsuccessful. As David Brink has argued, the internalists do not take the amoralist seriously enough.[9] It is not clear why a person who insists that there is an obligation to do X and yet is indifferent to X should be thought mistaken about what morality demands or else be using moral language in an inverted-commas sense. Surely, the same thing can be said about the theistic amoralist. There is no a priori reason why a person could believe that God approves of X and yet be indifferent to X. It is reasonable to suppose that whether a person is motivated to do what is their moral obligation is a contingent matter depending on their particular psychological state and the content of the obligation.

Another attempt to block amoral skepticism requires one to give up motivational internalism and adopt externalism instead. In the externalist view moral motivation would be based on contingent factors and the content of the particular moral obligation. The crucial question for a Christian morality is whether a plausible externalistic account is available.

Perhaps the most plausible way to develop such an account is through a theory of divine punishment and rewards. Theists would be externally motivated to act on their belief concerning what their moral obligations are since they would look forward to heaven's bliss if they do and would be afraid of hell's fire if they don't. From what we saw of Jesus' view in the last chapter, he often appealed to divine rewards and punishments. Although it might be argued that such considerations would not move everyone—some people might be irrationally willing to endure eternal damnation or forsake heaven—it is usually supposed that most theists are moved to comply. Yet, we know from history that many theists act immorally. As we have also seen, the homicide and crime rate is higher in the United States, a religious country, than it is in Western Europe and Scandinavia, where religion is far less predominant. It would seem that the threat of divine punishments and rewards does not work very well.[10]

It is well to remember that we do not know in many cases why theists are motivated to act, when they are motivated, let alone on what they believe their moral obligations depend. Is it really true that most Christians act morally because they believe they are complying with what they take to be the commands of God and are afraid of divine punishment or desire divine reward? Perhaps they act out of a long-standing habit or from social pressure. Perhaps they do so out of fear of secular punishment and desire for secular reward. Perhaps they think it is in their long-range secular interest to do so. Perhaps they have confusedly and implicitly rejected the Divine Command Theory and believe that God approves of certain actions because they are moral and are motivated to do the moral thing whether God approves or not.

In any case, there are several problems standing in the way of the Divine Punishment and Reward Theory of motivation that may account for its practical ineffectiveness. First, divine punishment and rewards are supposed to be rendered to human beings after death. For all but elderly theists, these punishments and rewards would be far in the future. Given human nature, one wonders how effective such a system of punishment and reward could be. Criminologists tell us that in order to be maximally effective, punishment and rewards must be immediate and certain. For most theists divine rewards and punishment are hardly immediate.

How certain are divine punishments and rewards? In the first place, as I have argued elsewhere, the sort of existence one would have in an afterlife is conceptually problematic;[11] the notion of divine punishments and rewards for the denizens of heaven or hell becomes conceptually problematic. Second, some parts of the New Testament assume that the purpose of heaven is not to reward people whose earthly lives and behavior warrants it; rather heaven is a gift of God's love for their faith in Jesus that is completely unmerited. In this view whether or not one ends up in heaven may have little to do with whether one has fulfilled one's moral obligations according to Christian theism. If such a view became widespread it would certainly undermine the motivational force of belief in divine punishment or rewards. Third, another good way to undermine the motivational force of a system of punishments and rewards is to question its justice. The more people suppose that a system is unjust, the more likely the system will have to be based on arbitrary sanctions and fear. To be sure, an unjust system could be highly effective. But in order to be so people would have to see the immediate and certain results of human obedience and disobedience. However, this is precisely what theists cannot see.

Is the divine system unjust? If going to heaven is a completely unmerited gift based on faith in Jesus and yet some go and some do not, it seems arbitrary and unfair. Millions of people, through no fault of their own, have never heard of Jesus or at least have never been exposed to Scripture. These people's failure to believe is hardly grounds for punishment. Suppose the reward of heaven is based not on belief but on moral behavior. Still this is unfair. Millions of people have not been exposed to the moral teachings of Jesus. That they do not live according to the biblical standards is not their fault. Moreover, even those who have been exposed may find the moral message of the Bible unacceptable on moral grounds. God, as portrayed in the Old Testament, is often cruel and arbitrary and, as we have seen, in the New Testament Jesus is pictured as having a flawed moral character.

I conclude that amoral skepticism is a plausible view with respect to theistic morality. Motivational internalism cannot block amoralism and although, in the abstract, externalism seems like a more plausible view, the Theory of Divine Rewards and Punishment seems to provide a rather uncertain and problematic theory of motivation. Consequently, the Christian amoralist has yet to be adequately answered.

PRAGMATIC MORAL SKEPTICISM

The fourth and last type of moral skepticism to be discussed here has to do with the goals of morality. In particular, Pragmatic Moral Skepticism is the view that although the achievement of some moral goal is essential to the moral life it is practically unobtainable. With respect to Christian ethics this skepticism concerns Christian Perfectionism, the theory that Christians must obtain ethical perfection.

The perfectionist view is most clearly manifested in the Sermon on the Mount (Matt. 5:17–45). There Jesus lays down impossible ethical standards not simply as goals to aim for that few if any humans will achieve but in order for there to be ideals to struggle toward. Jesus makes it clear that these strict ethical standards are essential for salvation. "For I tell you, unless your righteousness exceeds the scribes and Parisees, you will never enter the kingdom of heaven" (Matt. 5:20). By righteous conduct Jesus includes loving our enemies, not resisting evil but turning the other cheek, not being angry, not swearing, and not looking at a woman with lust in one's eye. Indeed, Jesus says that one must be perfect "as your heavenly Father is perfect" (Matt. 5:48).

Critics have correctly argued that given these strict goals it is hardly surprising that few Christians even try to follow the standards of the Sermon on the Mount. The utter unobtainability of the goals specified there generates cynicism. A practical Christian might well reason: "No human being could ever completely meet these standards. Yet unless I do I will not be saved. So why even try?"

How does Pragmatic Moral Skepticism differ from Amoral Skepticism? A Christian might believe that one can and should do what is morally required yet lack motivation. For example, a Christian might believe that she can follow Jesus' requirement to love her neighbor but lacks motivation to do this since she believes that whether or not she will be rewarded in heaven will depend not on her conduct but on God's gift. If, however, she is a pragmatic moral skeptic, she will believe that she cannot follow Jesus' standards, but if could, she would be highly motivated to do so.

CONCLUSION

That Christian theism results in four distinct types of moral skepticism again shows the superiority of the nonreligious foundations of morality developed in earlier chapters to the foundations of Christian theism. Christian theism combined with the Divine Command Theory leads to Moral Nihilism—the view that ethical statements are neither true nor false—if atheistic arguments are accepted. If atheistic arguments are not accepted, Christian theism results in Moral Epistemological Skepticism by virtue of the difficulty of establishing what God commands. In addition, Christian theism brings about Amoralist Skepticism by its externalist theory of divine rewards and punishments. Finally, Christian Perfectionism leads to Pragmatic Moral Skepticism.

NOTES

1. See also Michael Martin, *Atheism* (Philadelphia: Temple University Press, 1990), part I.

2. See ibid., part II.

3. I am, of course, not claiming that atheism is committed to either Weak Moral Nihilism or Strong Moral Nihilism since I do not hold that atheism is not committed to the Divine Command Theory.

4. Cf. Adolf Grünbaum, "The Poverty of Theistic Morality," http://www. infidels.org/library/modern/adolf_grunbaum/poverty.html. This essay was originally published in *Science, Mind and Art: Essays on Science and the Humanistic Understanding in Art. Epistemology, Religion, and Ethics in Honor of Robert S. Cohen*. Boston Studies in the Philosophy of Science, vol. 165 (Dordrecht, The Netherlands: Kluwer Academic Publisher, 1995), pp. 203–42.

5. See Greg Bahnsen, *Theonomy in Christian Ethics* (Phillipsburg, N.J.: Presbyterian and Reformed Publishing Co., 1984), chap. 21. See also Greg Bahnsen, *No Other Standard: Theonomy and Its Critics* (Tyler, Tex.: Institute for Christian Economics, 1991).

6. John Howard Yoder, "A Christian Perspective," in *The Death Penalty in America*, 3d ed., ed. Hugo Adam Bedau (Oxford: Oxford University Press, 1982), p. 370.

7. In what follows I am indebted to Douglas Krueger, *What Is Atheism?* (Amherst, N.Y.: Prometheus Books, 1998).

8. See David O. Brink, *Moral Reality and the Foundations of Ethics* (Cambridge: Cambridge University Press, 1989), p. 48. This has also been called a practical moral skepticism. See Robert Audi, ed., *The Cambridge Dictionary of Philosophy*, 2d ed. (Cambridge: Cambridge University Press, 1999), p. 590.

9. See David O. Brink, *Moral Realism and the Foundations of Ethics* (Cambridge: Cambridge University Press, 1989), pp. 45–50.

10. Cf. Adolf Grünbaum's discussion of motivational capacity of theistic morality in "The Poverty of Theistic Morality."

11. Michael Martin, "Problems with Heaven," July 22, 1997, http://www. infidels.org/library/modern/michael_martin/heaven.html.

PART THREE

THE MEANING
OF LIFE
WITHOUT GOD

— 11 —

INTRODUCTION
TO THE
MEANING
OF LIFE

INTRODUCTION

I n part 1 a nonreligious foundation of morality was defended and in part 2 a religious foundation of morality was criticized. This answers one aspect of a common charge against atheism: Objective morality presupposes a belief in God. It was shown that objective morality is possible without God and that basing objective morality on belief in God—in particular the Christian God—is problematic. However, this leaves another aspect of the charge against atheism unanswered: The meaningfulness of life is only possible with belief in God.

Part 3 of this book will examine the issue of whether life can be meaningful if God does not exist. This chapter will discuss what people mean when they ask, "What is the meaning of life?" or "Does life have meaning?" In the chapters to follow alternative accounts of the meaning of life will be explored and common objections to a nonreligious account of life's meaning will be refuted.

One thing that is clear from the start is that someone who poses the question "What is the meaning of life?" is not asking if the term "life" has a meaning. The definition of "life" is not at issue. The question does, however, require us to distinguish two senses of the phrase of "the meaning of life," one of which has to do with purpose and the other with value. Thus, when a person asks, "What is the meaning of life?" he or she might be asking what the purpose or purposes of life is or what value life has.

MEANING AS PURPOSE

Now it may be objected that it is one thing to speak of gestures, looks, customs, and dances as having some purpose and quite another to speak of life in this way. Gestures and the like are activities and activities usually have one or more purposes. But life is not an activity. How then can we legitimately speak of it having some purpose or purposes?

However, things besides activities can be said to have a purpose or purposes: for instance, tools, buildings, medicines, and roads. Indeed, these things were created for a purpose or purposes. In addition, certain biological processes, organs, and the like have functions or purposes. Thus, physiologists will say that the purpose or function of the heart is to pump blood. Furthermore, perhaps after all human life can be defined as an activity.[1] According to W. D. Joske, a diversity of goals and purposes characterizes the human life style. Thus, he argues,

> The human life style thus involves critical and reflective activity, and requires the use of practical and theoretical reason directed among other things, toward the discovery and achievement of ends which will not be seen to be futile when we learn more about our nature and the world.[2]

Despite the fact that we do not choose our fundamental drives and intellect, Joske argues that there is a point in construing the human life style *as if* it were an activity. First, human beings are not helpless and can opt out of life by suicide. Second, it may be possible in the future to change human nature through human intervention. Thirdly, "even if we are only playing a game of let's pretend when we construe human life as if it were a deliberately chosen activity, many people find satisfaction in playing the game. They find intellectual or aesthetic delight in discovering that if human life were a voluntary activity it could justifiably be chosen by rational creatures."[3]

Still, assuming there is no objection to talking about the purpose or purposes of life, a problem remains in identifying the *meaning* of life with the *purpose* or purposes of life if only because some purposes have no meaning. It is not inconsistent to say that human life has a purpose or purposes but that human life is meaningless. On the one hand, a purpose may have too little importance to equate with the meaning of life. Take, for example, stringing colored beads. Given this purpose, one would surely be justified in believing that human life has no meaning. Moreover, even if human life has a significant purpose or purposes, pursuing them might not be psychologically satisfying. For example, suppose that the purpose of human life is to contemplate abstract truths and that for most people such a purpose would provide no psychological satisfaction. For them human life would have no meaning.

In addition, if pursuit of a given purpose is futile, human life may be without meaning. Suppose Mary believes correctly that the purpose of human life is to create and promote beneficial practices and institutions and suppose that she finds this goal psychologically satisfying. But Mary is paralyzed and her body is racked with pain so great that she is unable to pursue this goal. In this case, her life will be without meaning. And finally, the purpose or purposes of life may either be arbitrary or else have no plausible rationale. Suppose a deity decrees that the purpose of life is to be saved from eternal damnation by writing poetry, but no plausible rationale is given for this purpose. Although this purpose is important, obtainable, and psychologically satisfying, life would still be meaningless.

The aforementioned problems suggest that the Purpose Meaning of life should be defined as follows:

> A human life has Purpose Meaning if and only if (1) it has a purpose or purposes, (2) this purpose or these purposes have significance, (3) this purpose or these purposes can provide psychological satisfaction, (4) it is possible to fulfill this purpose or these purposes, and (5) this purpose or these purposes are either not arbitrary or have a plausible rationale.

It is important to notice that conditions (3) and (4) relativize the meaning of life according to people's abilities, circumstances, and background. Purposes that can be achieved by one person might not be achievable by another and ones that provide psychological satisfaction to a given person might not provide it to another.

MEANING AS VALUE

Perhaps life has meaning without having any purpose or purposes. For example, it can be argued that enjoying music has no purpose, yet it is a valuable activity that is hardly meaningless. Can the same thing be true of human life? Might it have no purpose or purposes, yet be valuable, and therefore have meaning?

Let us define "Value Meaning" of life in this way:[4]

> A human life has Value Meaning if and only if it is, on the whole, good for the person who leads it.

Note that this analysis also relativizes the meaning of life. For whether a person's life is good on the whole for the one who leads it will vary from individual to individual. Notice too that Purpose Meaning and Value Meaning are independent: a human life can have Purpose Meaning and not Value Meaning or vice versa; a human life might have both Purpose Meaning and Value Meaning.

ANALYSIS OF THE ELEMENTS OF PURPOSE MEANING AND VALUE MEANING

Let us consider these two definitions of the meaning of life in more detail.

Purpose

To begin with, the purpose of human life can be considered in relation to four dichotomous but overlapping categories: (a) cosmic and terrestrial purposes, (b) single purpose and multiple purposes, (c) descriptive and normative purposes, (d) discovered and created purposes.

a. Cosmic and Terrestrial Purposes

It is important to distinguish between the purpose and purposes of life that are part of a larger cosmic plan and ones that do not have such cosmic implications. We are so used to the religious view of things that we suppose that if there is a purpose to human life, it must be of cosmic proportions. In the religious view, if it is not part of some grand plan for the universe, human life has no purpose. However, there is no reason to suppose that this view is true. The purpose or purposes of human life need have no cosmic implications, only human ones. Such purposes are very familiar and so much a part of a common sense view of life that they are overlooked.

For example, one of the purposes of the life of a health care professional may be to improve health care in her community. The purpose of a composer's life may be to write a lovely serenade. For a social activist it may be to reduce poverty in the world. And for a librarian it may be to improve library facilities in his town. These purposes have no cosmic significance. With the extinction of human life, there would be no purposes of this kind in the universe for if all human life ended, there would be no health care professionals, no composers, no social activists, no librarians to have purposes.

b. The Purpose and Purposes

It is usually assumed that there is a single unique purpose to life. But although this assumption may make sense when we are talking about a cosmic purpose, it is dubious when terrestrial purpose is at issue. Human beings have all sorts of purposes and to select a single one as *the* purpose does not do justice to reality. To be sure, under some conditions to speak of *the* purpose of life may make sense. Although humans have diverse *intermediate* purposes, there could perhaps be one *ultimate* purpose. However, although the idea is not wholly absurd, that there is or should be a single ultimate purpose in a nonreligious view remains to be seen. And it should be pointed out on the other hand that a religious point of view need not be committed to a single cosmic purpose. God might prescribe different purposes for different groups of humans or even multiple purposes for every human being.

c. Descriptive and Normative Purpose

It is also necessary to distinguish between descriptive and normative purposes. Descriptive purposes must in turn be divided into those whose end or ends that someone is in fact trying to achieve by his or her action, whether intentionally or on an unconscious level and those purposes where there is no implication that even unconscious intention is involved, as for instance when an institution, organ, or ritual is said to function within a certain system. There are also at least two types of normative purposes. On the one hand, a normative purpose can be the goal one should ethically be trying to achieve by one's action. On the other hand, it can be what a person, institution, or practice should be tending toward. Again in this second sense, there is no implication that intention is involved. Indeed, the purpose can perhaps best be achieved indirectly and unintentionally.

To say that descriptively the purpose of human life is X, can be to say that despite various subpurposes, in fact the ultimate aim of human beings is to achieve X. To say descriptively that X, Y, and Z are the descriptive purposes of life would mean that in fact in the final analysis human beings aim to achieve X, Y, and Z. On the other hand, descriptively speaking the purpose of life may not be a goal or goals but rather one or more basic functions of human life. In this case, intentional action toward some aim or aims is not at issue. Such descriptive functional claims are difficult to confirm and may all turn out to be false but there is no reason to rule them out a priori.

From a statement of life's descriptive purpose no normative conclusions can be drawn. Thus to say that the purpose of human life in the descriptive sense is X is not to say that people's basic aim *should* be X. Indeed, even if it is said that human life has no descriptive function or functions, it might still be claimed that human life *should* have a particular function or functions.

This independence of the normative from the descriptive has important implications for theological accounts of the meaning of human life as well as for claims about the purposelessness of human life in a godless universe. For example, the claim that the cosmic purpose of human life is to follow God's commands might have no normative implications for what human beings should do. It might simply mean that human beings have as their aim following God's commands. If so, one could then argue that they should have a different aim or aims. If the claim means that God has as his aim that human beings follow his commands, one might still believe that humans should not follow his commands. If there is no God and human life has no descriptive cosmic purpose, it may still be possible for someone to find or create a normative terrestrial purpose or purposes for human life.

d. Discovered and Created Purposes

A purpose can be discovered or it can be created. Moreover, some purposes might be created relative to someone's point of view and discovered relative to someone else's point of view. For example, if the universe has some cosmic purpose, it may be possible for human beings to discover it although relative to God's point of view this purpose is created.

In addition, some purposes may be discovered but not created by anyone, for example, the function of bodily organs. In particular, even the terrestrial normative purpose or purposes connected with the meaning of life may not be created by anyone. For example, if certain forms of moral realism are true, intrinsic values are not necessarily created by anyone. Insofar as the normative purpose or purposes connected with the meaning of life are based on such values, then neither are they. Yet, although terrestrial purpose or purposes need not be created, they certainly can be. Even if there is no God and human life has neither a discoverable cosmic descriptive nor a normative purpose or purposes, human beings can create either kind of terrestrial purpose or purposes.

The question arises of whether a created normative purpose can be objective and nonarbitrary. If by an "objective" purpose one means a purpose that can be argued for by giving impersonal and unbiased reasons for choosing it, then certainly a normative purpose can be created *and* be objective and not arbitrary. In another sense of "objective" to say that a purpose is objective is to say that it is a moral fact. Here too a purpose can be created since there is no reason why a moral fact cannot be.

If purposes are created and if different people or groups can create different purposes, this would mean that in principle the lives of different people or groups could have different meanings. However, the diversity that could be generated by creating different purposes of life for different people is neither necessary nor inevitable. For it is possible in principle that every rational human being who bases his or her creation on the same evidence and who considers the matter without bias would create the same purpose of life.

e. Significance

In order for the purpose of human life to bestow meaning of life the purpose must have significance. By this I mean that for life to be meaningful its purpose must not be trivial. However, this importance need not be in terms of positive value. Indeed, suppose life's purpose is to bring about human misery and unhappiness. This by itself would not show that life was without meaning. The purpose of life would still be important— although negatively so. What this entails is that in one sense the evilness of a Hitler or a Stalin is not necessarily an obstacle to their having lived meaningful lives. It is not inconsistent in this sense to say that Hitler's life was meaningful although incredibly evil.

However, there is a sense of Purpose Meaning in which such a claim seems paradoxical. In order to account for this let us define Positive Purpose Meaning.

A human life has Positive Purpose Meaning if and only if (1) it has a purpose or purposes, (2) this purpose or these purposes have positive significance, (3) this purpose or these purposes can provide psychological satisfaction, (4) it is possible to fulfill the purpose or purposes, and (5) the purpose or purposes are either not arbitrary or have a plausible explanation.

On Positive Purpose Meaning Hitler's life would not have meaning.

f. Psychological Satisfaction

It is possible that the most exalted normative purpose or purposes can provide no psychological satisfaction. The purpose may be too remote, abstract, unintelligible, or otherwise be unappealing for the average person to find satisfaction in its pursuit. On the other hand, as we have seen, some normative purposes need not be pursued directly. Suppose X is the normative purpose of life yet the direct intentional pursuit of X provides no psychological satisfaction. However, suppose that pursuit of Y does provide such satisfaction and that pursuit of Y tends indirectly to bring about X. Pursuit of Y rather than X would give meaning to life provided pursuit of Y was possible. Let us understand condition 3 of Purpose Meaning and Positive Purpose Meaning to allow for this indirect pursuit of a purpose.

g. Possibility of Fulfillment

Just because a purpose or purposes have great value and their pursuit can provide psychological satisfaction, striving to fulfill this purpose or purposes does not bestow meaning on life if it is impossible to achieve this goal. The impossibility of fulfillment may be the result of many factors, most of which can be separated into two broad categories. First, some factors prevent fulfillment because they are part of the human condition—at least of our present stage of development. For example, suppose the expansion of human culture to all parts of the galaxy has great significance and is supposed to be the purpose of human life. However, limitations of human mortality, technology, and resources make this purpose impossible to fulfill at the present time and in the foreseeable future. Consequently, its pursuit cannot at present confer meaning on human life.

Second, some factors prevent the fulfillment of the purpose of life because they are the limitations of certain human individuals or groups rather than being part of the human condition. For example, if part of the normative purpose of life were the contemplation of abstract truths, humans with severe mental retardation would not be able to fulfill this purpose. Consequently, their lives would be without meaning. Another example would be someone who is pursuing a significant purpose but because of ignorance or misinformation is using a means to it that makes it impossible to reach the goal.

The limitations of certain groups could affect the fulfillment of purpose in a religious worldview as well. If, for example, the purpose of life is to accept Jesus, then, for a large class of humans this purpose would be impossible to achieve. For the class of humans who either lived before Jesus was born and could not have received his message or else lived after he was born but by virtue of their education or geographical location in fact did not receive it life would have no meaning.

h. Neither Arbitrary nor Having No Plausible Explanation

In order to be meaningful the purpose of life must not be arbitrary and have no plausible rationale. For example, suppose the secular purpose of life was to look beautiful via the extermination of all flying insects. Prima facie such a purpose is arbitrary and has no plausible rationale. Without further explanation one would be justified in supposing, given this purpose, that life has no meaning.

Religious theories of the meaning of life must have a plausible rationale for the goal of life and the means of achieving it. Any suspicion of arbitrariness or irrationality with respect to the purpose of life and the way of accomplishing it casts doubt on the meaningfulness of life. Christianity, in particular, in order to provide Purpose Meaning must offer a plausible explanation of the incarnation and the resurrection of Jesus. Without this explanation these events make no sense and unless they do make sense the Christian goal of salvation through birth, death, and resurrection of the son of God makes no sense. This explanation is allegedly provided in the doctrine of the atonement that will be examined in a later chapter.

On the Whole Good for the Person Who Leads It

In judging the meaning of life in the value sense a religious people would take into account a person's earthly life and the person's afterlife. In contrast, atheists would judge it solely in reference to a person's earthly life taken as whole. But what does it mean to say that a person's life as a whole is good for the one who lives it? One plausible account based on the Ideal Observer Theory developed in chapter 3 is this: A person's life is valuable as a whole for this person if and only if this person was rational, fully informed, and unbiased, and the person would approve of his or her life as a whole. On account of the value meaning of life, meaning would vary from person to person. For some people life would have no value meaning and for others it would. Note too that the religious believer would have a particularly hard time deciding in this lifetime whether his or her life had value meaning since he or she would have no foreknowledge of the afterlife.

CONCLUSION

This analysis of the meaning of life can teach us some lessons that will be relevant for our future inquiries:

a. There are two senses of the meaning of a human life and human life could have one meaning without the other. Thus, even if atheism is incompatible with the purpose sense, it might still have meaning in the value sense. Whether a religious person's life has meaning in either sense must be shown and cannot be assumed.

b. The purpose sense of meaning is often identified with a cosmic purpose, but there is no reason for this. Atheism is compatible with purely human and terrestrial meaning in the purpose sense.

c. In an atheistic worldview (depending on what moral ontology one assumes) normative purposes connecting to the meaning of life in the purpose sense might or might not be created. If they are created, this does mean that they are not objective.

d. The purpose and value senses of meaning are relative to various factors. Whether or not the purpose of life is achievable and psychologically satisfying can vary from person to person. Moreover, in some atheistic accounts (but not all) the meaning of life itself can vary from human life to human life. In addition, meaning in the value sense is relative to the good of a person's life as whole, and thus varies from person to person. Regarding atheists' lives some might possess meaning in the purpose sense and others not. Some might have Value Meaning and others not. Some atheists' lives could have both Purpose Meaning and Value Meaning. And finally, relativism in connection with the meaning of life is not excluded by a religious point of view.

e. From the fact that a human life has a certain descriptive meaning, nothing follows about its normative meaning. In particular, a descriptive cosmic purpose has no normative implications for what the meaning of life should be.

NOTES

1. Cf. W. D. Joske, "Philosophy and the Meaning of Life," *Australasian Journal of Philosophy* 52 (1974): 94.

2. Ibid., p. 100.

3. Ibid.

4. Cf. Philip Quinn, "The Meaning of Life According to Christianity," in *Meaning of Life*, 2d ed., ed. F. D. Klemke (New York: Oxford University Press, 2000), p. 57.

12

TAYLOR'S ANALYSIS
OF THE
MEANING OF LIFE

In "Does Life Have a Meaning?" and "The Meaning of Life" American philosopher Richard Taylor explored the question of the meaning of life via an interpretation of the myth of Sisyphus.[1] In this chapter I will consider Taylor's often cited secular position. In particular, I will show that his three accounts of the meaning of life are problematic. In the first he wrongly excludes any life from being meaningful, in the second he allows almost any life to be meaningful, and in the third he too narrowly circumscribes the kinds of life that can be meaningful. I will also show that that the analysis provided here does not have these problems.

A MEANINGFUL LIFE AS A LIFE OF EVERLASTING SIGNIFICANT ACCOMPLISHMENTS

Taylor uses the myth of Sisyphus to portray a pointless and meaningless task. It will be recalled that because Sisyphus betrayed the gods, he was condemned by them to roll a rock to the top of a hill, whereupon it would roll back down. He was then compelled to begin again, and the rock would again roll back down the hill. This cyclic procedure would be repeated forever.

Taylor argues in the first part of "Does Life Have a Meaning?" that modifying certain details of the myth would not change its force in portraying this pointlessness and meaninglessness. Suppose that Sisyphus' rock was not heavy or that when the rock reached the top of the hill, it was allowed to roll down the other side. The myth's force would not be diminished. Nor does its force depend on the fact that Sisyphus continues this task forever. Taylor also argues that the situation would not be affected if the gods changed Sisyphus' motivation by making him like his task. Although he might embrace the task and it might appear meaningful *to him*, objectively it would still be meaningless.

Taylor grants however that changing other details of the myth would affect the meaningfulness of the task. Suppose Sisyphus rolled rocks up the hill and assembled them to make a beautiful and enduring temple. "His labors would then have a point, something would come of them all and although one could perhaps still say that it was not worth it, one could not say the life of Sisyphus was devoid of meaning altogether."[2]

What relevance has this myth to the question of the meaningfulness of life? In Taylor's view a meaningless life is one consisting of pointless activities. Even if life consists of a long, drawn out, and repetitive activity it has a meaning "if it has some significant culmination, some more or less lasting end that can be considered to have been the direction and purpose of the activity."[3] According to Taylor all animal life is meaningless in this sense. Pointing to the endless cycle of birth and death of animal life as a perfect example of meaningless activity, he says,

> One is led to wonder what is the point of it all, with what great triumph this ceaseless effort, repeating itself through millions of years, might finally culminate, and why it should go on and on for so long accomplishing nothing, getting nowhere. But then one realizes that there is no point to it at all, that it really culminated in nothing, that each of these cycles, so filled with toil, is to be filled only by more of the same.[4]

Unlike animals, humans have a history and are conscious of their activities. Nevertheless Taylor argues that human existence resembles that of Sisyphus: "We toil after goals, most of them—indeed, every single one of them—of transitory significance and, having gained one of them, we immediately set forth for the next, as if that one had never been, the next one being essentially more of the same."[5]

I have said that Taylor allows that Sisyphus' labor could be meaningful if, for example, it resulted in a beautiful enduring temple constructed from the rocks he rolled up the hill. But Taylor maintains that in order for the construction of the temple to have meaning it would have to endure forever. He says that for the temple to make any difference "it had to be a temple that would at least endure, adding beauty to the world for the remainder of time."[6] The implication he draws seems to be that human creations, although sometimes beautiful, are too transitory to give meaning to human life. Indeed, Taylor indicates that because they have decayed and crumbled, even the pyramids and other wonders of the ancient world are now mere "curiosities." As such they do not bestow meaning on the lives of their builders.

But what about religion with its hope of heaven and philosophy with its permanent goods such as Platonic changeless forms? Surely these do not crumble and have the permanence Taylor demands. Taylor says very little about them except, "When they fail to convince, then earthly ideals such as universal justice and brotherhood are conjured up to take their place and give meaning to man's seemingly endless pilgrimage, some final state will be ushered in when the last obstacle is removed and the last stone pushed to the hilltop." However, he says, "No one believes, of course, that any such state will be final, or even wants it to be in case it means that human existence would cease to be a struggle; but in meaning such ideas serve a very real need."[7] Although Taylor does not say so explicitly, he seems skeptical that religion, philosophy, or earthly human ideals can convincingly overcome the problem of the meaninglessness of life. It is not clear why he is skeptical, but one suspects that he doubts that the entities postulated by these theories—heaven, platonic forms, and universal ideals—really exist.

The conclusion of Taylor's argument can be easily summarized. Animal and human life have no meaning. Human life *could* have meaning if human activity intentionally resulted in permanent significant accomplishments. Unfortunately, it never does. To be sure, some human accomplishments are significant. Yet even they are transitory in the sense that they do not last eternally. Furthermore, subjective satisfaction with one's existence does not show that it is meaningful.

If one only reads the first part of "Does Life Have a Meaning?" one could capture Taylor's definition of the meaningfulness of life in this way:

(Def. 1) A life is meaningful if and only if it results in everlasting significant accomplishments.

Since Taylor claims that Definition 1 never applies, it follows that in his view no life is meaningful.

A MEANINGFUL LIFE AS A LIFE LIVED IN A WAY THAT IT IS NATURAL TO LIVE IT

In the last part of "Does Life Have a Meaning?" Taylor considers the meaningfulness of life in terms of what we strive for. He has previously rejected Sisyphus' life as meaningful in a scenario where Sisyphus strongly desires to roll the rock up the hill forever. Taylor now argues that the "meaning that this picture lacked was no meaning he and anyone could crave and the strange meaning it had was perhaps just what we are seeking."[8] Now we learn that there was no need to ask questions such as "what is it all worth if this is the final result?" Each day of toil "was sufficient to itself and so was life."[9]

Even the animal existence Taylor previously dismissed as pointless is now considered by him to be meaningful. "Their endless activity, which gets them nowhere, is just what it is, their will to pursue. This is its whole justification and meaning."[10] As far as a human being's existence is concerned,

> The point of his living is simply to be living in a manner that it is his nature to be living. He goes through life building castles, each one of these beginning to fade into time as the next is begun; yet it would be no salvation to rest from all of this. . . . What counts is that one should be able to begin a new task, a new castle, a new bubble. It counts only because it is there to be done and he has the will to do it. . . . The meaning of life comes from within us, it is not bestowed from without, and it far exceeds in both its beauty and permanence any heaven of which men have ever dreamed or yearned for.[11]

Taking these remarks into account one can define the meaningfulness of life in this way.

(Def. 2) A life is meaningful if and only if it is lived in the way it is natural to live it.

Now Taylor makes it clear that animals such as glowworms living in dark caves live meaningful lives. One wonders however whether it would be possible for these worms to live their lives in any way other than that which is natural to live them. His answer would seem to be "yes" since he suggests that even if migrating birds were well cared for in captivity, they would be condemned "for it is the doing that counts for them, and not what they hope to win by it."[12] Presumably caged birds that normally migrate would not be living natural lives; hence, their lives would be meaningless. By analogy glowworms that live in a laboratory would not be living in a way that for them is natural to live either so that their lives would be meaningless. It is not clear, however, how this idea of living lives it would be natural to live should be interpreted in the case of domesticated animals. For example, is a dairy cow living a life that is natural for it to live? Is an Eskimo husky who pulls sleds living a life that is natural for it to live?

What about human beings? What kind of life is it natural for us to live? From the little Taylor says he seems to identify a meaningful human life with a life of continuous striving and the only kind of human life he seems to rule out by implication is an inactive one. So perhaps to live a life of constant striving is to live a life in a way that is natural to live it. He says,

> What counts is that one be able to begin a new task, a new castle, a new bubble. It counts because it is there to be done, and he has the will to do it. . . . The meaning of life is within us, it is not bestowed from without, and far exceeds in both beauty and permanence any heaven of which men have ever dreamed or yearned for.[13]

What can one make of Taylor's apparent reversal in the second part of "Does Life Have a Meaning?" An uncharitable interpretation would be to say that he is confused and incoherent. However, he seems to base his thesis in the second part of his essay on what he says in the first part. In a more charitable interpretation he is simply saying that life is meaningless in one sense and meaningful in another and that he takes no sides as to which sense is to be preferred. But this interpretation conflicts with the fact that Taylor seems somehow to derive the second part of "Does Life Have a Meaning?" from the first part. The essay's two conflicting views are not simply juxtaposed but are somehow dialectally related.

Another suggestion is that in the first part of his essay Taylor is merely putting forth a plausible conjecture and that he overturns it in the second part. In other words, he can be interpreted as saying something like this: "One could plausibly argue that life is meaningless since it has no point and any accomplishments made within it are transitory and fleeting. But this may be too quick a judgment so let us reconsider things. Looked at in a different and more insightful way the meaning of life consists in its constant striving." The trouble with this interpretation is that no real argument is given for rejecting the position defended in the first part of his essay. The constant striving view is presented as a revised vision, not one derived from the problems with the eternal accomplishment view.

THE MEANINGFUL LIFE AS A CREATIVE LIFE

In any case, in "The Meaning of Life," a short essay that appeared over twenty years after "Does Life Have a Meaning?" Taylor presents a rather different view of the meaning of life. Once again using the myth of Sisyphus he argues, as he did in "Does Life Have a Meaning?" that the meaninglessness of Sisyphus' existence is not the hard toil he undergoes since a meaningless life can be one of easy tasks. Sisyphus' life is meaningless because it consists of tasks endlessly repeated.

According to Taylor, animal life is meaningless in just this sense.

> The robin you see today is doing exactly what those you saw as a child were doing, and the same as those seen by our distant ancestors. . . . Each generation replicates those that went before. It is an endless cycle that cumulates in nothing new, just more of the same.[14]

And Taylor says that this picture of animal life is to a large extent also a picture of human life:

> The lives of people are like clockwork, endlessly repetitive. They rise, do essentially the same things today they were doing yesterday and that

they will do again tomorrow, repeating this pattern year after year until, finally, they go to their graves leaving nothing behind of worth except a new generation to repeat the cycle.[15]

In their endless repetition human lives resemble the life of Sisyphus. Taylor stresses that it would make no difference if human beings did not complain about the unhappiness of their existence. "If we imagine Sisyphus enjoying what he is doing, perhaps as a result of a drug induced state, then that would add no meaning to his living. It would only show that, like most mortals, he has been rendered content with a meaningless existence."[16]

Now Taylor asks what we could add to this picture to convert it to one of a meaningful life. Suppose, he says, Sisyphus assembles his rocks into something of grandeur and beauty—an inspiring temple—"something that will inspire the generations of humankind for all time." But even this is not enough to create a meaningful life since Sisyphus may not know why he toils. "His life has no more meaning than that of an ox driven to do the same work."[17]

Suppose Sisyphus knows why he toils and can see the temple taking shape before his eyes. His existence would still be without meaning if he were in servitude. For his masters might allow him to see what was happening to the stones he was compelled to move but give him no role in planning the temple:

> Now let us take what is obviously the next step, supposing that Sisyphus not only moves the stones but it is he who places them by a plan he has created by thought and reason, and the result is an awesome structure of lasting beauty. Now here is a picture of a meaningful life.[18]

Taylor cautions us that we should not merely suppose that Sisyphus' life is meaningful because he has created a source of satisfaction. For if a man created a huge ball of string that gave him great satisfaction and impressed people with his energy and industry, this would not confer meaningfulness since huge balls of strings are of no real worth. On the other hand, Taylor assumes that Sisyphus' temple is "truly beautiful" and thus of real worth.

The answer to our question now lies before us. A meaningful life is a creative one, and what falls short of this lacks meaning to whatever extent. What redeems humanity is not its kings, military generals, and builders of personal wealth, however these may be celebrated and envied. It is instead that the painters, composers, poets, philosophers, writers—all who, by their creative power alone bring things about of great value, things which, but for them, would never have existed at all.[19]

Taylor goes on to argue that only human beings are creative and of these only a few are really capable of creativity. It follows that only a few humans live meaningful lives.

Taylor's position in "The Meaning of Life" can be stated as follows:

(Def. 3) A life is meaningful if and only if it creates something of great value.

Taylor argues that Definition 3 only applies to a relatively small number of people, for instance, composers, poets, philosophers, writers, and the like.

By implication Definition 3 rejects completely the striving view of the second part of "Does Life Have a Meaning?" It is not clear why Taylor rejects Definition 2 however. What he now advocates resembles Definition 1 albeit with two major differences.

In Definition 1, in order for a life to be meaningful it must result in a significant accomplishment. Although Taylor uses the creative act of building a temple as an example, he does not explicitly restrict significant accomplishments to significant creations. After all, a geological discovery can be a significant accomplishment, but it would not be considered a creation. Secondly, in "Does Life Have a Meaning?" he restricts these significant achievements to ones that last forever. The significance of creations in "The Meaning of Life" does not seem so restricted, however. Although Taylor there speaks of Sisyphus' creation inspiring generations of humankind "for all time," he assumes that actual painters, composers, poets, philosophers, and writers can lead meaningful lives even though their creations do not last forever.

EVALUATION OF TAYLOR'S VIEWS

Taylor's Definition 1 contrasts in interesting respects with my account of Positive Purpose Meaning. In the first place, Definition 1 is formulated in terms of life's significant accomplishments rather than its positive significant purposes. It implies that a life with a significant purpose has no meaning unless it accomplishes something significant. However, this seems overly harsh. Suppose Sisyphus' purpose in life is to construct a beautiful temple and, although it is not impossible for him to accomplish this task, he does not complete the task. Would it really be correct to say that his life was meaningless? This seems too strong. Moreover, Definition 1 does not take into account the need for psychological satisfaction. It seems mistaken to say that if Sisyphus derived no psychological satisfaction from constructing the temple, his life would be meaningful.

In addition, Taylor's Definition 1 has the serious implication that *no* life could be meaningful since the creations, discoveries, social reforms, and performances of any life are subject to change and eventual decay. As Bertrand Russell once said, "all the labors of the ages, all devotion, all the inspiration, all the noonday brightness of human genius, are destined to extinction in the vast death of the solar system, and the whole temple of man's achievement must inevitably be buried beneath the debris of a universe in ruins."[20] To be sure, this death will take millions of years to achieve. Nevertheless, it will take place. It should be noted that Positive Purpose Meaning has no analogous implication. In order to be meaningful the purpose of life need not be the achievement of something of everlasting importance.

Taylor's Definition 2 also contrasts in interesting ways with my notion of Positive Purpose Meaning. First, according to it human life need not have any significant purpose. Granted constant striving suggests a purpose or purposes but these can be trivial. Second, this constant striving need not be psychologically satisfying. And third, although striving suggests that there is a goal or goals being striven for, these may be impossible to accomplish.

If Taylor's Definition 1 errs on the side of stringency, his Definition 2 errs on the side of lenience. Whereas Definition 1 prevents any life from being meaningful since no life results in something of eternal significance, Definition 2 allows practically any life—even the life of the lowly glowworm—to be meaningful so long as it is a life that is natural to it. As previously noted, Definition 2 seems to exclude very little. With respect to animal behavior it seems only to exclude the lives of animals living in artificial environments.[21] With respect to human beings it is not clear if anything other than a life of inactivity is excluded. But constant striving does not seem to be a sufficient condition of meaningful existence. A person who strives ceaselessly all his life to achieve a trivial task such as blowing as many soap bubbles as he can cannot be said to have lived a meaningful life. Moreover, even if the striving were for a nontrivial purpose this would not be sufficient for a meaningful life. After all, the purpose may be impossible to accomplish. For example, suppose a man strives all of his life to show that arithmetic is complete. Although his purpose is far from trivial, as Gödel showed, his purpose is futile. One could plausibly say in this case that this man's life is meaningless. But even if the purpose is neither trivial nor futile a life of ceaseless striving is not sufficient for a meaningful life. Suppose a woman strives all of her life to be a good traditional wife and mother. Unfortunately, she hates the role and wants to be a brain surgeon. It is dubious that we could say her life was meaningful since she received no satisfaction from it.

Thus ceaseless striving is not a sufficient condition for a meaningful life and it is not a necessary condition either. Suppose a young mathematician makes a world-shattering discovery at the age of twenty-eight and relaxes for the remainder of her seventy-eight years. Suppose further that the original discovery was not the result of a great struggle but came quickly and effortlessly in a flash of genius. One might regret the waste of fifty years of inactivity and admire her less than other mathematicians who struggled more. But it seems unjust to suppose that her life is without meaning. The reason for this intuitive judgment appears to be that her life can fulfill the conditions of Positive Purpose Meaning: Her life had a significant purpose that was psychologically satisfying and which it was possible to fulfill nonarbitrarily.

Taylor's Definition 3 contrasts with my Positive Purpose Meaning in ways similar to Definition 1. Again, it is formulated in terms of life's creative accomplishments rather than its significant purposes. Thus it implies that a life with a significant purpose has no meaning unless it creates something of great value. Again this seems overly harsh. Moreover, like Definition 1, Taylor's Definition 3 does not take into account the need for psychological satisfaction. For these reasons alone my account is to be preferred. In addition Taylor's analysis has other problems.

Clearly Definition 3 is too narrow even in Taylor's own terms. Surely the important point of his temple building example is that Sisyphus do something important. After all, there are important scientific discoveries as well as inventions and creations. It seems arbitrary to limit the products of meaningful lives to what is created rather than found. Suppose that instead of creating a temple Sisyphus made an important scientific discovery or that he invented a labor saving device that would enable humans to transport heavy objects up hills with minimal effort. Would his life still be meaningless?

Limiting important achievements to creations has the absurd implication that great scientists such as Newton, Einstein, and Darwin did not lead meaningful lives. In a similar way, Definition 3 absurdly implies that inventors such as the Wright brothers, Marconi, Bell, and Edison led meaningless lives. But even if we expand Definition 3 to include scientists and inventors it is still too narrow. For example, there are also explorers, social reformers, and environmentalists. Is it really true that Columbus's life lacked meaning because it was not artistic, literary, or musical? That Martin Luther King's life was meaningless because he was not creative in the way that Taylor seems to have in mind? That environmentalist John Muir's life lacked significant purpose because he did not fit into Taylor's categories of a creative person?

Interestingly, Taylor, a philosopher, includes philosophers in the elite class of creative people who live meaningful lives. However, it is certainly debatable that the products of philosophers should be understood as creations. For example, many metaphysicians and ontologists would resist describing their work in this way. They would see themselves as specifying the structure of reality—as discovering—not creating. Some ethical philosophers as well would reject the creation terminology. Moral realists, for example, believe that their theories reflect the moral structure of the world. Creation language in ethics, they would argue, suggests moral conventionalism, which is precisely the view they reject.

Whereas builders of utopias might be thought of as trying to create a just or ideal society, social philosophers do not create such societies. Rather they try to discover what properties such societies have. Many epistemologists would say that they were discovering the answers to questions such as how knowledge is possible, not creating anything. Although aestheticians study the creations of painters, composers, poets, and writers, they themselves try to discover what makes a great work of art, piece of music, or literary work.

To be sure, elaborate philosophical theories are sometimes referred to as creations or constructions. If this only means that these theories are produced by human beings and are not found ready made in nature, there can be no objection to such talk. But insofar as these theories purport to be true and this truth is not determined by the theory, creation talk is just as misleading in philosophical contexts as discovery talk is in most musical and artistic contexts. Beethoven, for example, did not *discover* his Fifth Symphony.

The question also arises of what is to be included under the category of creation. In his list of creative people Taylor cites composers and writers. What about performing artists? Can it really be said that cellist Yo-Yo Ma leads a meaningless life because he "merely" plays someone else's compositions? Moreover, even if these presentations are considered to be creations, they cannot be the sort that Taylor has in mind. Although in "The Meaning of Life" he no longer requires creations to last forever, he seems to assume that the ones that give life meaning have at least some modest permanence. This is not true of performances. Unless they are recorded they are radically transitory: They end when the last note is played, the final word is spoken, or the ultimate dance step is taken. Following Taylor's idea to its logical conclusion one would be forced to say that Yo-Yo Ma would be leading a meaningless life were not his performances recorded for all posterity to enjoy, and that the great performers of the past did lead meaningless lives since their performance could not possibly have been preserved.

The products of the great chefs also have only the problem that their work does not last for it is pretty much agreed that they are wondrous culinary creations. To be sure, these creations could last for some time, say, in a frozen state. But normally they are intended to be consumed shortly after they are created. Are we to suppose that chefs live meaningless lives because of the short existence of their creations? This seems extremely implausible.

In addition, there is a very large class of human beings that Taylor overlooks, namely parents. Why they should be excluded from the class of creative people is not clear. Of course, it may be argued that parents do not live meaningful lives simply by virtue of having and rearing children. After all, the parents may be terrible, and the children may turn out badly. But the same thing is true of artists, poets, composers, and writers. Sometimes they produce bad paintings, worthless music, stupid poetry, and trashy novels. Taylor requires the creation to be of "great value" if it is to make the life of the creative person's live meaningful. But something similar could be demanded of parents. Surely, children with high moral values who grow up to be socially responsible adults are of great value. It would not be stretching the point to claim that on a generous interpretation of Taylor's view the parents of such children would be living meaningful lives.

According to Taylor's Definitions 1 and 3, animal lives and most human lives are meaningless since they are endlessly repetitive. Is this assumption true? Whether events in a life are considered to be repetitive or not is in part a function of how they are described. They can become varied, unique, and exciting under one description and uniform, homogeneous, and dull under another. According to Taylor, people "do essentially the same things today that they were doing yesterday and that they will do again tomorrow, repeating this pattern year after year until finally they go to their graves leaving nothing behind of worth except a new generation to repeat the cycle." Surely in many descriptions this is an inaccurate characterization of people's lives. People lead very different lives when they are babies and teenagers. They do different things in their teens and working years, and they do still different things when they are older and retired.

Of course, these differences can be eliminated by descriptions such as "X woke up," "X engaged in various activities including eating and eliminating bodily waste" and "then X went to sleep." Such descriptions would probably be accurate for most people at every stage of their lives and they can be used to make it seem as if the various stages of life are uniform. Moreover, many people's lives are varied even at the same stage, but they can be made to seem the same by homogenizing descriptions such as "X rose, went to work, came home, and went to bed." In addition, people's lives also vary enormously from culture to culture and from one historical period to the next. To be sure, descriptions are available that make the lives of an English aristocrat and an Australian bushman seem the same. However, there is no reason that such descriptions should be used.

CONCLUSION

My analysis of the meaning of life in terms of Positive Purpose Meaning has clear advantages over Taylor's problematic analysis. First, it is difficult to reconcile his three formulations of the meaning of life with one another. Second, his two formulations in "Does Life Have a Meaning?" are either too broad or too narrow. Third, his analysis in "The Meaning of Life" is also too narrow it that it restricts meaningful lives to those that are creative in a narrow sense of "creative." My analysis has none of these problems.

NOTES

1. Richard Taylor, "Does Life Have a Meaning?" in *The Meaning of Life*, ed. Steven Sanders and David R. Cheney (Englewood Cliffs, N.J.: Prentice-Hall, 1980), pp. 77–85; Richard Taylor, "The Meaning of Life," *Philosophy Today* 24 (summer 1999): 13–14.

2. Taylor, "Does Life Have a Meaning?" p. 79.

3. Ibid., p. 80.

4. Ibid., p. 81.

5. Ibid., p. 82.

6. Ibid.

7. Ibid., p. 83.

8. Ibid.

9. Ibid., p. 85.

10. Ibid.

11. Ibid.

12. Ibid.

13. Ibid.

14. Taylor, "The Meaning of Life," p. 13.

15. Ibid., pp. 13–14.

16. Ibid., p. 14.

17. Ibid.

18. Ibid.

19. Ibid

20. Bertrand Russell, *A Free Man Worship*. Quoted by Paul Edwards, in "Meaning and Value of Life," in Sanders and Cheney, *The Meaning of Life*, p. 89.

21. From the point of view of Taylor's Definition 1 it is unclear whether living in an artificial environment would always result in living a meaningless life. After all, laboratory animals might live very meaningful lives if they are subjects in a scientific experiment that results in great scientific advances. Indeed, the use of laboratory experiments on Animal A might result in great scientific advances that could further the interests of A. Thus, experiments on a glowworm in a laboratory might reveal the cause of a disease that is killing the worm in its natural state.

13

OBJECTIONS TO MEANING WITHOUT RELIGION

INTRODUCTION

Religious apologists do not accept the idea that an atheist's life can have meaning without God. Some argue that life without God has no purpose and that without a purpose life has no meaning. Others argue that human existence without an afterlife is meaningless. Even some nonbelievers such as Bertrand Russell have argued that the finitude of human creations and civilization deprives human existence of meaning. Still, other thinkers have maintained that human existence is absurd if God does not exist.

Is life without God meaningless or absurd? Do these arguments have any validity? What are the presumptions of such arguments? Do these arguments affect all atheists? Should atheism be abandoned if these arguments are accepted? These questions will be considered in this chapter.

BACKGROUND TO THE ARGUMENTS

We can approach the problem of whether life is meaningless without God by noting certain implications that seem to follow from a commonly ac-

cepted naturalistic and scientific view of the world. It is to this view of
the world that critics seem to be implicitly appealing when they attempt
to derive pessimistic implications from atheism.[1]

It is commonly accepted that if a naturalistic view of the world is true,
then all of the following are true:

1. There is no cosmic purpose.
2. Each human life is finite.
3. Human life in general is finite.

The acceptance of (1) seems to be entailed by the acceptance of naturalism. This acceptance not only rules out belief in a personal theistic God
but also in an impersonal purpose that guides our destiny. In contrast, (2)
and (3) are not entailed by naturalism per se. However, they seem overwhelmingly probable in the light of our present scientific evidence. Given
these three premises critics of atheism attempt to derive conclusions such
as the following:

4. Human life is meaningless.
5. Human life is worthless..
6. Human life is absurd.

The question is, given the facts described in (1), (2), and (3), are the pessimistic conclusions of (4), (5), and (6) justified?

Before we attempt to answer this question it is important to note that
atheism per se is not committed to the naturalistic worldview of science
that entails (1), (2), and (3). In particular, some nontheistic religions, for
example Jainism, deny (1), (2), and (3).[2] Moreover, one can be an atheist
and still believe in the immortality of the individual soul and in a grand
cosmic plan of salvation. Thus, only certain kinds of atheism can plausibly be accused of having pessimistic implications.

The second thing to note is that if pessimistic conclusions do follow
from a naturalistic atheism, such atheism is not necessarily false. A rational person might regret that a view so well justified by the evidence has
pessimistic implications but he or she should not abandon it simply for this
reason. If the evidence justifies pessimism, then we must be pessimistic. If
we are optimistic when pessimism is justified, we are irrational.[3]

THE MEANINGLESSNESS OF HUMAN LIFE

It is important to have before one's mind clear counterexamples to the religious thesis that life has no meaning in an atheistic worldview. So consider a medical researcher whose purpose in life is to find the cure of a deadly disease. Surely this purpose has positive significance. Let us assume that for this person medical research of this kind is psychologically satisfying. We can also presume that finding such a cure is scientifically possible. Moreover, given the needs of society, and the person's interests and talents, this purpose is hardly arbitrary and has a plausible rationale. In this case it seems plausible to say that the medical researcher's life has meaning in the purpose sense. Note that this judgment has nothing to do with religious belief.

Much the same thing can be said about meaning of life in the value sense. Consider a person with superior talents who lives a long, happy life devoted to his family, his writing, and his music. His life has been relatively free from worries, pain, and hardships. In this case too religion seems irrelevant to the plausible claim that his life has meaning.

Given examples such as these and countless more that can be cited, religious arguments have a heavy burden. They must show that nevertheless all human lives are meaningless without religion.

Perhaps one of the most important arguments that purports to show that life is meaningless without religion is the Argument from Cosmic Purpose. It can be stated as follows:

1. If naturalistic atheism is true, then there is no cosmic purpose or purposes.
2. If there is no cosmic purpose or purposes, then individual human lives have no meaning.
3. Naturalistic atheism is true.
4. Therefore, individual human lives have no meaning.

The analysis given in chapter 11 should quickly enable us to indicate the problem with this argument. Although meaning in the purpose sense can involve a cosmic purpose or purposes created by God, this is not necessary. It can also involve terrestrial purpose or purposes that are either discovered or created by human beings. Hence, premise (2) is false.

Perhaps something slightly different is intended, however. One might admit that people have terrestrial purposes and yet maintain that for life to have meaning these purposes must be justified. It might be argued that they are not and cannot be justified if there is no God: that if there is no cosmic purpose, any terrestrial purposes are arbitrary and must be so. This Argument from Arbitrary Justification can be stated as follows:

1. If naturalistic atheism is true, there is no cosmic purpose or purposes.
2. If there is no cosmic purpose or purposes, then there is no justification for terrestrial purposes.
3. If there is no justification for terrestrial purposes, then they are arbitrary.
4. Naturalistic atheism is true.
5. Therefore, terrestrial purposes are arbitrary.

What does it mean to say that terrestrial purposes are arbitrary? Presumably, it means that whatever purpose a person has is no better than any other terrestrial purpose. But premise (1) of this argument is false. Implicitly the Argument from Arbitrary Justification seems to be relying on reasoning similar to that which was criticized earlier in part 1 of this book, namely that if there is no God, moral anarchy is the correct moral position. Such reasoning is even less plausible here than it was in the context in which we initially encountered it. As we have seen, atheism does not entail moral anarchy. But supposing that it did, it would not follow that *all* purposes were arbitrary. It would simply show that all *ethical* purposes were arbitrary. Thus, if any purpose were *morally* permitted, the goal of avoiding life-threatening situations would still be a better *prudential* purpose than seeking such situations. Moreover, if atheism does not entail moral anarchy (as it does not), then some purposes would be better than others. Thus, for example, under normal circumstances not causing sentient beings needless pain would be a better moral purpose than causing sentient beings needless pain. Even if some form of ethical relativism were true, ethical reasons would not be arbitrary; the correctness would simply be relative.

THE WORTHLESSNESS OF HUMAN LIFE

So far we have seen that arguments for the meaninglessness of life in the purpose sense fails. However, critics of atheism also maintain that without God human life is meaningless in the value sense. In this sense a human life has meaning if and only if as a whole it is good for the person who leads it. But what does it mean to say that that life as a whole is good for the person who leads it? I suggested earlier that a person's life is good as a whole if, were the person rational, fully informed, and unbiased, he or she would as a whole approve of it. This account allows that the goodness of a person's life as a whole might vary from person to person. This could be the case for at least two different reasons. First, people's lives differ in regard to such things as hardships, pain, and happiness. These variations can affect how they would evaluate their lives as a whole. Second, since not all rational, fully informed, and unbiased people may desire the same thing, even if there were no variations, different evaluations could be made. As a result different people might evaluate their lives differently even if they were identical in terms of such factors as hardship, pain, and happiness.

Now some critics of atheism maintain that without God and the immortality that he provides human existence has no value. This Argument from Finiteness can be reconstructed as follows:

1. If naturalistic atheism is true, human life is not of infinite duration.
2. If human life is not of infinite duration, then it is not good as a whole.
3. Naturalistic atheism is true.
4. Therefore, human life is not good as a whole.

Here the problem is premise (2), for it is very difficult to see why one should believe it. Of course, it is possible for an individual to judge that her life is not good as a whole. If she were rational, she would judge the goodness of her life as a whole in terms of considerations such as her accomplishments, her efforts toward achieving certain worthwhile goals, and the moral style of her daily activities. However, the same sorts of considerations that enable some people to judge their lives as not good as a whole enables others to judge their lives as good as a whole. These considerations are not based on the length of the life. A relatively short life may be one of great value whereas a long one may be worthless. If there were immortal beings, they might lead worthless or worthwhile lives. One could not determine which simply from knowing that they were immortal.

Another argument for the worthlessness of life as a whole is based on the transitory nature of human achievements. The attitude that motivates this argument was well-stated by Bertrand Russell when he expressed profound regret that all the greatest achievements of humankind in art, literature, technology, and science will someday vanish from the universe. An argument against the possibility of Value Meaning of life in an atheistic worldview is based on the assumption that unless the fruits of human civilization last forever (at least in cultural memory) they are worthless. Consider then the Argument from the Transitory Nature of Things:

1. If naturalistic atheism is true, then the cultural and intellectual accomplishments of humankind in literature, art, technology, and science will not last forever.
2. Unless the cultural and intellectual accomplishments of humankind in literature, art, technology, and science last forever, they are worthless.
3. Naturalistic atheism is true.
4. Therefore, the cultural and intellectual accomplishments of humankind in literature, art, technology, and science are worthless.
5. If the cultural and intellectual accomplishments of humankind in literature, art, technology, and science are worthless, then human life itself is not good as a whole.
6. Therefore, human life itself is not good as a whole.

Premise (2) represents a major problem for this argument since it is hard to see how it can be maintained. The worth of literature, art, technology, science, and culture is surely not eternal. These serve various purposes and when these purposes are no longer possible they cease to have any value and may indeed become worthless. Premise (2) assumes that in order for something to have positive worth in one context it must have worth in all contexts. Nothing could be further from the truth. Indeed, such a view is not only false but in certain cases makes little sense. For example, with "the vast death of the solar system" (to use Russell's phrase) the whole notion of something having worth would have no meaning. However, it would not follow from this that before this "vast death" certain things had no worth.

The second problem with the Argument from the Transitory Nature of Things is posed by premise (5). I see no reason to suppose that if cultural and intellectual accomplishments are worthless, then individual human lives are not good as a whole. A mother who has raised intelligent, healthy, and morally upright children, a doctor who has devoted her life to caring for the indigent, a teacher who has spent her life teaching her pupils to be just and compassionate may lead worthwhile lives without anything being accomplished of cultural significance.

THE ABSURDITY OF HUMAN LIFE

So far in this book the concept of absurd has not been defined. However, the claim that human life is absurd is often equivalent to the claim that life is meaningless: to say that life is absurd often seems to mean just that life lacks purpose and value. If so, no new evaluation of the position is needed. However, sometimes a different sense of absurd is intended. Then, to say that life is absurd means that it is incongruous; that is, one aspect of life is out of harmony with another. In particular, Albert Camus and Thomas Nagel argue that human life is absurd in this latter sense.

Albert Camus maintained in *The Myth of Sisyphus* that the absurdity of human existence is a function of two things: the expectations of human beings and the reality that they find.[4] Human beings expect to live in a world that is rational and unified. What they find is a world which is neither. This tension between expectation and reality generates the absurdity of existence. Given Camus's sense of absurd, life is incongruous because of the tension between our expectation and reality.

Camus argues that for many people this absurdity is too much to bear. Some try to escape by physical suicide and some commit what Camus calls philosophical suicide in which by a leap of religious faith one assumes, despite the evidence, that the universe is rational and unified. Camus argues that such escapes are dishonest and unauthentic. One must live one's life with the full realization that human existence is absurd in defiance of the universe to which one is unreconciled.

Although atheists may approve of Camus's opposition to religious leaps of faith, they should not let his claim that human existence is absurd go unexamined. Putting aside Camus's recommendations on how one should live one's life in the face of the absurdity of human existence, the crucial question is, Is Camus's argument for the absurdity of human existence sound?

His Argument from Tension can be formulated in this way:

1. If humans expect the universe to be rational and unified and find neither rationality nor unity in the universe, then human existence is absurd.
2. Humans expect the universe to be rational and unified.
3. Humans find neither rationality nor unity in the universe.
4. Therefore, human existence is absurd.

The crucial premises are (2) and (3). Premise (2) does not seem to be true in the way that Camus intended and, although premise (3) is true in Camus's sense, it is trivial.

I know of no one who claimed that the universe is rational or unified in the senses Camus seems to have in mind. Consider, for example, what he says:

> If man realized that the universe like him can love and suffer, he would be reconciled. If thought discovered in the shimmering mirrors of phenomena eternal relations capable of summing them up and summing themselves up in a single principle, then would be seen an intellectual joy of which the myth of the blessed would be but a ridiculous imitation. That nostalgia for unity, that appetite for the absolute illustrates the essential impulse of the human drama. But the fact of that nostalgia's existence does not imply that it is to be immediately satisfied. For if, bridging the gulf that separates desire from conquest, we assert with Parmenides the reality of the One (whatever it may be), we fall into the ridiculous contradiction of a mind that asserts total unity and proves by its assertion its own difference and the diversity it claimed to resolve.[5]

In this quotation Camus seems to be suggesting at least three different respects in which the universe disappoints human expectation. First, the universe disappoints human expectation because it is not a sentient creature that can love and suffer. Furthermore, we cannot sum up all we discover about reality in a single principle. And finally, we want the universe to be a Parmenidian One and yet we notice that our minds are not part of the One.

One wonders who has these expectations. It is certainly not modern-day scientists, for they do not expect the universe to be any of the things Camus claims humans expect. Although an ideal of the unity of science is sometimes suggested as a heuristic principle of science and physicists continue to search for a unified theory of the physical sciences, no scientist supposes that everything could ever be summed up in a single principle or that the unity science seeks is like the Parmenidian One, let alone that the universe is irrational unless it loves and suffers. Moreover, if scientists did expect any of these things of the universe, they would surely be unwarranted. Although it may not be logically impossible for the Universe to have the properties that Camus says that humans demand, it is at least physically impossible and in any case is completely unnecessary for scientific inquiry.

We may conclude that if humans do demand or should demand what Camus says, there would indeed be a tension in human existence. But humans do not and should not.

Thomas Nagel has given a different argument for the absurdity of human existence.[6] Arguing that a philosophical sense of absurdity comes from the "collision between the seriousness with which we take our lives and the perpetual possibility of regarding everything about which we are serious as arbitrary, or open to doubt,"[7] he maintains that although as human beings we take our lives seriously, it is possible to take another vantage point outside ourselves. Unlike animals and inanimate things we can transcend our own limited perspective and see our lives *sub specie aeternitatis*. From this perspective, Nagel says, all we do appears to be arbitrary. Yet our ability to take this perspective does not disengage us from life and "there lies the absurdity: not in the fact that such an external view can be taken of us, but in the fact that we ourselves can take it without ceasing to be the persons whose ultimate concerns are so coolly regarded."[8] Nagel argues that it is futile to try to escape this position by taking some wider perspective that may give our lives meaning. In particular, he doubts whether belief in God and his cosmic purpose can eliminate the sense of the absurd. If we can step back from the purposes of individual life and doubt their point, it is possible to step back from the kingdom and glory of God and doubt its point as well: "What makes doubt inescapable with regard to the limited aim of the individual also makes it inescapable with regard to any larger purpose that encourages the sense that life is meaningless."[9]

Nagel's account, like Camus's, depends on the incongruous sense of absurd. He is saying that our everyday concerns are incongruous with the way we regard these concerns from an objective point of view. Thus, we regard our health, world peace, and our financial affairs with great seriousness. But if we regard them from the point of view of eternity, they seem unimportant and trivial. This is absurd. However, Nagel, unlike Camus, does not recommend a heroic defiance of the universe in face of this absurdity. This sort of dramatic response, Nagel says, fails to appreciate the "cosmic unimportance of the situation": "If *sub species aeternitatis* there is no reason to believe that anything matters, then that does not matter either, and we can approach our absurd lives with irony instead of heroism or despair."[10]

The Argument from *Sub Specie Aeternitatis* can be stated as follows:

1. When we view our life *sub specie aeternitatis*, our goals, aspirations, and the like seem arbitrary.
2. If our goals, aspirations, and the like seem arbitrary and we do not disengage from life, then our life is absurd.
3. We do sometimes view our life *sub specie aeternitatis*.
4. We do not disengage from life.
5. Therefore, our life is absurd.

But this argument, even if sound, gives no comfort to theists. For suppose that God exists and that his purpose in creating the universe and life was X. Nagel maintains that if we look at our life and X from *sub specie aeternitatis*, our life in relation to X seems arbitrary. So, if our lives are absurd in an atheistic world, they are, according to Nagel, equally absurd in a theistic one.

But is the argument sound? One problem is that premises (1) and (3) merely establish that our goals and aspirations *seem* arbitrary from a peculiar point of view of our life that we take in certain reflective moments. Perhaps it may seem to us in these reflective moments as if we are viewing our life *sub specie aeternitatis*. But we clearly are not—only an omniscient being can do this—and the perspective that we take should not be dignified in these terms. We are merely looking at our lives from another point of view in which our goals and aspirations have no importance. But why should one suppose that this point of view should be taken seriously?

To make this point clear and to reflect the true state of affairs, premises (1) and (2) should be replaced by these:

> 1'. When we view our life from what seems like *sub specie aeternitatis*, our goals, aspirations, and the like seem arbitrary.
>
> 2'. If our goals, aspirations, and the like seem arbitrary from what seems like *sub specie aeternitatis* and we do not disengage from life, then our life seems absurd from what seems like *sub specie aeternitatis*.

Given (1') and (2') we can derive the following:

> 5'. Therefore, our life seems absurd from what seems like *sub specie aeternitatis*.

But without further argument it is difficult to see why we should take the appearances specified in (2') and (5') seriously. Things may appear to us in all sorts of ways and from various apparent perspectives. For example, mystics claim that in what seems like the perspective of The Absolute, everything, including their lives, appears in complete harmony. If we take what they say to reflect reality, then it is difficult to take Nagel's vision of the absurdity of existence as reflecting reality. To only some of these ways that things appear to us and to only some of the apparent perspectives that we have do we give serious consideration. In the present case, why should we give such consideration to this apparent perspective and to the apparent reality shown from this perspective? In a sense, Nagel admits that how things appear from what seems like *sub specie aeternitatis* is unimportant and should not be taken seriously. Thus, he says that a vision of our lives *sub specie aeternitatis* has no practical implications: because of it we should not change our lives in any way. For example, both suicide and a heroic defiance would be unwarranted. After our vision of the absurdity of life we simply approach our life "with irony." However, it is difficult to see why even irony would be an appropriate response to this absurdity unless there was some reason to suppose that this perspective was a reliable one and, consequently, that the appearance of absurdity had some claim to truth. Yet this is precisely what has not been established.[11]

It must be concluded that if Nagel is correct, human life is absurd in both an atheistic and a theistic worldview. However, he has yet to show the validity of the perspective from which the judgments of absurdity of human life is made.

CONCLUSION

Once the claims that without religious belief life is without meaning, or devoid of value, or absurd, are clarified, the question is whether there are any good reasons to suppose that they are true. An examination of the arguments for these claims indicates that they are unsound. To illustrate the difficulties of assessing such claims further, in the next chapter I will consider a recent controversy generated by R. M. Hare's paper "Nothing Matters."

NOTES

1. See Michael Martin, *Atheism: A Philosophical Justification* (Philadelphia: Temple University Press, 1990), chap. 1.

2. See Umakant Premanand Shah, "Jainism," in *Encyclopaedia Britannica*, 15th ed. (Chicago: Encyclopedia Britannica, Inc., 1984), vol. 10, pp. 8–14; Ninian Smart, "Jainism," in *The Encyclopedia of Philosophy*, ed. Paul Edwards (New York: Macmillan and Free Press, 1967), vol. 4, pp. 238–39; E. Royston Pike, *Encyclopaedia of Religion and Religions* (New York: Meridian Books, 1958), pp. 203–205; Herbert Stroup, *Four Religions of Asia* (New York: Harper and Row, 1968), pp. 81–114.

3. This is not to say that the practical implications of a theory have no relevance in theory choice. There is an epistemological presumption that practical considerations should play no role in theory choice and there is a presumption that if practical considerations do play a role they should only be used when non-

practical considerations cannot decide. Since, as I have shown in *Atheism* (chapter 1) there are good nonpractical reasons for belief in atheism, there is a presumption that belief in atheism should not be based on whether it has pessimistic implications.

4. Albert Camus, *The Myth of Sisyphus and Other Essays*, trans. Justin O'Brien (New York: Alfred A. Knopf, 1955). Relevant selections of this work are reprinted in Sanders and Cheney, *The Meaning of Life* (Englewood Cliffs, N.J.: Prentice-Hall, 1980). See Albert Camus, "An Absurd Reasoning," in *The Meaning of Life*, pp. 65–75.

5. Camus, "An Absurd Reasoning," p. 69.

6. Thomas Nagel, "The Absurd," in Sanders and Cheney, *The Meaning of Life*, pp. 155–65.

7. Ibid., p. 157.

8. Ibid., p. 159.

9. Ibid., p. 160.

10. Ibid., p. 165.

11. Cf. Jonathan Glover, Review of Thomas Nagel, *The View From Nowhere*, *New York Review of Books*, April 9, 1987, p. 34.

14

THE
"NOTHING MATTERS"
ARGUMENT

INTRODUCTION

I n the last chapter many of the standard objections to the meaningfulness
of life without God were considered. However, another way of questioning if life has meaning given the truth of atheism is to claim that, if there
is no God, nothing matters. I will now critically consider this line of reasoning as it has been expressed in a contemporary controversy between
R. M. Hare, a British ethicist, and Quentin Smith, an American philosopher.

In a well-known essay entitled "'Nothing Matters'" Hare tells the
story of a young friend who, after reading Camus's novel *The Stranger*,
starts to act strangely.[1] His reading of the novel convinces him that
nothing matters, a view expressed by Meursault, the main character of
Camus's novel. This belief changes the young friend from a nonsmoking,
cheerful, vigorous, enthusiastic young man into a depressed chain smoker
who eats little and wanders aimlessly around the outskirts of Oxford.
Hare diagnoses the young man's problems as being based on linguistic
confusion and applies linguistic therapy to cure him. Critical of Hare's
"cure," Smith argues that the young man's depression is based on his
acceptance of ethical subjectivism.[2] Given this acceptance, says Smith,
the young man's depression is appropriate.

In this chapter I will show that both Hare and Smith are mistaken. Smith wrongly diagnoses the young man's problem and Hare's linguistic analysis fails to get at the basis of Camus's argument. It should be noted that Hare does not attempt to relate the claim that nothing matters to atheism despite the fact that Camus, an atheist, wrote *The Stranger* and Meursault expresses his claim that nothing matters in a dialogue with a priest.

HARE'S LINGUISTIC THERAPY

Using the techniques of linguistic analysis, in his essay Hare talks to his young friend and endeavors to show him that his belief is based on linguistic confusion. Hare convinces him that when we say something matters we are expressing concern about something. Having gotten the young man's agreement on this point Hare next convinces him that *someone's* concern is always expressed. One might say, "It matters very much that so and so should happen *to him*." Or if the words "to him" are left out, in the absence of any indication to the contrary, the concern expressed is of the speaker.

Having explained these points to his friend, the two men return to Camus's novel to consider the question of who is expressing unconcern for everything. According to Hare there are three possibilities: the character Meursault, the author Camus, and Hare's young friend. Hare then dismisses the idea that Camus himself is unconcerned about everything since it is obvious that as a novelist he is concerned about his own literary work. In Meursault's case Hare says that the authors of novels can put any sentiments they wish into the mouths of their characters. He maintains that although throughout most of the novel Meursault is depicted as a person rather given to unconcern, in a dramatic scene toward the end of the novel he acts violently, behavior which is inconsistent with unconcern. In any case, Hare argues that the sentiments of Camus's fictional character who is about to leave the world have no relevance for Hare's young friend who has the world before him. In fact, his young friend is concerned about many things. His real problem is to reduce to some order those things that really matter to him.

Hare conjectures that his young friend's confusion is based on a failure to understand that the word "matters" is used to express concern. His young friend thinks that mattering is something that things do "as if

'My wife matters to me' were similar to 'My wife chatters to me.'" As for people who understand this linguistic point and who still say that nothing matters, Hare believes that they are either hypocrites or psychologically abnormal. The majority of people feel concern for things.

SMITH'S CRITIQUE OF HARE

Smith argues that it is Hare and not his young friend who abuses ordinary language. "Nothing matters" has well-established ordinary uses. One of these is to indicate that nothing has intrinsic value and that "all values are subjective and projected by humans, who arbitrarily decide to regard this or that as valuable."[3] According to Smith, both Camus and Hare's young friend attempt to express this idea. This is what his young friend means by saying "Nothing matters."

Smith infers that Hare would say that the claim "Life is meaningless" is analogous to saying "Nothing matters" because values are not intrinsic properties of things. Hare would claim, says Smith, that the expression "Life is meaningless" is a misuse of "meaningless," since meaning is always meaning-for-somebody. The expression "Human life is meaningless," if it has any sense at all, expresses the idea that human life is meaningless to someone, for example, a person who is completely unconcerned about human life. In other words, Smith maintains that Hare holds that it is metaphysical nonsense to suppose that there is an objective sense of expressions such as "matters" and "the meaning or meaninglessness of human life."

Smith argues that despite what Hare claims about ordinary language, "Nothing matters" and "Human life is meaningless" have objective senses. He maintains:

> Indeed, this is immediately obvious, inasmuch as the question "What is the meaning of human life" is a part of ordinary use, and the two possible answers, whether they be true or false, are also part of ordinary use: "Human life is meaningless" and "The meaning of human life is [to do God's will, to do what is good, and so on]."[4]

Smith maintains that the situation of Hare's young friend is in fact one that Hare would inevitably find himself in given his view that there are no intrinsic values. If there are no intrinsic values, then there is "nothing in things that can ethically justify an action and enable a true belief to be an ethical motivation for acting. What I had normally taken to be objective ethical justifications to act were in reality arbitrary projections on my part. It seemed to me that certain things objectively ought to be done, but I recognize now that this seeming was delusive and so I slip into a nihilistic apathy."[5] The apathetic behavior of Hare's young friend is therefore quite appropriate given the man's beliefs. Smith argues that the only honest and sincere response to the relativity of value is apathy and people who profess ethical subjectivism and yet enthusiastically pursue certain ethical goals such as the alleviation of suffering are living compartmentalized lives.

Smith maintains that our first level (normative) moral beliefs tacitly assume objective moral facts; that is, they involve the notion of truth as correspondence to moral facts. But the belief in moral relativism in all its various forms—emotivism, prescriptivism, constructivism—on the second (meta) level is inconsistent with this assumption. Moral relativism on the second level entails moral antirealism which conflicts with the tacit assumption of moral realism made on the first level.

Smith points out that it is possible to argue that all first level moral beliefs are in error and only appear to correspond to moral facts. This construal would prevent any conflict between the normative and the meta levels of moral discourse. But it does not prevent despair from being the appropriate response to the realization that the assumption of moral realism on the first level of moral discourse is illusory.

Although an atheist, Smith does not explicitly relate the claim that nothing matters to atheism. However, it would have been easy enough for him to do so. He might have said that some people have wrongly associated atheism with subjective values. One consequence of this association is that if atheism is true, nothing matters. However, this association is mistaken and objective values are compatible with disbelief in God.

EVALUATION OF THE CONTROVERSY BETWEEN HARE AND SMITH

Smith is correct that the claim "Nothing matters" can be understood in terms of the denial that there are intrinsic ethical values. He is also correct that Hare tacitly assumes a subjective and relativistic view of ethical values. What is problematic about Smith's critique is the claim that Hare's young friend and Camus implicitly embrace this interpretation.

In the case of Hare's friend it is not clear why he thinks "Nothing matters," or—what amounts to the same thing—why his friend thought Meursault believes that nothing matters. To be sure, Smith's construction is not ruled out a priori. But if Hare's friend has read the novel carefully and has embraced Meursault's rationale, then it is clear that both Hare and Smith are mistaken.

In speaking to the priest at the end of the novel, Meursault says "Nothing, nothing had the least importance, and I know quite well why. He [the priest], too, knew why."[6] He goes on to indicate that nothing matters because everyone has the same fate, namely death:

> What difference could they make to me, the death of others, or a mother's love, or his God; or the way a man decides to live, the fate he thinks he chooses, since one and the same fate was bound to "choose" not only me but thousands of millions of privileged people who, like him, called themselves my brother. Surely he must see that? . . . All alike would be condemned to die one day; his turn, too, would come. And what difference could it make if, after being charged with murder, he were executed because he didn't weep at his mother's funeral, since it all came to the same thing in the end?[7]

Meursault's apathy has nothing to do with the subjectivity of morality. Even if morality were objective, Meursault would claim that human mortality would justify apathy. On the one hand, Smith's attempt to derive a justification of apathy from subjective morality may well be correct and perhaps this justification is the one that Camus *should* have used. But he did not use it. On the other hand, Hare's linguistic analysis seems to miss the point entirely. Even if Hare is correct that the expression "Nothing matters" expresses someone's—his friend's, Meursault's, Camus's—unconcern about everything, this does not get at the basis of the unconcern which is finite human life. Hare should have attacked this basis and tried to show that human mortality provides no justification for apathy.

Moreover, if we take into account Camus's long essay *The Myth of Sisyphus*, which was published in the same year as *The Stranger*, both

Hare's and Smith's interpretations seem mistaken. To be sure, some Camus scholars have maintained that in *The Stranger* and *The Myth of Sisyphus* Camus expresses the same position. Thus, Philip Thody maintains that "Meursault is a man who, apparently quite unconsciously, accepts the premise on which *The Myth of Sisyphus* is based."[8] But Thody's claim is questionable. In *The Myth of Sisyphus* Camus argues for the absurdity of life—not that nothing matters. Although in *The Myth of Sisyphus* Camus refers to the finitude of human life, he uses far more philosophical and abstruse arguments to justify the absurdity of life.[9] Nevertheless, the idea that nothing matters and the thesis of the absurdity of life have the following connection: Although Camus does not use the absurdity of life as a basis for the claim that nothing matters, presumably he *could* be have done so. Since life is absurd, one might argue, nothing matters. Of course, this rationale could only provide a good justification for the claim that nothing matters if life has been shown to be absurd and if it could be shown that the claim that nothing matters follows from the thesis that life is absurd.

Although neither Hare nor Smith evaluates the argument from mortality actually presented in *The Stranger* or the possible argument from absurdity presented in *The Myth of Sisyphus* for the claim that nothing matters, these are the lines of argument that they should have followed.

NOTHING MATTERS AND HUMAN MORTALITY

Rather than belief in subjective morality being the basis of Hare's young friend's depression, if he had taken Meursault seriously, the basis should be human mortality. Indeed, one might reconstruct Meursault's argument as follows:

1. If human existence is not of infinite duration, then nothing matters.
2. Human existence is not of infinite duration.
3. Therefore, nothing matters.

This argument is a variant of the Argument from Finiteness discussed in the last chapter. The problem with this argument is surely premise (1). It is very difficult to see why one should believe it. Of course, as Smith has suggested, it may be possible for an individual to judge rationally that nothing matters if he or she believes that there are no objective values. But human mortality is irrelevant to this judgment. Objective values are compatible with human life being finite. Yet it would be wrong to torture, rape, and steal even if humans did not live forever. Not torturing, not raping, and not stealing would matter morally very much if there were objective values.

Moreover, even if morality is not objective many things would matter from a prudential point of view. Perhaps if I embraced moral subjectivism, it would not matter morally to me if someone tortured strangers. Arguably it should not even matter morally to me if I were tortured since by hypothesis, torture is not objectively morally wrong. Nevertheless, it would certainly matter to me from a prudential point of view if I were tortured. From a prudential point of view there is no incompatibility in saying it does not *morally* matter if you torture but it matters to me if you torture me. This prudential concern is also independent of human mortality. Even if I had only six months to live, it would still matter very much to me if I were made to suffer before I died.

ABSURDITY AND NOTHING MATTERS

Does Camus's claim about the absurdity of life in *The Myth of Sisyphus* show that nothing matters? Although it is in error let us accept Camus's analysis and assume that in his sense the world does disappoint human expectations. This would not mean that nothing matters in either a moral or a prudential sense. The absurdity of the world in Camus's sense is compatible with objective moral properties. But then, it would matter morally if humans were needlessly caused to suffer. Moreover, even if moral objectivity is ruled out, the absurdity of life in Camus's sense would not show that nothing matters. Prudentially it would matter very much if someone caused me agony even if my expectations concerning the world were not and never could be fulfilled. For example, just because I am disappointed that the universe is not a Parmenidian One, it does not mean that it does not matter if I am made to suffer.

HARE'S "CURE"

Although Hare does not say so explicitly he implies that his linguistic therapy cured his young friend of apathy. If Hare's friend is cured, what are we to make of it? One thing we cannot make of it is that Hare's diagnosis of his friend's problem is confirmed. The alleviation of symptoms is compatible with therapies based on false premises. For example, simply talking to a sympathetic authority figure might eliminate a person's symptoms even if this figure were basing his or her discourse on a misunderstanding of the cause of the symptoms. Suppose he is cured. It is possible that Hare's young friend simply accepted Camus's authority and thus uncritically embraced Meursault's claim that nothing matters. This brought about his apathy. He did not see that this claim was based on the irrelevant premise of human mortality. When Hare enters the picture the young man accepts a new authority complete with false diagnosis. His acceptance of this new authority cures his apathy.

CONCLUSION

In Camus's *The Stranger* the character Meursault's claim that nothing matters is based on the premise of human mortality, not on the premise of subjective morality. Hare's attempt to undermine this claim by linguistic analysis fails because he misunderstands its basis. Smith's analysis fails for the same reason. Moreover, Camus's position in *The Myth of Sisyphus* is rather different from that in *The Stranger*. There he maintains that life is absurd. But his argument is dubious and, even if it is accepted, the absurdity of life fails to show that nothing matters. The important point for our purposes is, however, that Camus's claim that nothing matters is based on the very common *religious* thesis that without immortality life is meaningless. We have seen nothing to support this view.

NOTES

1. R. M. Hare, "Nothing Matters," in *The Meaning of Life*, ed. Steven Sanders and David R. Cheney (Englewood Cliffs, N.J.: Prentice Hall, 1980), pp. 97–103.

2. Quentin Smith, *Ethical and Religious Thought in Analytic Philosophy of Language* (New Haven, Conn.: Yale University Press, 1997), pp. 75–80.

3. Ibid., p. 77.

4. Ibid.

5. Ibid., pp. 77–78.

6. Albert Camus, *The Stranger*, trans. Stuart Gilbert (New York: Vantage Books, 1946), p. 152.

7. Ibid.

8. Philip Thody, *Albert Camus: A Study of His Work* (New York: Evergreen Books, 1957), p. 3.

9. Albert Camus, *The Myth of Sisyphus and Other Essays*, trans. Justin O'Brien (New York: Alfred A. Knopf, 1955). Relevant selections of this work are reprinted in Sanders and Cheney, *The Meaning of Life*. See Albert Camus, "An Absurd Reasoning," in *The Meaning of Life*, pp. 65–75.

PART FOUR

CHRISTIANITY
AND THE
MEANING OF LIFE

15

INTRODUCTION TO THE RELIGIOUS MEANING OF LIFE

Part 4 of this book will examine the thesis that religion can provide meaning to life. Although religious apologists frequently make this claim they do not usually explain how a religious perspective gives life meaning. In the first part of this chapter three general theories of religious meaning will be considered.[1] In the second part I will relate these theories to Phillip Quinn's recent discussion about the meaning of life from a Christian perspective. In later chapters I will evaluate specific problems arising from the claim that Christianity can provide meaning to life.

One general theory of religious meaning maintains that God has a plan for the world as a whole that can only be accomplished if each person discovers and completes the part God has assigned to him or her. According to the second theory, the world was created as an expression of God's glory, and as the extreme expression of his glory God redeems sinful human beings. The third theory is that human beings exist in this world in order to prepare themselves for the life hereafter—a life in another world that completes this life. The first two theories and most versions of the third assume that God exists and all three presuppose that there is an afterlife.

Although Karl Britton, an English philosopher, calls the first theory the "Protestant view,"[2] each of the three theories is held by some Protestants; indeed, some Protestants hold all three views of the meaning of life at the same time. In addition, it is possible for religious believers who are not Protestants to hold the "Protestant view." Rather than use this misleading label let us therefore call the first theory "the Divine Calling View," the second theory "the Redemption View," and the third theory "the Completion View." Although all three theories are quite general and have wider application than Christianity, the Redemption and the Completion views have special relevance to Christianity.

Before launching this discussion let me raise a general problem connected with all three theories of religious meaning, namely that each one construes the meaning of human life in terms of God's purpose. In particular, according to all these views the meaning of life is to realize God's purpose. But certain attributes of God seem to preclude this.

As God is usually understood, he exists beyond time. Yet a nontemporal being cannot engage in purposive activities. For example, it is inconceivable that a nontemporal being could adopt ends since such an activity takes time and occurs at a particular time. Furthermore, God is supposed to be absolutely simple. But how could a being be absolutely simple and yet assign different purposes to, for example, humans and animals? And finally, God is supposed to be unlimited. But how could an unlimited being have a purpose since to say that God is unlimited implies that no human term applies to God?[3]

In short, the properties of God preclude God's having purposes. Consequently, the meaning of life cannot involve fulfilling God's purpose or purposes. For the sake of the argument, however, I will assume in the rest of this chapter that the existence of God is compatible with God having purposes.

THE DIVINE CALLING VIEW

According to the Divine Calling View God made the world by an inscrutable act of will and human beings must cooperate and help complete this plan by fulfilling their divinely assigned roles. To each human being God has assigned a calling or role. The purpose of an individual's life is, then, to fill his or her calling or role, and the purpose of life in general is to fulfill God's plan. In other words, fulfilling one's divinely assigned purpose gives a person's life meaning and this helps fulfill life's purpose.

The theory has a number of problems, however.

a. Although God is supposed to have a plan, we have no idea what it is. But if we are ignorant of the plan, it is hard to see how we can know that we are contributing to it. Given the definition of Purpose Meaning developed earlier, it follows then life would have no meaning. The purpose of life could not be accomplished since humans would not know what the purpose was and would not be able to fulfill the purpose except by accident.

b. It may be answered that we can know that we are contributing to God's plan (whatever that may be) by fulfilling our calling since fulfilling our calling automatically furthers God's plan. But then the question arises of how we are to know that there is a connection between fulfilling our calling and furthering God's plan.

c. This question may be answered by saying that the connection is true by definition; that is, part of the meaning of fulfilling God's purposes is fulfilling one's calling. However, there does not seem to be any contradiction in asserting that one is fulfilling one's calling and not fulfilling God's plan. Yet there should be a contradiction if part of the *meaning* of fulfilling God's purposes is to fulfill one's calling.

d. In any case, how does one know what one's calling is? So that the claim is not empty, there must be some difference between *knowing* what one's calling really is and merely *thinking* that one knows. What is this difference? Again, according to the definition of Purpose Meaning, unless a person could know this, he or she could not achieve the purpose except by accident and life would have no meaning.

e. An assumption of this view is that God needs human cooperation to fulfill his plan. However, it is difficult to understand why an all-powerful God would need the cooperation of human beings to fulfill his plans.

f. Putting this problem of (e) to one side, it would seem likely that some human beings have not cooperated with God and have actually undermined God's plan. After all, some human beings have played roles in history that could hardly be part of God's plan; for example, some people have been professional killers and habitual child abusers. This problem would also seem to affect adversely the possibility of fulfilling the purpose of life, which in turn would fail to meet a condition of Purpose Meaning.

g. Moreover, if God were all-knowing, he would have known from eternity that his plan would not be fulfilled and yet despite this knowledge put this plan into operation. But why would God put a plan into operation that he knew would not work?

h. However, this would mean that even if all other human beings followed their true calling, they would not bring about God's plan even with God's help.

i. Consequently, following one's true calling would have no importance for giving life meaning since it would not help to bring about God's plan without the cooperation of others.

j. I see just two ways out of the problems specified in (h) and (i). First, advocates of the Divine Calling Theory might argue that according to God's plan some people do have the calling of, for example, being a professional killer. But this answer seems to conflict with God's goodness. Second, one might argue that God does not know beforehand that his plan will not be fulfilled because some people do not fulfill their calling. But this seems to conflict with God's omniscience. In any case, although God may not know before time t that his plan will not be fulfilled because of some people's failure to fulfill their calling before time t, he would know after time t. Yet he continues with his plan knowing it cannot succeed.

k. However, let us suppose that all of the above problems are waived. Still, it remains unexplained why God wants us to fulfill our calling. Without this explanation such a purpose seems arbitrary. Thus, another condition of Purpose Meaning is not fulfilled.

l. Finally, even waiving this problem still another condition of Purpose Meaning may not be satisfied, for some humans may get no psychological satisfaction at all from fulfilling their divine calling. If so, human life could not have Purpose Meaning.

THE REDEMPTION VIEW

In contrast to the Divine Calling View, the Redemption View does not put human beings in a pivotal position: although God's nature is largely beyond our ken he still has the central role. As Britton says, "God is complete and self-sufficient and cannot be said to *need* anything."[4] Although he created human beings there is no necessity for him to have done so. But the question arises then of why human beings were created. Advocates of this view say that we were created so that God could redeem us as an extreme expression of his goodness and glory.

As Britton has put it:

God made man to sin. Sin is unintelligible unless as a voluntary action: so then God made men to have and misuse free will. I shall not attempt to explain how Adam who was made by God came to sin; but in the divine plan this was intended:

Adae peccatum . . . O felix culpa!

Thereafter it is by sin and in sin that we are born and that sin is what God redeems men from. The sin is said to be voluntary but all those who are born of the flesh are born to sin. And everyone who (by the proper procedures) repents and is redeemed does so by God's power and to God belongs all the glory. The punishment of the unrepentant also redounds to God's glory.[5]

To be sure, God as part of his redemption is concerned about our happiness and moral virtue. But the purpose for which we are created has to do with completing *God's* glory and not with *human* achievement. Although God owes us nothing we owe him our gratitude and love. To those whom God redeems in his infinite mercy he bestows in the afterlife a gift of a vision of himself.

This view purports to answer both the question of why there is a universe at all and why there are human beings in such a universe. God created a universe for his glory and human beings are here in order to sin and be redeemed—again for God's glory. We live our lives according to this vision by repenting and obeying God.

There are, however, some problems with this view:

a. Why does God want to express his glory and goodness at all? Since he is infinitely good and glorious, what is the point?

b. Given that God wants to express his infinite glory and goodness why does he remain hidden? One would suppose that if God wanted to express his glory, he would reveal himself and his means of redemption so that there could be no doubt that there is a benefactor and who it is. Indeed, it seems inconsistent to say that X expresses his glory by doing Y but X keeps his identity and Y secret.

c. Why does God express his goodness and glory in this strange way? By analogy, we would find it perverse if a father (for his own glory) raised his children in such a way that he knew that they often chose to do bad things just in order to give them the opportunity to redeem themselves. It would become even stranger if we knew that this father could have prevented more moral trespasses in the first place, resulting in fewer sins, God could have made human beings that needed little moral redemption and who loved God for his infinite kindness in making them in this way. Why would not this express God's glory as much as the present situation?

d. If it is replied that God wants human beings with free choice, it can be answered that the combination of free choice and fewer moral evils is possible within a theistic framework.[6]

e. The problems specified above suggest that the reasons God redeems humanity are unexplained and seem arbitrary. This indicates that one of the conditions of Purpose Meaning is not fulfilled. Consequently, on the Redemption View life cannot have Purpose Meaning.

f. How does God choose to redeem sinful human beings? The most widely held answer in our Western theistic tradition is the one given by Christianity: by means of the incarnation, death, and resurrection of the son of God. However, as I will show in the following chapters, these doctrines have serious problems.

THE COMPLETION VIEW

According to the Completion View another world—an afterlife—is necessary for the completion of this earthly life. Justice demands it. This view has special relevance to those who have lost their lives before they have achieved their full potential, to those who have been so cruelly used by fate that they have not been able to realize their inherent powers, and to those who realize too late that they have made irreversible errors which prevent them from reaching their most cherished goals. In the afterlife justice will prevail and these individuals will be able to achieve their full potential, realize their inherent powers, and reach their cherished goals.

However, more than justice for such individuals may be involved. Britton suggests that there is also a question of natural economy that begins with humans as humans rather than individual human beings.[7] We all believe that life teaches us many things. Just as humans are learning to live, their lives are taken away. To many this is unnatural and can only be made to seem natural by the supposition that there is another life where what is learned in our earthly life is applied and completed. Without this supposition life is without point. Thomas Hardy expressed it in this way:

> A senseless school where we must give
> Our lives that we may learn to live!
> A dolt is he who memorizes
> Lessons that leave no room for prizes.[8]

On the other hand, the meaning of this earthly life is a stepping stone to the afterlife, a beginning of an odyssey that finds completion in the hereafter. The Completion View is often included as part of the Divine Calling View and, with modifications, as part of the Redemption View. In Christianity, the Completion View is merged with the doctrines of heaven and hell which in turn are closely associated with the doctrines of the atonement, the incarnation, the resurrection, the second coming, and salvation. In later chapters the Christian version of the Completion View will be considered. However, it is useful to consider this theory in its own right since many people, whatever other views they may hold, suppose that life makes sense only if the Completion View is assumed.

Here are some general problems with the Completion View:

a. The argument that justice demands that the injustices of our earthly existence be reconciled in the afterlife seems to be based on wishful thinking. There is no reason to suppose that it is true.

b. Furthermore, it is not clear how some injustices could be reconciled in the afterlife. Suppose a potentially great tennis player is paralyzed and cannot fulfill her potential. Are we to believe that she will be able to fulfill her tennis potential in the afterlife? Some accounts present the afterlife as nonspatial and its denizens as noncorporeal. Making nonsense of the fulfillment not just of athletic potential but also of *any* physical potential, this raises serious questions about whether the purpose of life can be achieved and, consequently, whether life has Purpose Meaning.

c. Let us suppose that the afterlife is spatial and that its denizens have bodies. Still in order for people to fulfill their potentials it would have to be very similar to earthly existence. Indeed, it would have to be so much like the latter that it would be devoid of all of its charm as an ideal place. For example, in order for a potentially great general to fulfill his promise there would have to be wars; in order for a potentially great detective to fulfill his promise there would have to be crimes.

d. The idea that we start to learn how to live in this life and that part of the natural economy is to apply this knowledge in a future life seems mistaken and even absurd. In the first place, some people die before they could have started to learn how to live in this life and some waste every opportunity to learn. Moreover, sages, pundits, and wise men and women have all learned how to live and apply what they know well in this life.

e. The Completion View fails to account for why we are supplied with so little information about how to prepare for the afterlife. One would suppose that if there were a God, we would be fully instructed about what to do, but we are not.

f. More importantly, there is no explanation of why the world is constructed in terms of this dualism: an earthly life and an afterlife. Since God is all-powerful he could establish his purpose in other ways. If the purpose is to learn how to live this could be accomplished without the dualism.

g. Finally, at best this theory only provides an answer to what the meaning of our earthly existence is. It gives no answer to the meaning of our complete life: our earthly life + our afterlife. What is the point of our complete life? If we want an answer to this question, a different theory is needed.

h. The last three points indicate that the Completion View fails another condition of Purpose Meaning. No plausible explanation is provided for the purpose of life specified by God.

CHRISTIANITY AND THE MEANING OF LIFE

Although all three theories can be found in Christian thought, those usually associated with Christianity are the Redemption View and the Completion View. One of the few explicit attempts to relate the meaning of life to Christianity can be found in a recent paper by Philip L. Quinn.

According to Quinn, two definitions are important in discussing religious views of the meaning of life:

AM. A human life has positive axiological meaning if and only if (i) it has positive intrinsic value, and (ii) it is on the whole good for the person who leads it; and

TM. A human life has positive teleological meaning if and only if (i) it contains some purposes that the person who lives it takes to be nontrivial and achievable, (ii) these purposes have positive value, and (iii) it also contains actions that are directed toward achieving these purposes and are performed with zest.[9]

Quinn maintains that AM and TM are independent: it is possible that a life could have both AM and TM, or lack both, or have one and not the other. When a life has both AM and TM Quinn say this life has complete meaning, which he defines as follows:

CM. A human life has positive complete meaning if and only if it has positive axiological meaning and positive teleological meaning.[10]

It should be noted that Quinn's two definitions, TM and AM, are similar to my own definitions of Positive Purpose Meaning and Value Meaning. However, one important difference is that Quinn's TM does not have a condition comparable to condition (5) of Positive Purpose Meaning; namely, that the purpose or purposes of life are either not arbitrary or have a plausible rationale. We shall see in the next chapter that this omission represents a serious flaw in his account.

Quinn argues that human life can be narrated and that such narratives can show that a human life has AM, TM, and CM. In Christianity, the gospel narratives of the life of Jesus have special importance in that they provide Christians with a paradigm to which they should conform their own lives as closely as circumstances allow.

Quinn says that there is no difficulty in supposing that the lives of imitators of Jesus have TM despite the suffering they are likely to contain. In his view there is, however, a difficulty in supposing that they have AM since for many people (including Jesus) their earthly life was not good. However, an afterlife for human beings affords them the opportunity to achieve AM and CM. This is the basic reason why the assumption of an afterlife is essential for achieving AM. Considered from the perspective of the Completion View, the afterlife enables human beings to have AM and thus complete their lives.

How is TM to be achieved in our earthly life according to Quinn? What are the nontrivial and achievable purposes with positive value associated with Christianity? After outlining what he calls "the cosmic metanarrative salvation history" of Christianity—the creation of humans in God's image, the incarnation, the death of the son of God, the resurrection, the redemption of sinful humanity, and the second coming of the kingdom of God—he says,

> The narrative of salvation history reveals some of God's purpose both for individuals and for humanity as a whole. Christians are expected to align themselves with these purposes and to act to further them to the extent that circumstances permit. Such purposes can thus be among those that give positive teleological meaning and thereby contribute to giving complete meaning to a Christian life.[11]

Quinn does not say exactly what purposes the metanarrative of salvation history reveals, let alone why he believes that they are nontrivial, achievable, and positive. However, one plausible interpretation is that he is assuming that Christianity is a special case of the Redemption Theory. The purposes he alludes to in the narrative salvation history are the purposes of redemption and salvation associated with the incarnation, death, and resurrection of the son of God. Since some of these doctrines and their bearing on TM will be considered in detail in other chapters in part 4 no more will be said about them here.

The Axiological Meaning (AM) of life is closely tied with the special case of the Completion View associated with Christianity: the afterlife and heaven in particular. This is because, according to Quinn, for most people their earthly life is not good on the whole. However, an afterlife in heaven would provide human beings with the opportunity to achieve AM. Presumably this is because no matter how bad one's earthly existence is, eternity in paradise will make up for it. One might look at it in this way: Suppose one's entire life for seventy years was a living hell. Looking back on one's life—earthly and spiritual—from the perspective of heavenly paradise one could truly say that one's life was good.

However, there are serious problems facing this view of the afterlife and of heaven in particular.

First, it is not obvious that it is correct to think that the joys of heaven can make up for a life of misery. To be sure, looked at from a utilitarian point of view the pain and suffering accrued in an earthly existence can be outweighed by the pleasure and happiness associated with the afterlife. However, it is plausible to suppose that some things that happen to people are incommensurable with their future pleasures and happiness. It is not unreasonable to say that nothing can make up for these invasions and assaults—not even heaven.

Second, let us suppose that heaven could make up for earthly suffering. What are the prospects of achieving AM via heaven? One should not suppose that just because one's earthly life was terrible things would be reconciled in heaven. According to the standard view of heaven, some people are sent there as a reward for something they do in their earthly existence. According to another theory, heaven is a gift of God that is completely unmerited. Indeed, for all Christians know, there may be few people indeed whose lives have AM.

Third, despite the common view of heaven as a place of eternal happiness, it might not be. Even if going to heaven rewarded a person, she might be so unhappy in heaven that her life as a whole would not be considered good. Why would a denizen of heaven be unhappy? She might realize that the fact that some people go to heaven and others do not is unfair and this realization would cause moral anxiety. But why suppose heaven to be unfair? If heaven is an unmerited gift of God, it seems arbitrary and unfair. A father who bestowed unmerited gifts on some of his children and not on others would be considered unjust and arbitrary. Surely much the same thing could be said about God if he were to act in a similar way. But suppose we accept the standard view that going to heaven is based on merit. It still seems unfair. Suppose that heaven is a reward for belief, for example in Jesus as the savior. As I will argue in more detail in chapter 17, millions of people through no fault of their own have never heard of Jesus or at least have not been exposed to Scripture. These people's failure to believe is hardly grounds for punishment, that is, lack of reward.

Moreover, even if people have been exposed to Christianity but have failed to believe, why should they be punished? Many nonbelievers reject the Gospel message for the good reason that the evidence shows the improbability of many of the major doctrines of Christianity: the resurrection, the virgin birth, and the incarnation.[12] Even if these doctrines are true and not improbable in the light of the evidence, rational people surely can fail to be impressed by the evidence. It would be going beyond what the evidence dictates—if not actually in conflict with the evidence—to accept Jesus as the son of God. Furthermore, even if nonbelievers have misevaluated the evidence and it does indeed provide solid grounds for belief, many nonbelievers sincerely believe that the evidence is lacking. Why would a good God want to withhold the gift of heaven to a sincere nonbeliever who might lack sufficient insight, knowledge, or analytical skills to appraise the evidence correctly?

Suppose the reward of heaven is based not on belief but on moral behavior as specified in the Bible. This is still unfair. Millions of people have not been exposed to the moral teachings of the Bible. That they do not live according to biblical standards is not their fault. Moreover, even those who have been exposed to the Bible may find its moral message unacceptable on moral grounds. God, as portrayed in the Old Testament, is often cruel and arbitrary and in the New Testament even Jesus is pictured as having a flawed moral character.[13] Moreover, even for those who accept the Bible the question is, What behavior should be rewarded? What the Bible teaches concerning morality is subject to various conflicting interpretations. But how in all fairness can heaven be a reward for following the correct moral standard of Scripture since it is unclear what this represents?

Fourth, let us suppose that universalism is true and eventually everyone goes to heaven. There is still a problem. Morally sensitive people might well see universalism as unfair. They might argue that it is unfair that everyone would be saved when some people have lived incredibly evil lives while others have lived wonderfully good lives. Thus, morally sensitive people would be unhappy and their lives would not be good as a whole. But then their lives would not have AM.

Fifth, even if universalism did not raise questions about fairness that do not adversely affect AM, it would adversely affect TM. For what is the point of heaven if everyone goes there eventually? What then is the meaning of earthly existence with its suffering and trials and tribulations? Human existence becomes apparently absurd and a deep mystery. Why do we have an earthly life at all? Why not *start* life in a heavenly state?

Sixth, Quinn says that one condition of a human life having AM is that it has positive intrinsic value. The term "intrinsic value" suggests that Quinn is contrasting a human life having instrumental value with a human life not having intrinsic value. But one important question is whether a human life can have intrinsic value in a Christian worldview. After all, according to the Redemption View God created human beings for his greater glory so they could sin and be saved through his infinite mercy. Insofar as human life has instrumental value for this end, the idea of a human life having intrinsic value makes little sense.

CONCLUSION

Although the Divine Calling View, the Redemption View, and the Completion View are stated as general accounts of religious meaning, they have special relevance to Christianity. All three theories face a general problem in that they assume that life has meaning in terms of fulfilling God's purpose. Yet the attributes of God preclude this. Setting aside this general problem, the theories have specific problems that belie the often-made claim that religion provides life with meaning. Phillip Quinn's analysis of the axiological and teleological meaning of life in Christian terms can be considered as a special case of the Redemption View and the Completion View. However, serious problems arise with his account of Christian axiological meaning. In subsequent chapters the problems about the Christian account of teleological meaning will be discussed.

NOTES

1. Karl Britton, *The Meaning of Life* (Cambridge: Cambridge University Press, 1969), chap. 2.
2. Ibid., p. 21.
3. I am indebted here to Thaddeus Metz, "Could God's Purpose Be the Source of Life's Meaning?" *Religious Studies* 36 (2000): 304–11.
4. Britton, *The Meaning of Life*, p. 38.
5. Ibid., p. 39.
6. Michael Martin, *Atheism: A Philosophical Justification* (Philadelphia: Temple University Press, 1990), chap. 15.

7. Britton, *The Meaning of Life*, p. 45.

8. Thomas Hardy, "Time's Laughingstocks," quoted in Britton, *The Meaning of Life*, p. 45.

9. Philip L. Quinn, "The Meaning of Life According to Christianity," in *The Meaning of Life*, ed. E. D. Klemke (New York: Oxford University Press, 2000), p. 57.

10. Ibid., p. 58.

11. Quinn, "The Meaning of Life According to Christianity," p. 61.

12. See chapter 8 in this volume and Michael Martin, *The Case against Christianity* (Philadelphia: Temple University Press, 1991), chap. 6.

13. See Martin, *The Case against Christianity,* chap. 6.

16

THE MEANING OF LIFE AND THE ATONEMENT

INTRODUCTION

So far we have seen Christianity can be plausibly interpreted as a special case of the Redemption View. A study of what Quinn called the narrative salvation history of Christianity indicates that from a Christian perspective redemption and salvation through the incarnation, death, and resurrection of the son of God give life meaning. In this chapter I argue that the lack of a plausible theory of the atonement prevents Christians from claiming that life is meaningful. My argument will be in two stages. First, I argue that having a plausible theory of the atonement is a necessary condition for Christians to reasonably claim that life is meaningful. Second, I will argue that no plausible theory of the atonement is available.

Stated more formally, the Argument from the Atonement is this:

1. In a Christian worldview in order for one to reasonably believe that life has meaning there must be a plausible theory of the atonement.
2. A plausible theory of the atonement must convincingly explain why Jesus was incarnated, died on the cross, and was resurrected.

3. There is no theory that convincingly explains why Jesus was incarnated, died on the cross, and was resurrected.

4. Therefore, in a Christian worldview one cannot reasonably believe that life has meaning.

Premise (1) is based on condition (5) of the definition of Positive Purpose Meaning introduced in chapter 12, and has considerable intuitive appeal. Premise (2) is simply an explication of premise (1). Premise (3) is the crucial premise and will be established by critically evaluating the most important theories of the atonement.

THE NECESSITY OF A PLAUSIBLE ATONEMENT THEORY

Recall that in chapter 12 I argued that condition (5) is a necessary condition for Positive Purpose Meaning. According to that condition the purpose or purposes of life must either be nonarbitrary or have a plausible rationale. Without this condition God's purpose could give positive meaning to life even if the purpose were arbitrary and unreasonable. For example, a deity could decree that the purpose of life is to be saved from eternal damnation by writing poetry, but give no plausible rationale for this purpose. In such a case one could not reasonably claim that life has Positive Purpose Meaning.

As we noted in the last chapter, Quinn's account of the Teleological Meaning (TM) lacked a condition that was equivalent to condition (5) in my definition of Positive Purpose Meaning. We can see now why this lack represents a serious flaw in his account. Without this condition a human life can have TM although the purpose is either arbitrary or there is no plausible rationale for the purpose. To use the same example as above: A human life would be meaningful if the purpose of life was to be saved from eternal damnation by writing poetry. This example would seem to meet all of the conditions of Quinn's definition of TA.[1] Yet one could not reasonably claim that life was meaningful under these conditions.

The doctrine of the atonement in Christianity can be construed as an attempt to meet condition (5) of Positive Purpose Meaning. According to Christianity, without the atonement life would have no meaning. The purpose of life is to be saved through faith in the son of God who was incarnated as Jesus, died on the cross, and was resurrected. But more must be said. For without some rationale for the incarnation, his death on the cross, the resurrection, and salvation by faith—what Quinn calls the narrative of salvation history—the entire process seems arbitrary and mysterious. Without some plausible rationale, this narrative of salvation history would no more provide meaning to life than would the hypothetical example of writing poetry in order to be saved from eternal salvation.

Thus Christian theologians have developed theories of the atonement that are designed to provide such a rationale: to provide a plausible account of why the incarnation of the son of God, his death on the cross, and his resurrection happened and why this was essential for human salvation. The question is whether any plausible accounts are available. Surely any plausible theory of the atonement must not fail two simple tests: It must explain why God sacrificed his son for the salvation of humankind and it must not make the sacrifice seem arbitrary.

THEORIES OF THE ATONEMENT

The reason why Jesus came to earth, died, and was resurrected is only hinted at in the New Testament.[2] Thus, in Matthew it is said that "the Son of man came not to be served but to serve, and to give his life as a ransom for many" (20:28). Also in Matthew, Jesus at the Last Supper is reported to have referred to "my blood of the convenant, which is poured out for many for the forgiveness of sins" (26:28). In John, John the Baptist proclaims of Jesus, "Behold, the Lamb of God, who takes away the sins of the world!" (1:29) In Romans it is asserted, "we also rejoice in God through our Lord Jesus Christ, through whom we have now received our reconciliation" (5:11). In Hebrews it is stated that Jesus was once offered "to bear the sins of many" (9:28). In 1 John it is maintained that Jesus is "the expiation for our sins, and not for ours only but also for the sins of the whole world" (2:2).

Vincent Taylor, a New Testament scholar, attempts to summarize and synthesize what the New Testament teaches concerning the atonement in the following way:

(1) The Atonement is the work of God in restoring sinners to fellowship with Himself and establishing His Kingdom in the world; it is the reconciliation of man and of the world to God. (2) It is the fulfillment of His purpose for man and the final proof of the greatness of His love, both revealing that love and expressing it for time and eternity. (3) The Atonement is accomplished in the work of Christ, whose suffering is vicarious, representative, and sacrificial in character; it is on behalf of men, in their name, and for the purpose of their approach to God. (4) The vicarious nature of Christ's ministry is one of the clearest elements in New Testament teaching, but its true content can be discerned only as its representative and sacrificial aspects are more closely defined. (5) The representative character of His death is disclosed by the fact that, in the greatness of His love for men, He identified Himself with sinners and in their service was completely obedient to the will of the Father, entering into and enduring in His own person the consequences of sin and the rejection and gainsaying of men. (6) The sacrificial significance of his death is suggested by the frequent use of the term "blood," by a limited use of analogies found in the ancient sacrificial system, by references to cleansing, redemption, and expiation, by allusions to the idea of the Suffering Servant, and by eucharistic teaching sacrificial in character. (7) The Atonement is consummated in the experience of men through faith-union with Christ, through sacramental communion with him, and in sacrificial living and suffering.[3]

Obviously, the passages from Scripture quoted above and even Taylor's summary leave many questions open. For example, how by dying on the cross did Jesus take away the sins of the world? And why in any case would God save sinful humanity through the death of his son? Taylor is certainly correct that the representative and sacrificial aspect of Jesus' ministry needs to be more clearly defined if he means by this that some explanation is required of why Jesus was sacrificed as a representative of sinful humanity. Through the centuries Christian thinkers have wrestled with these issues; indeed, in attempting to explain why Jesus died on the cross they have created a variety of theories of the atonement. Although a systematic critique of all of them would require a book-length treatment, let us briefly consider some of the historically most important types and their major problems.

MAJOR THEORIES OF THE ATONEMENT

The Ransom Theory

For approximately the first thousand years of Christianity's history the most popular theory of the atonement was the Ransom Theory. In the crude version held by early Christian thinkers such as Origen (185–254 C.E.), the theory assumes that the devil is in possession of humanity and that his rights of possession cannot be ignored. God consents to pay a price, the death of his own son, for the release of humanity. The devil accepts the bargain because he believes that he will have the son of God as his prize. However, God tricks the devil. God knows when he offers the devil the bargain that the devil will be unable to keep the son of God as a prize. Consequently, the son escapes the devil's powers and is reconciled with his father. In later, more sophisticated versions of the theory, for example Augustine's, the devil is deceived not by God but by his own inordinate pride. So the devil is justly overcome. Since the devil is not defeated by God's might, God's justice and righteousness are emphasized.[4]

There are obviously many problems with the Ransom Theory. First, crude versions explicitly attribute to God qualities of character that are unworthy of a divine being. If God is morally perfect, he will not deceive anyone, not even the devil. Second, even the more sophisticated versions make implausible assumptions, such as that the devil would be so blinded by pride as to believe that he is more powerful than the son of God. Third, the very idea of a devil, especially one that has gained a right of possession to human beings because of their sins, one that God must acknowledge and honor, strikes many modern readers as bizarre and implausible. Why would God believe that the devil has any moral claim on his creatures? After all, the devil is one of his creatures, one that has disobeyed him and sinned against him. Fourth, it is unjust for God to sacrifice his son for this ransom especially since it is not clear that no other alternatives existed. Since God is all-powerful and can do anything that is not logically impossible, God could surely have found other ways to achieve his ends. Finally, it is not clear in this theory why human beings must have faith in Jesus in order to be saved. Since in the Ransom Theory, after Jesus' death and resurrection human beings were out of the devil's clutches, it would seem that the way to salvation could simply have been to follow a life free from sin so as not to fall under the devil's control. What has faith in Jesus got to do with this? The ransom theory supplies no answer.

The Satisfaction Theory

Although the Satisfaction Theory was anticipated to some extent by earlier thinkers, it was Anselm who developed it in an explicit and sophisticated way in the eleventh century.[5] Anselm argued that God must save humanity and that he must do it via the incarnation and death of Jesus. To offer God his due, according to Anselm, is to follow his will. However, he argued that when God's creatures sin this is precisely what they do not do. The sins of God's creatures insult God and detract from his honor. There is, then, an obligation to restore God's honor and to undo the insult. This is satisfaction. However, only the death of the God-Man, Jesus, can give proper satisfaction. Only the God-Man is able, by his divinity, to offer something that is worthy of God and, by his humanity, to represent humankind. A mere human would be unable to give the proper satisfaction since this latter must be in proportion to the amount of sin and the amount of sin is infinite.[6] Furthermore, the death of the God-Man is not unjust since the son of God died completely voluntarily in order to restore God's honor. Those who accept Jesus' sacrifice are saved.

There are as many problems with this theory as with the Ransom Theory. First, it is certainly not obvious that the sin of humanity is infinite. The idea seems to be that since God is infinite, any insult to God occasioned by not following his will is an infinite wrong. But this would seem to mean that even if just one person committed a very small sin, an infinite wrong would have been inflicted and an infinite satisfaction would be necessary. This seems absurd. One also wonders: if not following God's will brings about an infinite harm, then would following God's will bring about an infinite good? If this is the implication, it seems mistaken for one would have supposed that only God himself can bring about an infinite good.

Second, it not clear why, if the wrong brought against God by humanity is infinite, it could not be properly satisfied by simply inflicting punishment on the sinners for eternity. The incarnation would not be necessary. Third, the death of Jesus, even though voluntary, seems unjust. Justice surely demands that at the very least the guilty party provide as much of the satisfaction as he or she can. Furthermore, a perfectly good person would not permit a completely innocent person to provide satisfaction on a voluntary basis even if the guilty party could pay nothing. Indeed, the very idea of God's pride being so wounded and demanding such satisfaction that the voluntary sacrifice of his innocent son is required, assumes a view of God's moral nature that many modern readers would reject.

Consider the following example from everyday life. Suppose the proper satisfaction for the wrong Smith inflicted on Jones is for Smith to pay $1,000 to Jones. But Smith can only pay $100. Evans volunteers to pay the entire $1,000 to Jones although Evans has done no wrong to Jones. Thus, Smith ends up paying nothing. Justice has surely not been served. At the least, Smith should have paid as much as he could. Furthermore, a saintly person would not accept Evans's offer. Such an individual would swallow his or her pride and would take an amount less than that which is due. But in Anselm's account humans do not provide any part of the satisfaction that is due God and God shows conspicuously unsaintly behavior by accepting vicarious satisfaction from his innocent son.

Fourth, in the Satisfaction Theory it is inexplicable why there has been only one incarnation and death of the God-Man and why it took so long for even this one event to happen. The birth and death of the God-Man is supposed to provide satisfaction for the dishonor that human beings have inflicted on God by sinning. But this satisfaction does not mean that people will no longer sin. In fact, Christians believe that since the birth and death of Jesus almost everyone has sinned. It would seem that the logic of this theory would necessitate at least one more incarnation and death of the God-Man in order to provide new satisfaction for the infinite wrong brought against God from the death of Jesus up until the present time. In fact, as history progresses it would seem that an indefinite series of births and deaths of the God-Man would be necessary to provide the satisfaction for the wrongs against God that occurred since the last incarnation of the God-Man. Furthermore, why did the son of God wait so long in order to sacrifice himself in the first place? After all, sin existed for tens of thousands of years before the coming of the God-Man.

Fifth, it is not clear in this theory why the death of the God-Man is necessary for satisfaction of an infinite wrong against God's honor. Why would not some other punishment suffice? If God's honor is infinitely

wounded by human sin, why could it not be appeased by the eternal punishment of the God-Man, Jesus? Why the death penalty? It would seem
much worse to punish Jesus for eternity than to kill him after only relatively little suffering. Even if one argues that death has a harshness that
no punishment can match, it is important to recall that Jesus was dead for
only a short time. It would have been a much harsher death punishment
if Jesus had remained unresurrected.

Finally, it is not clear why those who accept Jesus' sacrifice are saved.
Even supposing that Jesus' sacrifice provides satisfaction for the past
damage done to God's honor, why should faith in Jesus now save anyone?
And why should believers but not nonbelievers be rewarded?

The Acceptance Theory

Theologians in the Middle Ages were greatly influenced by Anselm's satisfaction theory but some of them developed it in ways radically different
from his. Consider the views of the thirteenth-century philosopher John
Duns Scotus. Whereas Anselm emphasized the necessity of the incarnation and death of Jesus for the salvation of humanity, Scotus argued that
all satisfaction derives from the arbitrary choice of God. The incarnation
was not necessary, according to Scotus, but was caused by the free choice
of God. Neither human sin nor the satisfaction which brought about the
death of Christ is infinite. It only becomes so by God's arbitrary choice.
Although Jesus as a man only experienced finite suffering, God freely
decided to accept this as satisfaction for the sins of humanity.

Scotus's theory of satisfaction—sometimes called the Acceptance
Theory since according to it the atonement depended on what God freely
accepts—certainly solved one of the main problems of Anselm's theory:
the difficulties of explaining why God acted in one way rather than another.
But it has problems of its own in that it fails to account for the incarnation,
death, and resurrection of Jesus. There is no apparent reason why God
should have chosen the way of salvation that he did choose. God might
have accepted any, or even no, satisfaction. Indeed, he might have chosen
to save humanity through the services of an angel or of a man who was not
divine.[7] Indeed, it seems that the way that God did choose can be criticized
on moral grounds. If there were alternatives open to God, it would seem
that he should not have to let his son sacrifice himself. But he did.

In sum, instead of providing us with an explanation of the incarnation, resurrection, and salvation, the Acceptance Theory makes them seem arbitrary and morally problematic.

The Penal Theory

In the Reformation theologians such as Martin Luther (1483–1446) and John Calvin (1509–1564) stressed the utterly sinful nature of humanity much more than did medieval thinkers. Justice, they argued, demands that sin must be punished and full compensation must be given to the injured parties. Thus, the attitude of a just God toward sinners can only be that of wrath. Only Jesus, the son of God, who as a man represents sinful humanity, can take on the infinite sins of the world and can be punished for these sins. With Jesus' punishment justice is satisfied and God's mercy toward humanity can be manifested. Jesus suffers as our substitute, making us righteous and free of sin. With faith we can grasp Jesus' victory over sin and be saved. Some reformed theologians such as Calvin combined these ideas with that of the elect. Those who have faith in Jesus and are, therefore, saved are the elect—the chosen ones—of God. Their faith comes as a gift of God through the Holy Spirit and those who are saved through this gift are predestined to have this gift bestowed upon them.

The Penal Theory has problems similar to those of the Satisfaction Theory. Indeed, most of the criticisms of the Satisfaction Theory are easily translated into criticisms of the Penal Theory. For example, it is certainly not obvious that the sins of humanity are infinite and that only the son of God can vicariously be punished for them. The only novel aspect of this theory is the Calvinist doctrine of the elect, which seems especially morally repugnant. Since faith in Jesus is an arbitrary gift it seems grossly unfair that only the elect should gain the kingdom of God.

The Government Theory

The Government Theory, which is usually associated with the seventeenth-century thinker Hugo Grotius (1583–1645), is in some respects a variant of the Punishment Theory.[8] However, according to it, God is not the administrator of some absolute and unchanging rules of justice nor is he bound by an ideal of justice or obligated to provide full compensation to injured parties. What is important, according to Grotius, is that God administers a good world government and this entails preserving public order. If in order to do this the rules of justice need to be relaxed, God has the right to do so. Divine punishment should be judged by its deterrent effect in bringing about public order. Jesus' punishment was justified on these grounds. Although it was not necessitated by the demands of absolute justice it was necessary for preserving public order and good divine government.

Why was it necessary even for this purpose? It was necessary, says Grotius, in order for God to show his hatred of sin as well as his clemency. Jesus' death on the cross vindicated the one but at the same time mercifully offered humanity a way of salvation through belief in Jesus.

There are several problems with this theory. First, Grotius seems to assume that God could not have preserved public order in any other equally effective way. However, since God is all-powerful it would seem that he could show his hatred of sin, give clemency to sinners, and mercifully offer humanity salvation in alternative ways that could have brought about public order just as well. Furthermore, alternative ways certainly seem preferable on grounds of justice since the way God chose involved the suffering and death of his innocent son. Finally, the facts of Jesus' death and resurrection would help preserve public order and good government only if they were known. However, before Jesus the world was ignorant of them. Why did it take God so long to make his message clear? For centuries after Jesus most of the world remained ignorant of them. Why did not God arrange things in such a way that the deterrent value of these facts was maximized? God's failure to communicate Jesus' death on the cross is hardly what one would expect of an effective governmental administrator interested in the deterrent effect of Jesus' example.

The Moral Theory

Although earlier writers hinted at a Moral Theory of the atonement, it was first developed explicitly by Peter Abelard in the twelfth century.[9] He argued that the cross is the manifestation of a love of God that inspires love in the hearts of human beings. But to love is be free from sin and to be reconciled with God. Thus, Jesus by his teaching and his example of love taught us and redeemed us from sin. Another important advocate of the

Moral Theory of the atonement was Faustus Socinus who in the sixteenth century rejected the traditional idea that one is saved through Jesus' suffering and death. According to Socinus, Jesus was sent by God to human beings so that he would "set forth to them the will of God Himself, and [that he] might establish an agreement with them in His name."[10] In this view the main function of Jesus is prophetic. He taught humanity the promise of God and gave them an example of a perfect life. The death of Jesus on the cross and his resurrection is important mainly as the completion of his perfect life. Without his death in obedience to God, his life would not have been able to stir human beings to follow his example. Further, when God resurrected Jesus from the dead and exalted him to a position at his right hand, Jesus became a high priest who offered freedom from sin and immortality in proportion to people's imitation of his example.

This theory also suffers from serious problems. First, if God were all-powerful and all-good, it would seem that he could teach humanity to love in a way that did not involve the innocent suffering of his son. Why would the ethical message of Jesus have been less effective if he had not suffered and died on the cross? Even if present psychological laws make this impossible, God could have created different laws. Second, it is not clear why Jesus' death and resurrection were a necessary completion to his perfect life. Many ethical and religious teachers have stirred people to follow their example without dying in the dramatic way that Jesus did. Buddha, for example, has been an ethical inspiration for millions. Furthermore, Jesus could have been exalted to a high priest who offers freedom from sin and immortality in proportion to people's imitation of his example without his undergoing suffering and death. Finally, this theory provides no account of how people who have never heard of Jesus could be inspired to love, be free from sin, and obtain immorality.

Thus, this theory provides no explanation of the Christian doctrines of the incarnation and the resurrection and it calls into question the goodness of God by making it difficult to understand how people who have never heard of Jesus could be able to gain freedom from sin and immortality.

The Christus Victor Theory

In his influential book *Christus Victor* Gustaf Aulén (1879–1978) presents what he calls the classical theory of the atonement which, he says, can be found in the New Testament and the writings of the fathers of the ancient Church.[11] In his analysis, the Ransom Theory seems to be a variant of this classical theory and should not be confused with the classical theory itself. The essence of the classical theory, according to Aulén, is the dramatic victory of Christ over the evil powers to which humanity has become enslaved, especially sin, death, and the devil. In this victory God through Christ not only frees humanity from death, sin, and the devil but also is reconciled to himself.

However, although this theory does not have some of the obvious problems of the Ransom Theory, a crucial question is not answered. Why was victory achieved by means of the sacrifice of the son of God? An all-powerful God could have "defeated" sin, death, and the devil without this sacrifice. An all-good God in a battle with evil should have followed the rules of just war. In just war theory one should choose a means to victory that has the fewest unjust results. The defeat of evil presumably could have been achieved without sacrifice of his son. Why then did he choose to sacrifice him? Since this sacrifice seems objectionable on moral grounds, one wonders whether it is compatible with God's moral perfection. Furthermore, it is not clear why in order to defeat sin, death, and the devil the son of God must be incarnate in a human being. Surely an all-powerful God could accomplish this without being incarnated.[12] In addition, there is the problem of why faith in Christ is the only means or even a means to salvation. Aulén maintains that the saving victory of Jesus over sin continues into the present, indeed that it is an eternal victory.[13] But why? It is certainly not obvious why or how Christ's victory could be eternal unless God arbitrarily willed it to be. But in that case God could have arbitrarily willed the defeat of sin, death, and the devil without either the incarnation or the resurrection.

The Mystical Theory

Mystical interpretations of the significance of Jesus' death and resurrection go back to Paul, who declared "I have been crucified with Christ; it is no longer I who live, but Christ who lives in me" (Gal. 2:20). Some early church fathers such as Irenaeus in the second century explicitly embraced the Ransom Theory but also spoke of Jesus making men one with God.[14] In the Middle Ages philosophers such as Aquinas explicitly held a form of the Satisfaction Theory, but used mystical language to explain the union of Christ, who was the head of Church, with the Church's members: "The Head and the members are as it were one mystical Person, and so Christ's satisfaction pertains to all the faithful as to His own members."[15] Reformed thinkers such as John Calvin, although advocating the Penal Theory, spoke of a mystical union of Christ with the members of the church: "He, in short, has deigned to make us one with Himself, therefore do we boast that we have fellowship in righteousness with Him."[16]

These and other Christian thinkers wished to maintain that an essential part of the atonement is a mystical identification or union with Jesus' death and resurrection. Does this supplement to the traditional theories help solve their problems? On the contrary, it may make them more acute.

First of all, there is a problem with the mystic union itself. What epistemological status does it have? Can we even make sense of the paradoxical language of mysticism? What could it possibly mean to say that Jesus and we are one? If we put these questions aside, however, and accept the meaningfulness and epistemological legitimacy of such experiences, there are other problems.[17]

Mystical identification with Jesus' suffering and death hardly helps the ethical problems faced by the theories discussed up to this point. The problem of the injustice of God inflicting pain on his innocent son remains despite a mystical union with Jesus. Indeed, the union should bring the injustice home in a most poignant way for we would feel directly the injustice of Jesus' suffering and death if we were one with him.

Nor does the Mystical Theory account for the problem of why God chose to operate in the way he did when other alternatives were not clearly ruled out. If mystical union with God is important or even necessary for salvation, why does it need to be achieved with the incarnated, crucified, and resurrected son of God? Why not a mystical union with God directly? And if a mystical union with the incarnated son of God is necessary for salvation, why must he suffer and be resurrected? Why could we not simply have a mystical union with an incarnated son of God who does not suffer and die?

The idea of a mystical union does not help solve the problem of the arbitrariness of the other theories either. The need or desirability of a mystical union of humanity with an incarnated, crucified, and suffering God is still determined by the free arbitrary choice of God. But God could have chosen that the path to salvation did not depend on any mystical union; indeed, he could have made it essential for salvation that there not be such a union.

Nor does Mystical Theory help explain why a mystical union is essential for teaching people to love. Even if present psychological laws make loving impossible without a mystical union with God, God could have created different laws. Furthermore, even if we follow Socinus in believing that Jesus was exalted to a high priest who offers freedom from sin and immortality in proportion to people's imitation of his example, a mystical union with him does not seem necessary for this imitation and, hence, for salvation.

Finally, the problem of salvation for non-Christians becomes even more acute in the Mystical Theory. Non-Christians have a hard enough time being saved by believing in the incarnation and resurrection of Jesus. However, if a mystical union with Jesus' suffering and death is also essential, non-Christians could not possibly fulfill the requirements.

POSSIBLE CRITIQUES OF THE ARGUMENT FROM THE ATONEMENT

Premise (3) of the Argument from the Atonement—that there is no theory that convincingly explains why Jesus was incarnated, died on the cross, and was resurrected—might be rejected for one of two reasons. First, one might object that my criticisms against the various theories only show that they are implausible to me, not that they are implausible to Christians. Second, one might admit that God's acts are sometimes arbitrary, so it is not surprising that his actions with respect to the atonement are.[18] However, this does not mean that life is not meaningful.

With respect to the first point surely it makes the notion of plausibility too subjective and relative. Presumably any plausible theory of the atonement acceptable to rational Christians would not fail either of the two tests mentioned above: It must explain why God sacrificed his son for the salvation of humankind and it must not make this sacrifice seem arbitrary. Whether I am correct that all theories of the atonement fail, one of these tests is, of course, the crucial issue. For example, it has been argued that the Ransom Theory can be defended against my criticisms.[19] But I gave five reasons why this explanation should be problematic even for thoughtful Christians. These criticisms cannot be ignored.

With respect to the second point, one could reject completely any criticism that God's actions in sacrificing his son seem arbitrary. One could reason that Christians should be prepared to admit that some of God's actions *seem* arbitrary since they should admit that God's actions *are* sometimes arbitrary. One might go so far as to claim that only thing I have shown is that arbitrariness is not acceptable to me.

But this reply has problems. First, most traditional theories of the atonement have not supposed that God's actions in sacrificing his son are arbitrary. Rather they have held that God's action can be explained in terms of his reasons.[20] In other words, people who expound these theories *assume* nonarbitrariness. Thus, nonarbitrariness is not just what is acceptable to me. Second, the view that God's choices are arbitrary has traditionally been an obstacle to Christian faith and has not been accepted by many Christians. Third, Christian thinkers have often avoided appeal to God's arbitrary choice in theological theories since it weakens explanatory power of these theories. Last, and most important, to admit that the atonement was arbitrary seems tantamount to admitting that there was no good reason for God to choose it and that human life that is based on this choice is without meaning. How can an arbitrary choice confer meaning on life?

CONCLUSION

In order for Christianity to provide an adequate and acceptable account of the meaning of life it must provide a plausible theory of the atonement. However, the historically important theories of the atonement all have serious problems. In particular, they either fail to explain why God sacrificed his son for the salvation of sinners or else make the sacrifice seem arbitrary. These problems provide good reasons for accepting premise (3) of the Argument from the Atonement: There is no theory that convincingly explains why Jesus was incarnated, died on the cross, and was resurrected.

NOTES

1. First, it would meet condition (i) since people would surely take being saved from eternal damnation by writing poetry nontrivial and achievable. Being saved from eternal damnation is very important and is achievable by poetry writing. Second, it would meet condition (ii) since being saved from eternal damnation is a positive value. Third, it would met condition (iii) since writing poetry is an action aimed toward achieving salvation from damnation and it certainly could be learned to be performed with zest. Indeed, the motivation to be saved from damnation could supply the zest.

2. See Alan Richardson, *An Introduction to the Theology of the New Testament* (New York: Harper and Brothers, 1958), chap. 10; William J. Wolf, "Atonement," in *The Encyclopedia of Religion* (New York: Macmillan Publishing Co., 1987), vol. 1, pp. 495–96.

3. Vincent Taylor, *The Atonement in New Testament Teaching*, quoted in William J. Wolf, *No Cross, No Crown: A Study of the Atonement* (Garden City, N.Y.: Doubleday and Company, Inc., 1957), pp. 90–91.

4. L. W. Grensted, *A Short History of the Doctrine of the Atonement* (London: Manchester University Press, 1920), chap. 3. Some commentators argue that Augustine did not hold even a sophisticated ransom theory. See Joseph M. Colleran's Introduction to Anselm, *Why God Became Man and the Virgin Conception and Original Sin*, trans., introduction, and notes by Joseph M. Colleran (Albany, N.Y.: Magi Books, 1969), p. 44.

5. Grensted, *A Short History of the Doctrine the Atonement*, chaps. 4, 5, 6.

6. Colleran in Anselm, *Why God Became Man*, pp. 44–45.

7. Grensted, *A Short History of the Doctrine the Atonement*, pp. 161–63.

8. Ibid., pp. 292–302.

9. Ibid., pp. 103–105.

10. Ibid., p. 287.

11. Gustaf Aulén, *Christus Victor: A Historical Study of the Three Main Types of the Idea of Atonement*, trans. A. G. Herbert (New York: Macmillan Co., 1967).

12. Aulén says that the incarnation is a "necessary presupposition" of the atonement but he gives no argument for this contention. See Aulén, *Christus Victor*, p. 151.

13. Ibid., p. 150.

14. Grensted, *A Short History of the Atonement*, p. 58.

15. Ibid., p. 156.

16. Ibid., p. 219.

17. Michael Martin, *Atheism: A Philosophical Justification* (Philadelphia: Temple University Press, 1989), chap. 6 and p. 219.

18. For these sorts of criticisms see Steven Davis, "Is Belief in the Resurrection Rational? A Response to Michael Martin," *Philo* 2, no. 1 (spring–summer 1999): 51–61.

19. Ibid.

20. One notable exception is the Acceptance Theory of Duns Scotus.

— 17 —

THE MEANING
OF LIFE
AND
SALVATION

INTRODUCTION

Acentral doctrine of Christianity is that one is saved through faith in Jesus. Thus, the Athanasian Creed says, "whosoever earnestly desires to be saved must above all hold the content of the Catholic Faith" and further affirms that unless one keeps this faith whole and undefiled "he shall perish in eternity." The Catholic Faith, according to the creed, is the content of the creed itself. The Nicene Creed is less explicit. However, in affirming belief in one Lord Jesus Christ, the only-begotten son of God, "who for us men and our salvation came down from heaven," died on the cross, was resurrected, ascended to heaven, and will come in glory and in judgment, it certainly suggests that salvation comes through faith in Jesus. The creed does not explicitly say what this belief in "one Lord Jesus Christ" consists of, although it is natural to infer that a necessary condition for salvation through faith in Jesus is belief in the content of the creed itself. Although the Apostles' Creed is the least explicit of the creeds and in fact says nothing directly about salvation, given what we understand of the use of the creed by Christian churches, it is natural to suppose that belief in it is considered by most Christians to be at least a necessary condition for salvation through Jesus Christ.

Commentators have also stressed the importance to Christianity of salvation though Jesus. Thus, Jaroslav Pelikan argues in an article on Christianity in the *Encyclopedia of Religion*,

> Neither the belief in God as Trinity nor the dogma of Christ as divine and human in nature nor the doctrine of humanity as created in the image of God but fallen into sin is, however, an end in itself for Christian faith. As a religion of redemption, Christianity presents itself as the message of how, through Christ, reconciliation has been achieved between the holiness of God and the sin of fallen humanity.[1]

And John Hick maintains in the *Encyclopedia of Philosophy*,

> At its primary level of belief Christianity claims that by responding to God's free forgiveness, offered by Christ, men are released from guilt of their moral failure (justification) and are drawn into a realm of grace in which they are gradually re-created in character (sanctification). The basis of this claim is the Christian experience of reconciliation with God, and, as a consequence, with other human beings, with life's circumstances and demands, and with oneself.[2]

Although the importance of the doctrine of salvation to Christianity is undeniable, what exactly is it? Is there one clear doctrine of salvation or are there several that are incompatible? What are the problems with the Christian view(s) of salvation? Before we answer these questions the relation of salvation to the Christian meaning of life must be considered.

MEANING AND SALVATION

In the last chapter we saw that theories of the atonement either fail to explain why God sacrificed his son for the redemption of sinners or else make the sacrifice seem arbitrary. In themselves these difficulties make rational belief in the meaningfulness of the Christian life impossible. Now in Christianity the doctrine of the atonement is closely connected to the theory of salvation. According to a commonly accepted view, God in his infinite mercy saves sinful human beings through the incarnation, death, and resurrection of his son, that is, via the atonement. However, the

Christian doctrine of salvation is just as problematic as the doctrine of the atonement; indeed, in some respects it is more so. As I will show in what follows, the New Testament contains conflicting accounts of how a person is to be saved, none of which is plausible. As a result it is impossible in practice to follow the New Testament teaching in order to achieve salvation. But since being saved is the entire point of the Christian life, life cannot possibly be meaningful in a Christian worldview.

Separating the practical from the theoretical issue enables us to formulate two arguments that challenge the meaningfulness of Christianity: the Argument from Conflicting Theories and the Argument from Implausibility.

Stated formally, the Argument from Conflicting Theories is this:

1. In order to lead a meaningful life in a Christian worldview, it is necessary to know which path leads to salvation.
2. In order to know which path leads to salvation, there cannot be inconsistent accounts of salvation.
3. There are inconsistent accounts of salvation.
4. Therefore, one cannot lead a meaningful life in a Christian worldview.

The only controversial premise in the Argument from the Conflicting Theories is premise (3). Premises (1) and (2) not only have intuitive appeal but also are in accord with condition (iii) of Quinn's Teleological Meaning (TM). This condition states in part that a meaningful life also "contains actions that are directed toward achieving these purposes." However, in order for actions to be directed to any purposes it must be known which actions will achieve success. But this is impossible to know if inconsistent actions are specified. In what follows I will defend premise (3).

However, even if one waives the inconsistencies and the practical issue, there are the implausibilities of different accounts of salvation. Surely for life to be meaningful in a Christian worldview the path of salvation must be intellectually plausible. Lack of plausibility should rationally undermine a person's belief that life is meaningful in a Christian worldview. Stated more formally, the Argument from Implausibility is this:

5. In order for one to reasonably believe that life has meaning in a Christian worldview there must be a plausible account of salvation.
6. There is no plausible account of salvation.
7. Therefore, one cannot reasonably believe that life has meaning in a Christian worldview.

Since premise (5) is based on condition (5) of Positive Purpose Meaning it has intuitive appeal. Recall that this condition specifies that the purposes of life must not be arbitrary or without a plausible explanation. Hence, the only controversial premise is premise (6). Although I do not pretend to consider here all extant theories of salvation, I will consider the most important ones historically. Showing fundamental problems with these theories should give us good grounds to suppose that no extant theories are adequate.

NEW TESTAMENT DOCTRINES OF SALVATION

Clearly the source of the Christian doctrine of salvation is the New Testament. But what does the New Testament teach? In the synoptic Gospels, John, and Paul's letters one can discern four different views. The first, presented in the synoptic Gospels, is that one is saved by following a strict ethical code that goes beyond the Jewish laws. According to the second, which was also presented in the synoptic Gospels, one is saved by making great sacrifices in following Jesus. The third maintained by Paul and John is that one is saved by having faith in Jesus. Paul seems to suppose that this is sufficient and necessary only for those people who lived after Christ came to earth. The fourth suggested in Paul's letters is that one can be saved before Christ came by following the Jewish laws.

1. Although Jesus' message about salvation in the synoptic Gospels is not completely clear, he teaches both that one can be saved by following a very strict moral code and that one can be saved by giving up everything and following him. Let us consider these ideas in more detail.

The first three gospels teach that salvation is closely connected with belief in the imminence of the Kingdom of God (Luke 10:9, Mark 13:30). In what will the Kingdom of God consist? Although the account is sketchy these gospels indicate that God will rule the Earth, the son of man will come and pronounce judgment, the dead will be resurrected, and Satan and the demons will lose their power.[3] But how is one to participate in this coming kingdom of God? How is one to be saved? Is belief in Jesus sufficient for salvation? Is it necessary?

It is not clear according to these gospels if belief in Jesus is either sufficient or necessary for salvation. Some of the pronouncements of Jesus indicate that much more is involved and, indeed, that even exemplary moral conduct independent of faith can be sufficient. For example, in the Sermon on the Mount Jesus proclaimed that in order to enter the kingdom of heaven not one of the commandants must be relaxed and a person's righteousness must exceed that of the scribes and the Pharisees (Matt. 5:19–20). He suggested that those who will find salvation are few since following what he teaches is so very hard (Matt. 7:13–14). Yet he said that those who hear his words and do not follow them are like a house built on sand and will fall down in times of floods, rain, and wind (Matt. 7:24–27). Indeed, when Jesus was later asked by a young man what one must do to have eternal life, he replied, "if you would enter life, keep the commandments" (Matt. 19:17). Yet when he was pressed to specify which commandments, he went beyond them by saying that one must sell what one possesses and give to the poor. And he proclaimed to his disciples that it will be easier for a camel to go through the eye of a needle than for a rich man to enter the kingdom of heaven (Matt. 19:21–24; cf. Luke 18:18–25).

These passages suggest that it is possible to enter the kingdom of God by simply adopting a strict moral code that few people indeed can follow (Luke 13:24); in fact they suggest that it is impossible to enter the kingdom without adopting such a code. Yet New Testament scholars do not commonly adopt this interpretation, perhaps because they have been influenced by the doctrines of salvation of John and Paul.[4] In any case, in some parts of the synoptic Gospels salvation through faith in Jesus is, to say the least, not well developed and the favored doctrine is salvation through following a strict moral code.

2. Other passages in the synoptic Gospels suggest that salvation can be achieved by renouncing everything and following Jesus and that behaving according to a strict moral code is not necessary to salvation.[5] After hearing Jesus' proclamation about the impossibility of entering the

kingdom of heaven if one is rich, the disciples are dismayed and ask, "Who then will be saved?" (The import of the question seems to be that Jesus' ethical standards for salvation are so high that no one, including his disciples, can meet them.) Jesus answers that with men this is not possible but with God all things are possible. Peter points out that they have given up everything and followed him. Jesus assures them that everyone who has left family and lands "for my name's sake" will enter the eternal life (Matt. 19:25–29; Mark 10:29). Jesus then tells the parable of the house-holder and the vineyard workers. The workers are paid the same amount of money whether they work the whole day or a part of it and the workers complain about the unfairness of this. But the householder argues, "Am I not allowed to do what I choose with what belongs to me? Or do you begrudge my generosity?" (Matt. 20:15)

One obvious reading of this passage is that to give up everything and follow Jesus is sufficient for salvation. God, like the householder, can choose whom to reward. Just as the vineyard workers who have labored all day may get no more earthly reward than those who have only worked part of a day, people who have followed a strict code of ethics all their lives may get no more heavenly reward than those who have only recently given up everything and followed Jesus. On the other hand, there is nothing in what he says to indicate that those following the strict code that Jesus specifies will not be saved.[6] Rather, Jesus can be interpreted as saying that following this code is not the only way to be saved.

Thus, according to the synoptic Gospels, salvation is a two-track affair: It can be obtained through adherence to a strict moral code that few can follow or by following Jesus. This second track is also difficult, but in a different way: It involves great personal sacrifice but not the rigors of following a strict moral code.

It should be noted that the first two paths of salvation would make it extremely difficult to fulfill condition (iii) of Quinn's Teleological Meaning that states in part that the actions directed to fulfilling the purposes of life "are performed with zest." Following a strict moral code or renouncing everything and following Jesus are hard enough to do. But Quinn's condition (iii) implies that life would have no meaning unless they were done with zest.

3. Both John and Paul indicate that salvation is achieved only through faith in Jesus. However, even here there are differences in what they

assume this faith consists of.

We have seen that the Athanasian Creed maintains that unless one keeps the faith "whole and undefiled" one shall perish in eternity. This idea is clearly taught in the fourth gospel except that John does not seem to demand belief in the Trinity:

> For God so loved the world that he gave his only Son, that whoever believes in him should not perish but have eternal life. For God sent the Son into the world, not to condemn the world, but that the world might be saved through him. He who believes in him is not condemned; he who does not believe is condemned already, because he has not believed in the name of the only Son of God. . . . He who believes in the Son has eternal life; he who does not obey the Son shall not see life, but the wrath of God rests upon him (John 3:16–36).

In many other passages in John this same message is given: One is saved only through Jesus. "I am the way, and the truth, and the life; no one comes to the Father, but by me" (John 14:6). What does believing in Jesus involve? In his reply to Nicodemus, Jesus indicated that in order to enter the kingdom of God one must be born anew (John 3:7). But is being born again the result of believing in Jesus? What exactly does it consist of? It is not implausible to suppose that John taught that being born again is brought about by believing in Jesus and that believing in Jesus involves some sort of ethical transformation. Jesus says, "he who believes in me will do the works that I do" and "if you love me, you will keep my commandents" (John 14:12–15). "This is my commandment, that you love one another as I have loved you" (John 15:12).

Thus, there is no suggestion in John, as there is in the first three gospels, that salvation can be achieved by following a strict ethical code. Indeed, no strict ethical code is even suggested. Nor is it implied directly that if one sacrifices everything to follow Jesus one is saved quite independently of following some strict code of ethics. Rather one is saved only by believing in Jesus. It is not clear that this involves sacrificing everything and following Jesus although it seems to involve some spiritual rebirth that may involve an ethical transformation in which one manifests the love that Jesus manifested for his disciples. There is no suggestion in John that Jesus had narrow sectarian goals of salvation as there is in some of the first three gospels. On the other hand, John, like the synoptic Gospels, threatens punishment. He indicates that the wrath of God will rest on anyone who disobeys the son of God.

Salvation by following a strict ethical code seems to be completely foreign to Paul's understanding: "For we hold that a man is justified by faith apart from works of the law" (Rom. 3:28). "Therefore, since we are justified by faith, we have peace with God through our Lord Jesus Christ. Through him we have grace in which we stand and we rejoice in our hope of sharing the glory of God" (Rom. 5:1–2). Paul argues that because of Adam's sin everyone became a sinner but because of Jesus' death we are given the gift of being free from sin and are reconciled to God. Paul sometimes seems to be saying that faith in Jesus makes it impossible for us to sin. He maintains that our old sinful self was crucified with Jesus and we are no longer in bondage to sin (Rom. 6:6–11). On the other hand, he urges Christians not to sin (Rom. 6:12–16).

But what, according to Paul, is one supposed to believe when one has faith in Jesus Christ? It is not completely clear. He certainly thought that Jesus was resurrected on the third day, but there is no reason to suppose that Paul had knowledge of the details of the Gospel story of the trial and crucifixion. So if for Paul faith in Jesus involved belief in his resurrection, this involved less in terms of the content of belief than it did in the creeds. Nor is there any reason to think that Paul believed in other doctrines specified in the traditional creeds of Christianity. Thus, Paul probably did not believe in the virgin birth since he does not mention this. Indeed, some scholars have argued that it is not completely clear whether Paul believed that Jesus was the son of God, although there is little doubt that he believed that Jesus and God were closely related.[7] Consequently, it is not clear that for Paul, in contrast to the creeds and John, faith in Jesus involved belief in the virgin birth and the incarnation.

4. Paul seems to suppose that until Jesus came men were under the law but the coming of Jesus annulled the law: "So that the law was our custodian until Christ came, that we might be justified by faith. But now that faith has come, we are no longer under a custodian" (Gal. 3:24–25). This suggests that people before Jesus could have been saved by strictly following the Jewish law but afterward they could only be saved through Jesus. This seems to conflict with Jesus' statement in the synoptic Gospels that more than following the Jewish law is needed for salvation

but that by following a strict moral code that goes beyond the Jewish law salvation can be achieved. But what about the people who did not hear of Jesus after he came? In his letter to the Romans Paul asks, "But how are men to call on him in whom they have not believed? And how are they to believe in him of whom they have never heard? And how are they to hear without a preacher?"(10:14) Paul seems to assume that people have now heard since the voices of preachers have "gone out to all the earth and their words to the ends of the world" (10:18).

In conclusion, the first, second, and fourth routes to salvation seem to be salvation by works while the third involves salvation by faith alone. Certainly the third route is the one most commonly associated with Christianity. However, it is not clear exactly what besides belief it involves. Even when one concentrates only on the cognitive dimension of faith there are unclarities. In particular, the creeds seem to demand belief that defines everything in orthodox Christianity, from the virgin birth to the second coming, from the resurrection to the incarnation. On the other hand, John seems to demand only belief in the incarnation while Paul seems to demand only belief in the resurrection. Neither John nor Paul, unlike the creeds, demands belief in the virgin birth or the Trinity.

The practical implication of the above considerations for the meaning of life in a Christian worldview is devastating. Since the meaning of life in a Christian worldview depends on salvation and there is no consistent doctrine of salvation, obtaining meaning in one's life is impossible. In short, premise (3) of the Argument from Conflicting Theories is supported and the conclusion that one cannot lead a meaningful life in a Christian worldview is vindicated.

EVALUATION OF THE DOCTRINE

So far we have argued that the Argument from Conflicting Theories is sound. But what about the Argument from Implausibility? As noted, the crucial premise in this argument is premise (6): There is no plausible account of salvation. Is there any reason to think that (6) is true? There are problems that make the Christian doctrine of salvation implausible and consequently undermine the meaning of life in a Christian worldview.

The Dependency on Other Christian Doctrines

One fundamental problem with the doctrine of salvation by faith in Jesus is its close dependency on questionable doctrines such as the incarnation, the resurrection, the virgin birth, the atonement, and the second coming. As I have argued elsewhere, there is good reason to suppose that Jesus was not the son of God, was not resurrected from the dead, was not born of a virgin, and will not come again.[8] However, salvation through faith certainly presupposes that at least some of these doctrines are true and must be believed if one is to be saved. Thus, the Athanasian Creed proclaims that Jesus is the son of God and that in order to be saved one must believe this. John maintains that unless one believes in Jesus one is condemned and belief in Jesus presumably involves belief that he is the son of God. Paul's idea of salvation through Christ certainly presumes belief in the resurrection.

Furthermore, the two routes to salvation suggested in the synoptic Gospels only make sense if some of the basic doctrines of Christianity are assumed. The route to salvation by following a strict ethical code that goes beyond following Jewish law is indirectly dependent on dubious Christian doctrines. Many aspects of this strict ethical code outlined by Jesus make sense only if it is presumed that the end of the world is near. Of course, if we had independent reason to suppose that the son of God proclaimed this code, then perhaps we might have grounds for following it. But this would presuppose another dubious assumption of Christianity, namely, that Jesus is the son of God. The second track to salvation of giving up everything and following Jesus also presupposes dubious Christian doctrines. It would be irrational to give up everything and follow Jesus if the basic doctrines of Christianity are improbable.

The Incompatibility with Belief in an All-Good God

It is important to see that to reject the four routes to salvation outlined above is compatible with belief in an all-powerful, all-knowing, and all-good God. Indeed, there is good reason to suppose that salvation by these routes is incompatible with such a belief.

Surely an all-good God would not want his creatures to follow the implausibly strict ethical code laid down by Jesus. How could a good God want us to have no concern for the future since many of the most serious problems of our time, for instance, world hunger and environmental pollution, are in part the result of lack of concern? How could an all-good God condemn people for being angry with someone or punish a person with the fires of hell for calling someone a fool? (Matt. 5:21–22) Nor would it seem that an all-good God would want people to sacrifice in the name of Jesus if the evidence indicates that he is not what Christians claim. Surely an all-good God does not demand irrational action.

There is also another issue indicated in chapter 15 that calls into question the compatibility of the Christian doctrine of salvation with an all-good God. The four routes to salvation outlined above neglect the status of people who have not had the opportunity either to follow Jesus' strict moral code or to sacrifice in Jesus' name or to have faith in Jesus or to follow the Jewish laws. People might lack these opportunities for many different reasons, the most obvious being that they were born in the wrong time or the wrong place. A Chinese woman in the second century B.C.E., an American Indian living in the eighth century C.E., and a Black African in the second century C.E. would have had no opportunity to be saved in any of the ways outlined above. They would not have heard of Jesus' strict ethical code, they would not have known about Jewish law, they would have had no opportunity to sacrifice in Jesus' name since they would have never heard of Jesus, they would have had no opportunity to have faith in Jesus even if that involved only believing that Jesus existed.

Paul was clearly wrong to suppose that news of Jesus had reached the ends of the Earth by his time. Even today there are many people in the world who have little or no exposure to Christianity or the Jewish laws. For these persons also salvation is apparently impossible. Furthermore, there is also the possibility of intelligent extraterrestrial life. Indeed, some astronomers suggest that the existence of such life is extremely likely somewhere in the vastness of the galaxy. Such creatures would not have the opportunity of being saved and this also is unfair and is incompatible with an all-good God.

MORRIS'S SOLUTIONS

Thomas Morris points out that "the scandal of particularity" is an old theological worry: How can humans who either lived and died before the time of Christ or lived since the time of Christ in different religious cultures and traditions be held accountable for not responding to him?[9] Concern about the salvation of extraterrestrial intelligent beings, Morris argues, is a variant of this problem. He offers four different possible solutions.

Morris first suggests a solution favored by Eastern Church fathers in which the incarnation "somehow metaphysically transformed our nature." This process known as deification would not be transmitted by any physical causation but could touch any rational creature "whatever their location in the space-time continuum. One divine incarnation would serve for the salvation of all the universe."[10] Morris admits that this model "has not been a very popular understanding of salvation made available by Christ. Dominant models of salvation have required a response on the part of the created individual being saved."[11] Surely he is correct but he fails to note that the reason it is unpopular is because it seems out of keeping with what the Bible teaches.

The second solution Morris proposes is based on his rejection of what he takes to be the questionable assumption that it would be necessary for God to save all rational creatures through the incarnation of Christ:

> In principle, it seems that a Christian could hold that the divine economy is such that we human beings are offered salvation through the incarnation of God as Jesus, but that other rational beings may offer salvation through some completely different sort of means not involving a divine incarnation at all.[12]

Morris's argument has several problems. First, he seems to be talking in this passage only about the possibility of alternative means of salvation for extraterrestrial beings. For his solution to work it must also hold for human beings—earthlings—who have not had the opportunity to have faith in Jesus. Second, as we have seen, there is scriptural evidence that Paul and John understood the salvation of human beings to occur only through Jesus. In Paul's case this was tempered by the stipulation that salvation was possible without Jesus before he came by following Jewish law. The two routes specified in the synoptic Gospels would also exclude members of other religious cultures and ancient times from salvation. If there were alternative means open to members of different cultures, then one would have supposed that Jesus and his disciples would have said so. Once we start postulating alternative means of salvation why not suppose that even people raised in Christian homes could be saved without faith in Jesus? But if this is allowed, what is the point of the incarnation? Third, Morris gives no reason to suppose that there are alternative means that are available to people in different religious cultures and ancient times. He only implies that such means are possible. But what reason do we have to suppose that in fact some means of salvation was available to, say, a fourteenth-century Australian Aborigine? What could it have been?

Morris's third solution is that knowledge of the incarnation may not be propagated by natural causes and may not be had in this life. God may either offer knowledge of the incarnation directly to his rational creatures or offer it in the next life. Now it is, of course, possible that God could give his rational creatures knowledge of the incarnation directly. But there seems to be no reason to suppose that in general this has happened or is happening. For example, we have no evidence that Chinese of the third century B.C.E. had knowledge of the coming incarnation of Christ. Furthermore, it seems likely that this amazing knowledge would have been recorded in Chinese history if it was at all widespread.

This leaves us with the afterlife. Of course, there is no way we can here and now determine what we will know in the afterlife or even whether there is an afterlife. But the proposal that a rational creature who did not know of the incarnation in this life would be informed in some later life and be provided with the opportunity to be saved seems to be an act of desperation to protect the doctrine of Christian salvation from refutation, not a serious proposal. In any case, why would God wait until the afterlife to provide people with this opportunity? Certainly there is no scriptural support for the view that such knowledge will be provided in the afterlife.

The fourth solution offered by Morris is that God could have been incarnated many times and thereby has given every rational creature an opportunity for salvation. Thus, God could have been incarnated in all of the planets inhabited by rational creatures and in all of the great civilizations of the earth. Arguing that there are no logical obstacles to multiple incarnations, Morris suggests that perhaps multiple incarnations on other inhabited planets would be necessary. For it might be maintained that in order for God to save his creatures through being incarnated he must share all the kinds of experiences that they experience. However, in order to save extraterrestrials who are likely to have different sensory apparatus, different brains, and radically different experiences multiple incarnations might indeed be necessary.

The conceptual problems of this theory aside,[13] is there any reason to suppose that extraterrestrial incarnations have occurred? Unfortunately one must wait for interstellar space exploration to verify the hypothesis that extraterrestrial cultures have been blessed with divine incarnations. However, it should be noted that Morris's suggestion is in principle capable of such verification. Presumably if such incarnations had occurred they would be likely to be believed by the creatures of these cultures and evidence would be cited to justify their beliefs.

But there is a more immediate problem. Morris suggests that in order to save human beings God through the incarnation of his son must experience all the trials, tribulations, temptations, and suffering of human beings. But how could God have been successful in doing this in one single incarnation here on Earth? Relatively speaking, Jesus experienced very little of the intense suffering that human beings have undergone. For example, a Jew in a concentration camp, a starving mother and her child, a person dying from cancer without painkillers surely experiences more and different kinds of suffering than Jesus did. Jesus knew nothing personally of the degradation experienced by women and minorities, of the horrors of war, of the terrors of Nazism. In order for Jesus to have really experienced the many and varied sufferings of humanity God would have had to have been incarnated many times in human form. One would simply be insufficient. Yet surely there is no evidence that he has been incarnated more than once in human form. Indeed, all of the evidence suggests that he was not incarnated at all. Consequently, this way of handling the scandal of particularity is not viable.

Finally, it should be noted that Morris seems only to consider salvation through faith in Jesus. However, we have seen that the New Testament offers at least four salvation tracks. The difficulty of reconciling the goodness of God with the means to salvation is inherent in all of these. At best Morris provides solutions to the problem inherent in one. In fact, either his solutions do not succeed or else they succeed only by changing the original doctrine of Christian theory of salvation.

I conclude that Morris's defense of Christian doctrine of salvation is not successful.

CATHOLIC DEFENSE

The Catholic Church has given much thought to the salvation of infidels. The crucial question is whether Catholic thinkers have been able to interpret the Christian doctrine of salvation in such a way that infidels are not unjustly relegated to hell without at the same time making the incarnation irrelevant. Father Maurice Eminyan in his comprehensive study of this subject maintains that the Church's doctrine of the salvation of infidels can be divided into two parts: from the origin to the discovery of America and from then to the present day.[14] During the first period the Church was concerned about how the millions of pagans living before Christ could be saved. According to Father Eminyan the Church fathers utilized a passage from Paul. "Ever since the creation of the world his invisible nature, namely, his eternal power and deity, has been clearly perceived in the things that have been made. So they are without excuse" (Rom. 1:20). According to Father Eminyan they concluded from this that "the chosen people, therefore, were not the only beneficiaries of God's divine plan of salvation. The same argument was used in regard to the pagans who lived after Christ, although these were even more inexcusable, for, insisted the early Apologists, the echo of the Gospel preaching had already reached the farthest limits of the Earth."[15] St. Thomas "also believed that at least an echo of the Gospel had reached the farthest limits of earth in his time. If, by any chance, there should yet be any person still invincibly ignorant of the truths that are necessary for salvation, God would send him a missionary to teach him these truths."[16]

However, with the discovery of America theologians were again faced with the concrete problem of salvation of the infidels. Reformers such as Luther and Calvin held that explicit faith was absolutely necessary for salvation. According to Father Eminyan, "For Luther, the absence of a missionary among infidels was a sure sign of their reprobation. Calvin went further: in order to render infidels more deserving of condemnation God has left them a few traces of truth."[17] The Catholic doctrine was different. The doctrine of the Council of Trent as interpreted by theologians such as Suarez was that explicit faith in Christ and the Trinity is strictly speaking necessary for salvation. However, since the obligation to believe in these two doctrines "derives from a positive law promulgated by the Gospel, faith in voto (i.e. implicit faith)" in these two doctrines will suffice for salvation whenever "the Gospel itself has not yet been divulged and there is therefore invincible ignorance."[18]

Although there have been some movements in the Church that have proclaimed that infidels cannot be saved at all, these have been condemned as heresies and there has been a tendency away from the doctrine of explicit faith. Father Eminyan cites as an example of this tendency Father Perrone, a professor at the Roman College, who in the last century advocated the opinion that the American Indians before the sixteenth century were in exactly the same situation as the Romans were before the Christian era: their implicit faith in Christ the Mediator was contained in their adherence to a providence capable of coming to man's rescue.[19]

More recent Catholic theologians who have wrestled with the problem of the salvation of infidels have proposed similar solutions. Having implicit faith can save infidels. They have been provided revelation in some hidden ways,[20] which they can accept or reject. What these hidden ways are seem to vary from theologian to theologian. For some they involve merely providing supernatural and positive values in their otherwise false religions; for others they involve knowledge of the ultimate human end at the dawn of human reason; for others a divine offer of salvation in the instant of death; in still others an interior inspiration in the minds of good infidels.

There are several problems with the Catholic doctrine. First, the utilization of Paul's statement in Romans seems strained. The rest of the passage says that "for although they knew God they did not honor him or give thanks to him but became futile in their thinking and their senseless minds became darkened" (Rom. 1:21). It is certainly not clear that Paul was suggesting that people could be saved simply by honoring God and giving thanks to him, although he may have thought this was necessary for salvation. After all, if this is all that was necessary, what was the point of the incarnation?[21] Further, it is surely overly optimistic to suppose that all the people who existed before Christ "clearly perceived God's eternal power and deity in the things that have been made." St. Thomas's view that the echo of the Gospel had reached the farthest limits of Earth in his time was mistaken as was his view that God will send a missionary to any infidels who have not heard of the Gospel. After all, many millions of Indians died before missionaries were sent.

Although Luther's and Calvin's doctrines concerning the infidels were harsh, they certainly seemed to reflect the implications of the New Testament doctrine better than the official Catholic doctrine of faith in voto. The emptiness of the doctrine is illustrated well in Father Perrone's claim that one has implicit faith so long as one believes "in a providence capable of coming to man's rescue." What infidels are excluded from this doctrine of salvation? Perhaps only atheists, agnostics, and skeptics. If so, one wonders why. These people may have good reasons for not accepting a beneficent providence. Why should they not be saved? In any case why should only infidels who have not heard of the Gospel be allowed to be saved in the way Father Perrone suggests? People in our time and in Christian societies may have good reasons for not accepting the Gospel.[22] Why should they not be saved by faith in voto? On the other hand, if this is allowed why did God come to Earth? Surely we have come a long way from Peter's worried question in Matthew 19: Who then will be saved? If Father Perrone is taken seriously neither the rich man nor Peter need have been worried. Belief in a beneficent providence would have sufficed.

Recent Catholic theological thought allowing for the salvation of infidels for a wide variety of reasons goes even further than Father Perrone does in diluting the idea of Christian salvation, and the same problems can be raised about it. There is no New Testament justification for this broad interpretation of salvation. There is no good reason why only infidels and not wayward Christians are provided with these alternative means of salvation. It is unclear that even this broad doctrine applies to all worthy infidels. An atheist could be an extremely moral person and yet not accept supernatural values, not believe that humans have any ultimate end, reject the offer of salvation at death because he or she believes there are good reasons for supposing it is illusory, and not respond to some spiritual inspiration for similar reasons. But why should such a person not be saved? After all, his or her response is rational and honest.

In sum, either the Catholic doctrine of faith permits too many people to be saved, making the incarnation unnecessary, or it forbids the salvation of too many, calling into question the infinite goodness of God. Thus, this doctrine no more than Morris's adequately explains how the Christian doctrine of salvation can be reconciled with belief in an all-good God without seriously modifying the doctrine.

CONCLUSION

The Christian paths to salvation have serious problems that adversely affect the meaning of life in a Christian worldview. The conflicting doctrines of salvation in the New Testament make seeking life's meaning through salvation practically impossible. This problem aside, the doctrines presume at least some of the dubious doctrines of Christianity. Furthermore, the doctrine of salvation is incompatible with an all-good God. Rational creatures who lived before Jesus as well as those who lived after Jesus but were not exposed to his teaching would not be saved. On the other hand, if one alters the doctrine in order to solve this problem of particularity, one wonders why anyone needs to have faith in Jesus to be saved.

NOTES

1. Jaroslav Pelikan, "Christianity: An Overview," in *Encyclopedia of Religion* (New York: Macmillan, 1987), vol. 3, p. 356.

2. John Hick, "Christianity," in *The Encyclopedia of Philosophy*, ed. Paul Edwards (New York: Macmillan and Free Press, 1967), vol. 2, p. 107.

3. Werner Georg Kümmel, *The Theology of the New Testament* (Nashville: Abingdon Press, 1973), pp. 34–35.

4. See, for example, Alan Richardson, *An Introduction to the Theology of the New Testament* (New York: Harper and Brothers, 1958), pp. 79–83.

5. G. Ryder Smith, *The Bible Doctrine of Salvation* (London: Epworth Press, 1946), p. 144 seems to suppose that the actions that Jesus recommended to the young man for salvation and the actions of the disciples that will gain them salvation amount to the same thing. To be sure, the disciples have given up their wealth in following Jesus and a rich young man is advised to give up his wealth. But the young man has not been advised to follow Jesus and the disciples are not advised to follow the commandments strictly.

6. Leon Morris, *New Testament Theology* (Grand Rapids, Mich.: Academic Books, 1986), p. 128 maintains that the parable teaches that one does not merit salvation by good work. However, Jesus says that if the rich man followed the commandments and gave up everything to the poor, he would be saved; that in this case his good works would bring about salvation. I am inclined to think therefore that Jesus was advocating in this passage two ways to salvation.

7. Ibid., p. 48.

8. Michael Martin, *The Case against Christianity* (Philadelphia: Temple University Press, 1991).

9. Thomas V. Morris, *The Logic of God Incarnate* (Ithaca, N.Y.: Cornell University Press, 1986), pp. 170–86.

10. Ibid., p. 176.

11. Ibid.

12. Ibid., p. 177.

13. Ibid.

14. Maurice Eminyan, S.J., *The Theology of Salvation* (Boston: Daughters of St. Paul, 1960), p. 19.

15. Ibid.

16. Ibid., p. 20.

17. Ibid.

18. Ibid., p. 21.

19. Ibid., p. 22.

20. Ibid., p. 28.

21. Cf. Charles Watts, "The Death of Christ," reprinted in *An Anthology of Atheism and Rationalism*, ed. Gordon Stein (Amherst, N.Y.: Prometheus Books, 1980), p. 217.

22. Martin, *The Case against Christianity*; Michael Martin, *Atheism: A Philosophical Justification* (Philadelphia: Temple University Press, 1990).

18

THE MEANING
OF LIFE
AND THE
RESURRECTION

INTRODUCTION

I argued in chapter 16 that there is no plausible theory of the atone-ment. Yet without one the Christian worldview makes no sense and the incarnation, death, and resurrection of Jesus are all pointless. But now let us suppose for the sake of argument that a plausible theory of the atonement is available. Unless there is good reason to suppose that the resurrection occurred, life in the Christian worldview would still be without meaning. Indeed, the truth of the resurrection is pivotal to both the Christian worldview and the meaning of a Christian life. In this chapter I will argue, however, that there is no good evidence that Jesus arose from the dead; consequently, that there is no reason to suppose that life has meaning in a Christian worldview.

Stated more formally, the Argument from the Resurrection is this:

1. In order for one to be able to believe reasonably that life has meaning in a Christian worldview, there must be good reason to believe that the resurrection occurred.
2. There is no good reason to believe that the resurrection occurred.

3. Hence, one is not able to believe reasonably that life has meaning in a Christian worldview.

The only controversial premise in the Argument from the Resurrection is (2). In what follows I will show that there are good grounds for believing that (2) is correct.

BACKGROUND

Orthodox Christianity assumes that Jesus was crucified on the orders of Pontius Pilate and was then resurrected. Thus the Apostles' Creed proclaims that Jesus "suffered under Pontius Pilate, was crucified, dead, buried; he descended into hell; the third day he rose again from the dead." The Nicene Creed, in turn, maintains that Jesus "was crucified also for us under Pontius Pilate; He suffered and was buried; and the third day he rose again according to Scriptures."[1]

Furthermore, the resurrection has been considered by Christians to be a crucial element of Christian doctrine. Thus nearly two thousand years ago Paul proclaimed,

> If Christ has not been raised, then our preaching is in vain and your faith
> is in vain. We are even found to be misrepresenting God. . . . If Christ
> has not been raised, your faith is futile. (1 Cor. 15:14–17)

Many contemporary Christians seem to agree. Hugh Anderson, a New Testament scholar, writes,

> With all assurance we can say that, save for Easter, there would have
> been no New Testament letters written, no Gospels compiled, no
> prayers offered in Jesus' name, no Church. The Resurrection can
> scarcely be put on a par with certain other clauses in the Apostles'
> Creed—not if the New Testament is our guide. . . . Easter, therefore, is
> no mere addendum to other factors in the story of Jesus Christ; it is con-
> stitutive for the community's faith and worship, its discipleship and
> mission to the world.[2]

Terry Miethe, a Christian philosopher at Oxford, has in turn maintained, "'Did Jesus rise from the dead?' is the most important question regarding the claims of the Christian faith."[3]

THE IMPROBABILITY OF THE RESURRECTION

One argument against the existence of the resurrection is the following:[4]

1. A miracle claim is initially improbable relative to our background knowledge.
2. If a claim is initially improbable relative to our background knowledge and the evidence for it is not strong, then it should be disbelieved.
3. The resurrection of Jesus is a miracle claim.
4. The evidence for the resurrection is not strong.
5. Therefore, the resurrection of Jesus should be disbelieved.

Let us call this the Initial Improbability Argument. Premise (3) is granted by Christians and later in this chapter I will defend premise (4). Since Christian apologists might maintain that the argument fails because of the implausibility of premise (1), I will begin with it.

Why should premise (1) be accepted? Traditionally a miracle is defined as a violation of a law of nature caused by the intervention of God. The improbability of miracle claims in this sense of the term can be understood in the following way: Let us suppose for the sake of the argument that theism is true. Can we then expect God to intervene in the natural course of events and violate a natural law? We cannot. If theism is true, then miracles in this intervention sense are *possible* since there is a supernatural being who *could* bring them about, but it does not follow that such miracles are more likely than not to occur.[5] Indeed, God would have good reason for never using miracles to achieve his purposes. For one thing, a violation of the laws of nature cannot be explained by science and, indeed, is an impediment to a scientific understanding of the world. For another, great difficulties and controversies arise in identifying miracles. Whatever good effects miracles might have, then, they also impede, mislead, and confuse. Since an all-powerful God would seem to be able to achieve his purposes in ways that do not have unfortunate effects, I conclude that there actually is reason to suppose that the existence of miracles is initially improbable even in a religious worldview.

For the sake of argument suppose now that we assume with Christian apologist Richard Swinburne that miracles in the traditional sense are probable given God's existence. This assumption is perfectly compatible with the thesis that in any particular case a miracle is unlikely. Consider the following analogy: It is overwhelmingly probable that in a billion tosses of ten coins all ten coins will turn up heads at least once, but it is extremely unlikely that in any given case all ten coins will come up heads. In the same way, even if it is correct that, given the existence of God, some miracles are probable, it might be extremely unlikely that in any given case a miracle has occurred.

I say "might be" rather than "would be" because the occurrence of miracles, unlike the occurrence of ten heads in ten tosses of a coin, might not be rare. If miracles were as plentiful as dry days in the Sahara Desert, my analogy would be misleading. However, as far as religious believers are concerned, violations of the laws of nature are relatively rare. Even if 10,000 violations of natural laws were to occur every day, in relation to the total number of events that occur their relative frequency would be very low. So given the background belief that miracles are rare—a belief that is held even by theists—it follows that a claim that a particular event is a miracle is initially improbable.

There is another sense of miracles, however, according to which God sets up the world so that an unusual event serves as a sign or message to human beings without violating a law of nature. This nonintervention sense of the term is meant to cover the following sort of case. Suppose that God arranges the world so that at a certain time in history the Red Sea parts because of a freak wind. Although no violation of a law of nature has occurred, this event conveys a message to religious believers; for example, that the Jews are God's chosen people and that God takes a special interest in them.

Now there is a way of interpreting a miracle claim in the nonintervention sense that makes a miracle extremely probable. If a theist maintains that *most* events which are governed by the laws of nature are arranged by God to serve as signs or to communicate messages to human beings, then miracle claims are initially probable. But this way of understanding miracles tends to trivialize the notion. Nonintervention miraculous events are usually *contrasted* with the great majority of other events. For the typical believer in nonintervention miracles, most events are not arranged by God to convey some message. Thus, the initial probability of nonintervention miracles is low in terms of the background theories of the typical religious believer.

So far I have argued that miracle claims are initially improbable even on the assumption of theism. Indeed, relative to background beliefs that are shared by atheists and believers alike, for example belief in the uniformity of nature, miracles are rare events. In addition, from a historical point of view, miracle claims, when understood as violations of laws of nature, have often been rejected by religious believers themselves. Even thoughtful believers in miracles admit that *most* miracle claims turn out to be bogus on examination; that in most cases of alleged miracles no law of nature has been violated and no action of God need be postulated. Even they say that relatively few claims ultimately withstand critical scrutiny.

For example, although the Catholic Church has investigated thousands of claims of miracle cures at Lourdes, it has rejected most of these as unproven.[6] Indeed, the number of officially designated miracles at Lourdes is less than seventy. Inductively, therefore, any new claim made at Lourdes is initially likely to be spurious. The same is true of other miracle claims: Sophisticated religious believers consider most to be invalid. Thus, for example, Stephen T. Davis, a well-known Christian philosopher and apologist and believer in miracles, argues that "naturalistic explanations of phenomena ought to be preferred by rational people in the vast majority of cases."[7] His position is perfectly compatible with both the existence of miracles and the possibility of obtaining strong evidence for them. It does imply, however, that even on the assumption of theism *initially* any given miracle claim is incredible and that to overcome this initial improbability strong evidence must be produced.

THE RESURRECTION AND GOD'S PURPOSE

So far I have shown that, in general, particular miracle claims are initially unlikely even in a theistic framework. Is the claim that Jesus arose from the dead an exception to this rule? Could God have had special purposes that made it necessary to cause the resurrection? Could it be the case that although any ordinary miracle claim is initially unlikely, the claim that the resurrection occurred is initially likely? What special purpose of God would make the resurrection initially likely?

According to Swinburne, it is likely that God who created human beings would make it possible for them to atone for their sins and, consequently, it is likely that God's son would become incarnated as a human and would die in order to do this.[8] Earlier I argued in detail that all the historically important theories of the atonement either fail to explain why God sacrificed his son for the salvation of sinners or else they make the sacrifice seem arbitrary. But for the sake of argument let us suppose that it is likely that God would sacrifice his son for the redemption of humanity. Still it would not follow that the incarnation and the resurrection are themselves likely. These are *particular* historical events that occurred at *particular* times and places. However, God could have become incarnated and have died for sinners on an indefinite number of other occasions. There does not seem to be any a priori reason to suppose that he would have been incarnated and have died at one particular time and place rather than at many others. Consequently, even if *some* incarnation and resurrection or other is likely, there is no a priori reason to suppose that he would have become incarnated and have died as Jesus in first-century Palestine. Indeed, given the innumerable alternatives at God's disposal it would seem a priori unlikely that the incarnation and the resurrection would have taken place where and when they allegedly did.

Consider the following analogy, which I adapt from one used by Swinburne. Suppose a parent has decided to pay her child's debts.[9] Suppose that this parent can do this in an enormous number of different ways and that there is a wide time span in which the parent can act. Suppose we know of no reason why the parent might use one of these ways rather than another or act at one time rather than another. Although it is likely, given the parent's decision, that she will pay her child's debt in some way at some future time, it is unlikely that she will settle her child's debt by a cash payment on July 8 of this year. Indeed, it is initially improbable that she will do so. Similarly, given all of God's options, it is initially unlikely that his son would have become flesh and then have died in the way he is portrayed to have done in the Scriptures.

POSSIBLE REBUTTALS TO THE CLAIM OF LOW INITIAL PROBABILITIES[10]

a. The Particular Time and Place Argument

I claim that the probability of the resurrection is initially low even if God exists since the resurrection occurs at some particular time and place. One possible rebuttal to my argument is that it would make the probability of any future event absurdly low.

In order to answer this charge it is important to notice that my argument is a special case of a more general and familiar point: The more specific a hypothesis the less its initial probability while the less specific a hypothesis the greater its initial probability. For example, it is more probable initially that a king will be drawn from a deck of cards than that the king of hearts will be drawn, it is more likely initially that a bird will be seen in my backyard than that a bluebird will be seen, it is more initially probable that I will receive a phone call at some time or other in the next year than that I will receive one on July 4 at 2 P.M., it is more likely that I will receive a letter today from somewhere or other in the United States than that I will receive one from New York City.

Unspecific claims often but not always have a rather high initial probability and specific claims a very low initial probability. For example, given the background knowledge about my health, the unspecific claim that I will get a cold sometime in the next decade is very likely while the claim that I will get a cold on October 5, 2005, is initially unlikely. On the other hand, given our background knowledge the unspecific claim that some human or other will turn into a fish at some time or other in the next hundred years is initially improbable even though the specific claim that Dan Rather will turn into a swordfish on July 4, 2003, is even more unlikely initially. In contrast, the specific claim that July 4, 2001, in Phoenix, Arizona, will be hot and sunny is initially likely but not as likely as the less specific claim that some day or other in the next century it will be hot and sunny somewhere in Arizona.

Seen in this light, my Particular Time and Place Argument should cause no puzzlement. Now let us suppose that relative to Christian supernaturalism's background beliefs the following rather unspecific claim is initially probable:

1. Some redeeming event or other has occurred or will occur at some time and place on Earth.

This statement is unspecific in just the sense considered above.

The statement does not specify how God plans to redeem humanity. Resurrection is merely one among many ways of redemption. Moreover, if the redeeming event is a resurrection, the statement does not specify the form the resurrection would take and when or where it would take place. In addition, in contrast to a hot and sunny day in Arizona, this redeeming event is unique and singular: There is only one such event of this kind. In short, although (1) may be initially probable, both

2. There was a redeeming resurrection of Jesus in first-century Palestine

and the equivalent of (2)

2'. The resurrection occurred

are initially improbable.

Thus, my example of a particular hot and sunny day in Phoenix indicates that one cannot argue that the initial probability is low for virtually any future event. Moreover, an indefinite number of examples similar to my Phoenix one can be given.

b. The Free Will Objection

Another possible rebuttal to the thesis that the probability of the resurrection is initially low is based on the following example. Steven Davis argues

> This is why the rarity of resurrections (which everyone will grant) cannot be equated with improbability. Suppose I want to buy a car, and I enter a lot where there are a thousand cars for sale, of which only one is red. Now what is the probability that I will buy the red one? Clearly, that probability is not just a function of the infrequency of red cars in the sample. This is obviously because my selection of a car might not

be entirely random as to color. Indeed I might freely choose to buy the red car precisely because of its uniqueness.[11]

This car lot example attempts to show that since God's choice of the resurrection is free, the initial probability of the resurrection is not low. However, consider the initial probability of a person's free choice of the only red car in the lot of nonred cars from the point of view of onlookers who do not know this person's preference for red cars. The initial probability of choosing this car from a lot of thousands of cars is very low. Of course, if the onlookers knew the person's color preferences this initial probability would change. By analogy, God's choice to enact some redeeming miracle or other is a free one. But, as far as supernaturalists are concerned, God has numerous options and any *particular* one such as the resurrection is initially improbable. Perhaps if Christians knew God's preferences this would change. But they do not. They only believe that God wants to redeem humanity.

c. Another Objection to the Low Initial Probability Claim

Another possible objection to my argument that the initial probability of the resurrection is that I assume background beliefs shared by both naturalists and supernaturalists rather than ones shared only by Christian supernaturalists, for instance:

5. God wants to redeem human beings.

However, allowing (5) as part of the background belief still makes (2'), the resurrection occurred, initially improbable. Indeed, redemption can occur without any resurrection at all, let alone the resurrection of Jesus in first-century Palestine.

EVIDENCE FOR THE RESURRECTION

So far I have defended both premise (1) of the Initial Improbability Argument that a miracle claim is initially improbable relative to our background knowledge and a special case of that premise, namely that the initial probability of the resurrection is low. But premise (4) that the evidence for the resurrection is not strong also needs to be defended, for Christians not only argue that the initial probability for the resurrection is not low. They also argue that there is strong evidence for the resurrection. Assuming that my argument so far is sound, this evidence has to be very strong indeed to overcome the initial improbability. If a claim is initially incredible, then the evidence has to be overwhelming to override this. The sort of evidence that apologists typically provide will be considered in what follows.

The General Insufficiency of the Evidence for the Resurrection in the Strong Sense

Some apologists maintain that Jesus' resurrected body has supernatural properties such as being able to walk through walls and move instantaneously from one place to another. Let us call this the strong sense of the resurrection and being brought back to life without necessarily having supernatural properties the neutral sense of the resurrection. Most arguments offered by Christian apologists, even if free from other problems, give no support to the resurrection in the strong sense.[12] For example, appeal to the empty tomb, the conduct of the disciples, many of the postresurrection appearances, and the rise of Christianity at best support the resurrection in the neutral sense. Indeed, the only evidence for the resurrection in the strong sense seems to be *some* descriptions of Jesus' postresurrection appearances. This means that the entire burden for the claim that Jesus was resurrected in the strong sense rests on a few descriptions.

Now someone might grant the view that Jesus was resurrected in the neutral sense but deny that he was resurrected in the strong sense. The question then is whether alternative accounts, when they are not restricted to explanations of reports of Jesus walking through walls and the like, are as low in probability as apologists thinks. Obviously, a priori it is more likely that one or another of the alternative accounts will explain these few reports than that one or another will explain the empty tomb, the conduct of the disciples, all of the postresurrection appearances, the rise of Christianity, and so on. However, even if one supposes that one is talking about Jesus' resurrection in the neutral sense, the case is not strong.

Evidence of the Empty Tomb

Apologists frequently point out that the empty tomb story appeared in all four Gospels. Yes, but what historical accuracy do these stories have?[13] Well-known New Testament scholars such as Crossan and Gerd Lüdemann, argue that the traditional biblical accounts are unlikely.[14] Given Roman crucifixion customs, Jesus was probably not buried at all; even if Jewish customs were followed, his enemies probably buried Jesus ignominiously in an unmarked grave.[15] The traditional story of Jesus' burial, according to Crossan, was likely inspired by the hope of a decent burial rather than by historical truth. Lüdemann points out that Jesus' disciples did not know where he was buried, for "given the significance of tombs of saints in the time of Jesus, it can be presupposed that had Jesus' tomb been known, the early Christians would have venerated it and traditions about it would have been preserved."[16] Many other New Testament scholars agree.[17]

Although apologists attempt to meet the objection that Jesus was either not buried or was buried in an unknown grave, their defense is unconvincing.[18] They say that although such scenarios are possible, they are highly improbable. For example, it could be maintained that the claims about the empty tomb would not have had much apologetic value if they had been made years after the event since opponents could have objected that the tomb was lost. However, for all we know, this is precisely what critics did maintain. Zealous disciples are not always persuaded by arguments or by strong negative evidence.

Apologists also argue that the empty tomb could not have been invented by later Christians since the tomb was discovered by women whose value as legal witnesses in the culture of the day was very low. However, in Jewish society women *were* qualified to give testimony if no male witnesses were available.[19] Moreover, the care and anointing of bodies was women's work at that time so it is to be expected that a writer of fiction would depict women as the ones who went to seek Jesus' body.[20] Other explanations of why the presence of women in the empty tomb story is compatible with its being fictional can also be given.[21] It should be noted that one cannot assume uncritically that the women in the story are presented *as* witnesses. Other interpretations are possible.[22]

Apologists also maintain that Christians could not have falsely claimed that the tomb was empty for their enemies could have produced Jesus' body. However, this assumes that Jesus was buried and that the place of burial was known. In addition, this objection assumes an interest in Christianity, which first-century non-Christians probably did not have. For instance, Jewish sources did not mention the resurrection, let alone try to refute it.

Also it is important to remember that even if the tomb had been opened it is quite possible that the body of Jesus would not have been identified. First, all corpses were wrapped and it is unlikely that anyone at the time would have violated the body in order to identify it.[23] Second, if the body was unwrapped, it is uncertain that it could have been identified. As Robert Price has pointed out, "the only estimate the New Testament gives as to how long after Jesus' death the disciples went public with their preaching is a full fifty days later on Pentecost! After seven weeks, I submit, it would have been moot to produce the remains of Jesus."[24] In this period of time Jesus' corpse might well have decayed sufficiently to make identification impossible. In addition, the estimate of fifty days might be wrong since, for all we know, the empty tomb stories may have emerged many months after Jesus' death.

Apologists reject the argument that if the place of Jesus' burial had been known it would have been venerated, as was the custom in the case of the tombs of saints; since it was not venerated it was not known.[25]

The Argument from Veneration can be explicated as follows:

a. If the empty tomb stories are true, the location of the tomb was known.
b. If the location of the tomb was known, it is likely that Christians would have venerated the tomb shortly after Jesus' resurrection.
c. Christians did not venerate the tomb shortly after Jesus' resurrection.

d. It is not likely that the empty tomb stories are true.

Notice that in this argument the empty tomb story is not *presumed* to be false. Rather the case is *argued*. The crucial premise of the argument is (b), which is based on analogous cases, such as the veneration of the tombs of saints of the time. It would be strange indeed for apologists to assume that Jesus' followers would not have venerated his tomb because they believed he had risen from it. Indeed, one would suppose that venerating the tomb is precisely what they would have done given their belief. "Here," they would have likely said, "is where Our Lord rose from the dead. Let us worship here!" Moreover, centuries after the Jewish war a site was picked out and venerated and even today the Holy Sepulchre Church in Israel proudly claims it harbors the tomb of Jesus. However, there is good reason to suppose that such a claim coming many years after Jesus' death is suspect, and in fact it is rejected by most biblical scholars.[26] Thus, there are good grounds to accept premise (b) and, since (b) is the only controversial premise, there is good reason to accept the Argument from Veneration.

The Evidence of the Conduct of the Disciples

In addition to the evidence of the empty tomb, apologists sometimes appeal to the conduct of Jesus' disciples to refute alternative accounts of what happened to Jesus' body. One such account is the deliberate fraud theory; that is, that Jesus' disciples stole Jesus' body and pretended that Jesus was resurrected. Apologists argue that the behavior of the early Christians indicates that they sincerely believed that the resurrection was true. However, there are not just two alternatives: either the resurrection was a deliberate fraud or it was true. People down through the ages have sincerely believed strange and irrational things despite the evidence. Their beliefs have been based on self-delusion and wishful thinking in which legends grow, feed on themselves, and are mistaken for reality. As Richard Carrier has shown, there is abundant evidence that the Roman Empire was filled with "kooks and quacks of all varieties, from sincere lunatics to ingenious frauds, that there was no end to the fools and loons who would follow and praise them."[27] In addition to many alleged minor messiahs and miracle workers there were major figures such as Apollonius, Peregrinus, and Alexander who claimed to have divine powers and drew large followings. Carrier concludes his analysis by saying that the age of Jesus "was not an age of critical reflection" but rather an era filled with "con artists, gullible believers, martyrs without a cause, and reputed miracles of every variety. . . . Even if [the gospel stories] were false in every detail, there is no evidence that they would have been rejected as absurd by a people largely lacking in education or critical thinking skills. They had no newspapers, telephones, photographs, or public documents to check a story.[28]

Later centuries also contained examples of human credulity. Consider the growth of the movement associated with Sabbatai Sevi, a seventeenth-century Jewish messianic pretender who eventually converted to Islam. Because of his conversion, the movement associated with Sevi suffered a setback but surprisingly it did not die away. Indeed, within weeks of his public appearance a surge of miracle legends appeared.[29] In this case and in many others religious disciples were not deliberately perpetrating a fraud and yet their beliefs were completely out of touch with reality.[30]

Apologists might argue that if the resurrection story was invented within the lifetime of eyewitnesses to the events, they could have easily refuted the false claims. But as Price points out, such a view of the apostles is anachronistic since it assumes them "to be a sort of squad of ethnographer-detectives, ranging over Palestine, sniffing out legends and clamping the lid on any they discover."[31] In any case, apologists could argue that such a refutation was not accomplished for if it had been, Christianity would not have prospered. But the assumption that religious believers would have given up their beliefs in the light of negative evidence is mistaken. Consider what happened to religious movements such as the Seventh-Day Adventists, Jehovah's Witnesses, and Sabbatainism. Negative evidence had no effect on the zeal of the followers of these movements. In the case of Sevi the efforts of the chief apostle, Nathan of Gaza, could do nothing to stop true believers from producing a legend complete with stories of miracles.[32] In any case, the detailed story of the resurrection seems to have been unknown to Paul *and* other early Christian letter writers and the Gospel stories with all their details appeared generations after Jesus' death when many eyewitnesses were either dead or very old.

The Evidence of Agreement between Gospels and Legends

Apologists could maintain that despite many discrepancies in the New Testament account, there is agreement on many of the details concerning the death and resurrection of Jesus and no resurrection text questions these. Indeed, one might suggest that even the discrepancies themselves "testify in a left-handed way to the accuracy of the essential story: if the Resurrection of Jesus were a story invented by the later Christian Church, or by certain members of it, no discrepancies would be allowed."[33]

To doubt the reality of the resurrection is not necessarily to assume that the Christian Church deliberately invented the story. The story might be in large part legendary and legends, although not true, are not intentionally created. Various versions of the same legends might well agree on the main points but vary widely in detail. Their discrepancies do not testify in a left-handed way to their historical accuracy concerning the points on which they agree, but rather to the piecemeal and fragmentary way in which legends grow.

Briefly, the case for a legend explanation of the resurrection rests on these points:

a. There is no independent confirmation of the details of the resurrection story from pagan and Jewish sources.

b. There is no independent confirmation of the details of the resurrection story from Paul or other earlier Christian writers. This does not necessarily show that Paul and these other writers did not know these details. Perhaps. But this mere possibility does not provide independent support.

c. The legend theory predicts that later accounts of a growing legend would have more details. Gospel versions of the resurrection have more details than earlier ones.

d. We know from other historical cases of growing legends that the zealous followers of a religion dismiss negative evidence and are not fazed by rational arguments. It is thus hardly surprising that the Gospels contain no "inner circle controversy," over the resurrection—the crucial Christian belief.[34] Any adverse eyewitnesses or arguments would have been ignored and their claims would have been supressed. One might argue that such irrationality is unusual and that "most sensible folk change their beliefs in the face of powerful evidence"[35] and cite the fact that many former religious believers gave up their religion after being exposed to negative arguments. But surely the history of religion—from Mormonism to American religious leader Father Divine, from Jonesville to Heaven's Gate, from Jehovah's Witnesses to the followers of Sabbatai Sevi—is filled with cases of irrational dogmatic belief on the part of zealous followers. Yes, most sensible folk change their minds in the face of powerful evidence. But it simply begs the question to suppose that most religious believers—including early Christians—are sensible folk.

e. The legendary nature of the resurrection is to be expected given that many resurrection myths[36] were common in Jesus' era and before.[37] Ancient heroes such as Romulus and Hercules were rewarded by being taken up into heaven and made divine beings. Romulus' ascent was seen by "eyewitnesses." In other cases the hero's ascent was shown by the lack of bodily remains. Sometimes the hero might return to Earth and appear to his friends. Similar legends have been associated with more recent or contemporary personages such as Apollonius of Tyana, the prophet Peregrinus, and the Emperor Augustus.[38]

According to some apologists, doubters and skeptics of the resurrection in the Gospel stories themselves testify to the truth of the stories. But this is questionable. In some legends the skepticism of characters is used as a literary device to stress the reality of miracles performed by the hero.[39] Given this background, it is not surprising that the resurrection story would develop complete with skeptical characters.

Moreover, it hardly seems to matter that the Christian story might have some elements not found in the Jewish tradition. There are other traditions not mentioned, including Egyptian, Zoroastrian, and Greek, that might have influenced Christian legends. However, suppose that it is shown that Christianity has elements not found in any other tradition. Legend-making is to some extent creative. From the fact that a story contains elements that cannot be traced to older myths and legends nothing follows about whether these elements reflect historical reality. One might dismiss the relevance of these myths to Christianity since, one could argue, non-Christian myths are wild fairy tale–like stories where the Christian stories of the resurrection "are understated, realistic, firmly grounded in historical settings and events of the first century."[40] However, this is a distortion. In Mark there is the wonder of the darkness at noon and the rending of the temple veil. Matthew outdoes Mark by adding an earthquake and the resurrections of numerous "saints" who appear in Jerusalem. How one can suggest that these stories are understated and realistic whereas the apotheosis stories of Apollonius, Empedocles, Romulus, and so on are overstated and unrealistic defies all understanding.

Evidence that Resurrection Appearances Are Not Hallucinations

Apologists might claim that many factors indicate that the resurrection appearances of Jesus were not hallucinations: The disciples were not expecting the resurrection, the idea of the resurrection of one individual before the end of the world was not found in the Jewish tradition, the resurrected Jesus was not immediately recognized, some who saw him doubted, many different people saw the risen Jesus at different times and in different circumstances, and there were none of the usual causes such as drugs, lack of food, water, sleep, and so on. Apologists also seem to reject the idea that one person's hallucination could start a chain reaction among other members of the group.[41]

However, the historical reality of the resurrection is not the only alternative to the hallucination theory. Stories about Jesus' appearances in the Gospels may be legends that cannot be completely traced to hallucinations.

Moreover, it is not clear that the hallucination theory can be so easily dismissed. Hallucinations plus legends can explain more than either phenomenon can taken in isolation. Despite what is sometimes suggested, collective hallucinations are well-known phenomena and there is every reason to suppose that they can occur without "usual causes" being present. Moreover, we know that one hallucination can trigger others. The history of witchcraft indicates that people who were thought to be bewitched had hallucinations that caused those around them to have hallucinations also.[42] In the case of Sevi the visions of his followers were infectious, one person's vision triggering hundreds of others.[43] In a series of visions of the Virgin Mary in Dordogne, France, in 1889 one child's vision triggered similar visions in other children, and then in a large number of peasants.[44]

One cannot argue that hallucinations are ruled out by the fact that neither Jesus nor his disciples were expecting the resurrection, that Jesus was not immediately recognized, and that different people in different times and circumstances saw him. With respect to the first point we know from the gospels that people did believe in the resurrection of individuals before the general resurrection at the end of time. The public appearance of Jesus was interpreted as the resurrection of John (Mark 6:14) and some suspected that John was the Messiah (Luke 3:15).[45] Furthermore, the apologists' argument assumes that the historical account is accurate. What if part of the story is legendary? Legends of the time and earlier suggest that heroes are resurrected, ascend to heaven, and sometimes return to Earth. So was it really true that the disciples could not expect some sort of resurrection? These legends also indicate that skepticism is used as a literary device to authenticate miracles. The stories of the initial failure to recognize Jesus surely could function in a similar way.[46] Moreover, the evidence cited here shows that collective hallucinations do not always occur in a particular place or in one group of people.

Evidence of the Rise of Christianity

Apologists argue that only the historical reality of the Resurrection can explain why or how the Christian Church came into existence proclaiming the resurrection. Without the reality of the resurrection, one might argue, there would not have been a Christian movement or at least it would have taken a different form. The faith of disciples was new, not traceable to Jewish sources, and not explicable by Jesus' life or teachings. The real resurrection provides an explanation of the Easter faith, namely, that "the disciples saw the risen Lord, . . . and interpreted their experience in a theologically novel way."[47]

However, why suppose that the reality of the resurrection is the only explanation of the rise of Christianity? Surely, there is at least one other: Early Christians believed deeply but falsely that the resurrection had occurred. They *thought* that the disciples saw the risen Jesus and they interpreted their beliefs theologically at least partly in terms of the myths and legends of their times. We have no more need to appeal to the reality of the resurrection to explain the rise of Christianity than to appeal to the reality of the revelation of the Book of Mormon to Joseph Smith by the Angel Moroni to explain the rise of Mormonism.[48]

Moreover, there is a plausible naturalistic explanation for why some groups in the early Christian Church advocated a physical resurrection. As Elaine Pagels has argued, a physical interpretation of the resurrection gave "orthodox" Christians political advantages over Gnostic Christians who stressed subjective spiritual experience.[49]

In conclusion, in the light of my criticisms readers must ask themselves if apologists have really shown that the historical evidence is as low as they suppose relative to alternative theories such as the hallucination theory or the legend theory.

OTHER FACTORS AFFECTING CREDIBILITY

There are three other factors adversely affecting the credibility of the resurrection story and thus the probability of premise (4).

Inconsistencies in the Empty Tomb Stories

One factor is that there are numerous contradictions in the Scriptural account of the resurrection. According to some apologists there are only "a few" inconsistencies that are difficult to harmonize and in any case all of the accounts are in agreement on the "main" points. But consider the following contradictions connected with the empty tomb. They are not a few, and as far as I know, they have not been reconciled. Moreover, they are connected to major points such as who were the first witnesses to the empty tomb and what was seen in and around the empty tomb by these witnesses.

In Matthew, when Mary Magdalene and the other Mary arrive toward dawn at the tomb there is a rock in front of it. There is a violent earthquake and an angel descends and rolls back the stone. "And behold there was a great earthquake; for an angel of the Lord descended from heaven and came and rolled back the stone and sat upon it" (Matt. 28:2). In Mark, the women arrive at the tomb at sunrise and the stone has been rolled back: "And very early on the first day of the week they went to the tomb when the sun had risen and they were saying to one another, 'Who will roll away the stone for us from the door of the tomb?' And looking up they saw that the stone was rolled back, for it was very large" (Mark 16:2–4). In Luke, when the women arrive at early dawn they find the stone has already been rolled back. "But on the first day of the week, at early dawn, they went to the tomb, taking the spices which they had prepared. And they found the stone rolled away from the tomb" (Luke 24:1–2).

In Matthew, an angel is sitting on the rock outside the tomb (Matt 28:2) and in Mark a youth is inside the tomb: "And entering the tomb, they saw a young man sitting on the right side dressed in a white robe, and they were amazed" (Mark 16:5). In Luke, two men are inside: "While they were perplexed about this, behold, two men stood by them in dazzling apparel" (Luke 24:4).

In Matthew, the women present at the tomb are Mary Magdalene and the other Mary: "Now after the sabbath, toward the dawn of the first day of the week, Mary Magdalene and the other Mary went to see the sepulchre" (Matt. 28:1). In Mark, the women present at the tomb are the two Marys and Salome: "And when the sabbath was past, Mary Magdalene, and Mary the mother of James, and Salome brought spice, so that they might go and anoint him" (Mark 16:1). In Luke, Mary Magdalene, Joanna, Mary the mother of James, and other women are present at the tomb: "Now it was Mary Magdalene and Joanna and Mary the mother of James and the other women with them who told this to the apostles" (Luke 24:12).

In Matthew, the two Marys rush from the tomb in great fear and joy, run to tell the disciples, and meet Jesus on the way: "So they departed quickly from the tomb with fear and great joy, and ran to tell the disciples. And behold Jesus met them and said 'Hail!' " (Matt. 28:8–9) In Mark, they run out of the tomb in fear and say nothing to anyone: "And they went out and fled from the tomb; for trembling and astonishment had come up on them; and they said nothing to any one, for they were afraid" (Mark 16:8). In Luke, the women report the story to the disciples who do not believe them and there is no suggestion that they meet Jesus: "And returning from the tomb they told all this to the eleven and to all the rest . . . but these words seemed to [the apostles] an idle tale, and they did not believe them"(Luke 24:9–11).

Given these various accounts what should one believe? Can the Gospel according to John help one decide? Unfortunately, John contradicts much of the three other gospels. (John 20:1–18). According to John, only Mary Magdalene comes to the tomb and she does so when it is still dark, although all three other gospels state it was somewhere near dawn, and therefore at least somewhat light out. She sees that the stone has been moved and rushes to tell Simon Peter and the other disciples who apparently take her story seriously since they run to the tomb. This directly conflicts with the accounts of Mark and Luke. In John, before Mary Magdalene runs to tell Simon Peter and the disciples, she sees neither angels nor a youth, thus contradicting the other three gospels. Moreover, since there is no report of her entering the tomb before she tells Simon Peter and the disciples, Mark and Luke are hard to reconcile. Only after she returns to the tomb with the disciples, and they inspect the tomb and find linen wrapping and a head napkin, and then leave, does she, while standing outside weeping, see two angels inside the tomb. This, of course, differs from the three other gospels. At this point, according to John, she also sees Jesus, whom she does not at first recognize. This also contradicts the other gospels.

Lack of Independent Confirmation

Given all these uncertainties we need independent confirmation of the resurrection, yet this is lacking both from Jewish and pagan sources.[50] Independent confirmation is also lacking from the New Testament sources. The genuine Paulian epistles and the earlier non-Paulian letters provide no details about the burial, and what is said there is compatible with Jesus not being buried in a tomb.[51]

This lack of independent evidence needs to be accounted for. Interestingly enough, although some apologists try to make Paul's views compatible with the Gospel's empty tomb stories, they do not attempt to explain the lack of independent confirmation from earlier non-Paulian letters let alone from Jewish and pagan sources. This failure to explain the lack of independent confirmation also adversely effects the credibility of the resurrection.

The Reliability of Testimony

It is well known from psychological experiments that eyewitness testimony is often unreliable. Eyewitness testimony is influenced by what psychologists call "post-event" and "pre-event" information. In the case of Christianity, for post-event information we can read "early Christian beliefs" and for pre-event information we can read "prior messianic expectations."[52] Moreover, we know from other religious movements such as Sabbatai Sevi's that eyewitnesses in such movements tend to be unreliable. Why should we expect the situation to be different in the case of Christianity?

It should be noted that I do not claim that the probability of a witness's testimony is based simply on the probability of that witness telling the truth and the initial probability of the event in question. It is also based on many background factors including whether testimony is confirmed by other independent witnesses and sources. This independent confirmation is lacking in the case of the resurrection. Moreover, I do not deny that the probability of an alleged event must also be determined in the light of the probability of the witnesses reporting as they did had the event not taken place. This latter determination would involve assessing alternative accounts. My point is that in the case of the resurrection these alternative accounts can have a fairly low probability and yet rational belief in the resurrection would still be impossible.

RATIONALITY: COMPARATIVE AND NONCOMPARATIVE

So far I have assumed that to say that belief in the resurrection is rational for Christians is to say that the probability of the resurrection relative to background theories and historical evidence is more than 50 percent. This means that if the falsehood of the resurrection relative to our background and the historical evidence is more than 50 percent then the resurrection is not rational for Christians. Let us call this the Noncomparative Sense of Rationality.

However, it could be maintained that even if I have shown that the falsehood of the resurrection has a higher probability than the truth of it relative to our background and the historical evidence, this does not settle the question of the rationality of the resurrection for Christians. The resurrection still may be more probable than any specific alternative hypothesis. Clearly this objection proposes a different meaning of rationality from the Noncomparative Sense. In this sense, to say that the resurrection is rational for Christians is to say that the probability of the resurrection relative to background theories and historical evidence is higher than that of any *specific* alternative hypothesis. Let us call this the Comparative Sense of Rationality. Note that Comparative Sense of Rationality is compatible with a disjunction D of specific alternative hypotheses that does not entail the falsehood of the resurrection and is more probable than the resurrection.

Two points can be made concerning this shift to the Comparative Sense of Rationality. The first is that it has strange and paradoxical implications that even many Christians might find hard to accept. One such is that it implies that Christian belief in the resurrection is rational even if the probability of the resurrection relative to background theories and historical evidence is .000000000000000001 so long as all specific alternative hypotheses have a lower probability. So, paradoxically even if the falsehood of the resurrection is virtually certain, in this sense of rationality belief in the resurrection could still be rational.

Second, I cannot see that anything has been done to establish that the probabilities of all specific alternatives to the resurrection are less than the probability of the resurrection. Given the low initial probability of the resurrection, the weakness of the historical evidence, the unreconciled consistencies, the unreliability of eyewitness evidence, is it really the case that, say, the legend explanation has a lower probability than the resurrection?

A critic might object that I have not specified the details of alternative accounts to the resurrection. But is this really necessary? It is certainly not necessary when we are debating the Noncomparative Sense of Rationality of the resurrection. Here it is enough to provide general considerations indicating that alternative accounts are not worthless. Even in relation to the Comparative Sense of Rationality it is not always necessary.

Consider an entirely different context: Suppose a ship called the *Santa Marie* disappears in the Bermuda Triangle. Someone proposes a hypothesis H to explain this disappearance consisting of a detailed story of the disappearance of the *Santa Marie* that involves UFOs and parallel universes. Suppose a specific alternative explanation A is that the *Santa Marie* sank in a storm but no details are provided in A since none are known. The mere vagueness of A and lack of detail does not necessarily mean that A is less probable than H. Its probability would depend on other factors: the initial probabilities of H and A, evidence of a storm in the area during the relevant time, and so on. In a similar way, the vagueness of some alternative account of the historical evidence, despite what a critic might believe, does not necessarily indicate that it has a lower probability than the resurrection.

CONCLUSION

Without the truth of the resurrection life is meaningless in a Christian worldview. However, there is no good reason to suppose that the resurrection did occur. First, the initial probability of the resurrection is very low—even in a Christian worldview. Thus, premise (1) of the Initial Improbability Argument is justified. Second, in order to override this the evidence for the resurrection must be very strong. But it is not. Consequently, premise (4) is also justified.

Possible objections to my critique of the resurrection fail. Moreover, the thesis that Jesus was resurrected in the strong sense is not supported by most of the evidence usually cited by apologists. In addition, even supposing that apologists argue that Jesus was resurrected in the neutral sense, the evidence presented is not strong. Furthermore, unreconciled inconsistencies in the biblical account of the resurrection, the failure to independently confirm the Gospel account, and background evidence indicating the unreliability of eyewitness reports further weakens the apologists' case.

NOTES

1. The Athanasian Creed does not say that Jesus was crucified under Pilate but only that he "suffered for our salvation, descended into Hades, rose again of the third day."

2. Hugh Anderson, *Jesus and Christian Origins* (New York: Oxford University Press, 1964), pp. 186–87.

3. Terry Miethe in *Did Jesus Rise from the Dead? The Resurrection Debate, Gary Habermas and Antony G. N. Flew,* ed. Terry Miethe (San Francisco: Harper and Row, 1987), p. xi.

4. See Michael Martin, *The Case against Christianity* (Philadelphia: Temple University Press, 1991), chap. 3; Michael Martin, "Why the Resurrection is Initially Improbable," *Philo* 1 (spring–summer 1998): 63–74; Michael Martin, "Reply to Davis," *Philo* 2 (spring–summer 1999): 62–76; Michael Martin, "Christianity and the Rationality of the Resurrection," *Philo* 3 (2000): 52–62.

5. Antony Flew makes a similar point when he says that "the defining characteristics of the theistic God preclude all possibilities of inferring with benefit of particular revelation, what a God might be reasonably be expected to do." See Antony Flew, *God: A Critical Inquiry* (La Salle, Ill.: Open Court, 1984), p. 145.

6. Michael Martin, *Atheism: A Philosophical Justification* (Philadelphia: Temple University Press, 1990), pp. 202–207.

7. Stephen T. Davis, *Risen Indeed* (Grand Rapids, Mich.: Eerdmans, 1993), p. 13.

8. See Richard Swinburne, *Revelation* (Oxford: Clarendon Press, 1992), pp. 71–72.

9. Ibid., p. 71.

10. See Stephen T. Davis, "Is Belief in the Resurrection Rational? A Response to Michael Martin," *Philo* 2 (spring–summer 1999): 51–62; Steven T. Davis, "The Rationality of the Resurrection for Christians: A Rejoinder," *Philo* 3 (2000): 41–51.

11. Davis, "Is Belief in the Resurrection Rational?" p. 58.

12. For more details on this argument, see Robert Greg Cavin, "Is There Sufficient Evidence to Establish the Resurrection of Jesus?" *Faith and Philosophy* 12 (1995): 361–79.

13. For a detailed evaluation of the evidence see Jeffrey Jay Lowder, "Historical Evidence and the Empty Tomb Story," http://www.infidels.org/library/modern/jeff_lowder/empty.html.

14. John Dominic Crossan, *Who Killed Jesus?* (San Francisco: HarperCollins, 1996), chap. 6; Gerd Lüdemann, *What Really Happened to Jesus?* (Louisville, Ky.: Westminister John Knox Press, 1995), pp. 22–24.

15. For more details see Lowder, "Historical Evidence and the Empty Tomb Story," pp. 1–5.

16. Lüdemann, *What Really Happened to Jesus?* p. 24.

17. For example, over 70 percent of the members of the Jesus Seminar, a group of nonfundamentalist New Testament scholars devoted to the historical study of Jesus, have maintained that the gravesite of Jesus was unknown and that the empty tomb stories are a creation of Mark. See "The Jesus Seminar Voting Record," *Forum* new series 1, no. 1 (spring 1998): 231–32.

18. Davis, *Risen Indeed*, pp. 81–82.

19. John Wenham, *Easter Enigma: Are the Resurrection Accounts in Conflict?* 2d ed. (Grand Rapids, Mich.: Eerdmans, 1992), pp. 150–51. I owe this point to Jeff Lowder. Moreover, Davis's argument assumes that if later Christians invented a story, they would only have used epistemic criteria. But this is not necessarily so. Crossan suggests an entirely different explanation. Crossan, *Who Killed Jesus?* pp. 181–88. See Kathleen E. Corley, "Women and the Crucifixion and Burial of Jesus," *Forum* new series 1, no. 1 (spring 1998): 163–80; G. A. Wells, *The Jesus Legend* (La Salle, Ill.: Open Court, 1996), pp. 60–61.

20. I owe this point to Keith Parsons.

21. Martin, "Why the Resurrection Is Initially Improbable," p. 75.

22. Robert Price wrote in a personal communication, "the empty tomb story reflects and derives from myths and rituals of Isis and Nephthys seeking the corpse of Osiris to anoint it after Set's betrayal and murder. They anoint the body and bring it back to life!" He points out interesting parallels between the Osiris myth and Gospel stories and suggests that Mark got hold of these stories and adapted them to his own purposes. Crossan also suggests an explanation in which the women are not considered as witnesses. See Martin, "Why the Resurrection Is Initially Improbable," p. 75, n. 11.

23. Lowder, "Historical Evidence and the Empty Tomb Story," p. 11.

24. Robert Price, "By This Time He Stinketh," http://www.infidels.org/library/modern/robert_price/stinketh.html.

On the authority of his brother-in-law who is "an eminent pathologist" Davis says that in "normal cases, especially where the body is buried and where local climate is dry as opposed to humid, corpses are identifiable by sight alone for much longer than that." Apparently, authorities disagree. A retired pathologist, John Nernoll III, consulted by Lowder, maintained that in cave temperatures (65 degrees or less) in the Middle East, in several days decomposition will render a face nearly unrecognizable. Even recently dead bodies will have distortions in the facial structures that render them unrecognizable to relatives. This is a well-known caveat in forensic circles. It is never a good idea to rely just on sight recognition of most corpses for identification; fingerprints, dental records and other forms of I.D. are always the standard. Needless to say, in Jesus' day such methods were unavailable. For more details see Lowder, "Historical Evidence and the Empty Tomb Story," p. 11.

25. Cf. Lowder, "Historical Evidence and the Empty Tomb Story," p. 13.

26. See Dan Bahat, "Does the Holy Sepulchre Church Mark the Burial of Jesus?" *Biblical Archaeology Review* (May/June 1986); Gabriel Barkay, "The Garden Tomb—Was Jesus Buried Here?" *Biblical Archaeology Review* (March/April 1986).

27. Richard Carrier, "Kooks and Quacks of the Roman Empire: a Look into the World of the Gospels," http://www.infidels.org/library/modern/ richard_carrier/kooks.html (accessed 1997).

28. Ibid.

29. See Gershom Scholem, *Sabbatai Sevi: The Mystic Messiah* (Princeton, N.J.: Princeton University Press, 1973), pp. 252, 265, cited by Robert Price, *Beyond Born Again*, chap. 5, http://www.infidels.org/library/modern/robert_price/beyond_born_again/.

30. Davis argues that there was not enough time for a legend to grow but in

the Sevi case as well as in many other historical cases it is clear that legends can develop in a short period of time. For example, see the examples provided by Price, *Beyond Born Again*, chap. 5.

31. Price, *Beyond Born Again*, chap. 5.

32. Ibid.

33. Davis, *Risen Indeed*, p. 181.

34. There is, of course, the Jewish objection reported in Matthew 28 that the disciples stole the body. But how seriously this is to be taken is completely unclear given the fact that the Roman guards at the tomb were reported to have fallen asleep on duty and yet claimed to know what happened when they were asleep. This story most likely reflects the Jewish polemic as of Matthew's time, that is, late first century–early second century. It is too late to provide information about what the original non-Christian critics might have said. The Jewish criticism can be understood as granting the empty tomb for the sake of argument and then explaining it away.

35. Davis, "The Rationality of the Resurrection for Christians," p. 49.

36. In "Reply to Davis," n. 18, in citing ancient parallels to the resurrection I mention the Old Testament stories of Enoch and Elijah who were taken up to be with God and left no traces. Davis points out that they were not said to have been raised from the dead. Very true. But I did not say they were. The close analogy between being taken up without a trace and being resurrected remains and is not discussed by Davis. See Davis, "The Rationality of the Resurrection for Christians," p. 47.

37. For example, the Sumerian goddess Innana and the Thracian god Zalmoxis. See also resurrection stories from ancient mythology, for example, Demeter, Dionysos, Persephone, Castor and Pollux, Isis and Osiris, and Cybele and Attis. (I owe these references to Richard Carrier, personal correspondence.) There are also Old Testament stories of Enoch and Elijah who were taken up to be with God and who left no traces. (See Price, *Beyond Born Again*, chap. 6.)

38. Price, *Beyond Born Again*, chap. 6.

39. Ibid.

40. Davis, "The Rationality of the Resurrection for Christians," p. 47.

41. Davis, *Risen Indeed*, p. 183, n. 30.

42. Martin, *The Case against Christianity*, pp. 93–95.

43. Scholem, *Sabbatai Sevi*, pp. 417, 446, cited by Price, *Beyond Born Again*, chap. 6.

44. George Barton Cutten, *The Psychological Phenomena of Christianity* (New York: Scribner's Sons, 1908), pp. 65–66, cited by Price, *Beyond Born Again*, chap. 6.

45. Price, *Beyond Born Again*, chap. 6.

46. Ibid.

47. Davis, *Risen Indeed*, pp. 184–85.

48. Jeff Lowder used this example in personal correspondence.

49. I owe this point to Jeff Lowder. See Elaine Pagels, *The Gnostic Gospel* (New York: Random House, 1979).

50. Martin, "Why the Resurrection Is Initially Improbable," p. 71.

51. Lowder, "Historical Evidence and the Empty Tomb Story," p. 5.

52. Robert M. Price, *Beyond Born Again*, chap. 5. See also E. F. Loftus, *Eyewitness Testimony* (Cambridge, Mass.: Harvard University Press, 1979).

CONCLUSION

In the preceding chapters I showed that the commonly held beliefs that without God life has no meaning and objective morality is impossible are mistaken. Moreover, I have argued that from the standpoint of the dominant religious perspective in our culture, namely Christianity, there are serious obstacles to developing an objective ethics and having a meaningful life.

Of course, my theses leave unanswered the questions of why so many people in this culture are so misinformed about these issues and what can be done about this misinformation. The first question seems rather easy to answer. Most people are misinformed because they are raised in a culture where religious morality and meaning are uncritically accepted and nonreligious morality and meaning are misunderstood and rejected. From TV to popular religious books, from religious sermons to statements of people in high places, antiatheistic and proreligious messages seep into our consciousness. Counterarguments such as those presented in this book are rarely, if ever, heard. Few people in our society know any atheists, let alone articulate atheists who defend the positions taken in this book. Small wonder then that the views I argue for are not widely accepted.

The second question is easy enough to answer in principle: People must be reeducated. But it is difficult to apply in practice. How can they be reeducated when a religious perspective dominates the popular media; our national leaders, including the president of the United States are antiatheists; and religion pervades every aspect of life? Atheistic organizations are, relatively speaking, socially weak, financially impoverished, and politically cloutless. This is not to say that no efforts can or should be made. For example, atheists can write letters to their local newspapers challenging religious perspectives and claims, develop Web sites[1] and public radio programs where their messages are aired, run for political office *as atheists*,[2] defend their positions in oral and written debates,[3] advertise their views, organize political lobbies, and write books and articles defending their positions.[4] However, given the strength of religion in our society the limitations of these efforts should not be underestimated.

I need hardly say that this book has theoretical and practical limitations of its own. One is that my critique of religious morality and meaning is restricted to Western theism and mainly to Christianity. I hope however that others will carry on where I have left off and critically consider the morality and meaning provided by Eastern and non-Christian religions. Another limitation is that although I have defended a nonreligious *metaethics* I have not attempted to develop a nonreligious *normative* ethics. There are many normative ethical systems that are compatible with the metaethical views that I defend and I leave it to others to develop and defend such systems.[5] Finally, although I have argued in general terms that life can be meaningful without God, I have not attempted to develop and defend a particular secular philosophy of life. Again I leave this to others.[6]

Nevertheless, although there is work left to be done, there is no need to underestimate what has been accomplished here: Given the arguments of this book, Christian theists can no longer correctly claim that objective morality and a meaningful life are impossible from an atheist perspective or that Christianity has established objective morality and the meaningfulness of life.

NOTES

1. One example of this is the Secular Web, an on-line community of nonbelievers (http://www.infidel.org/).

2. Edward Tabash, a Los Angeles attorney, ran for political office in Cali-

fornia as an avowed atheist, but was not elected. I am not aware of any avowed atheists being elected to political office.

3. Jeffery Lowder, Edward Tabash, Keith Parsons, and Dan Barker among others have publicly debated theists.

4. For example, philosophers Kai Nielson, Robin Le Poidevin, Keith Parsons, Antony Flew, and Quentin Smith have written books defending atheism.

5. For example, David Brink in *Moral Realism and the Foundations of Ethics* (Cambridge: Cambridge University Press, 1989) has developed an objective utilitarian position that is compatible with the metaethics I adopt in this book. See also Paul Kurtz, *Forbidden Fruit: The Ethics of Humanism* (Amherst, N.Y.: Prometheus Books, 1988).

6. For example, see some of Paul Kurtz's work, for example, *The Fullness of Life* (New York: Horizon Press, 1974), and Sidney Hook, *Pragmatism and the Tragic Sense of Life* (New York: Basic Books, 1974).

INDEX